THE RADICAL IMPULSE

Music in the Tradition of the Indian People's Theatre Association

THE RADICAL IMPULSE

Music in the Tradition of the Indian People's Theatre Association

SUMANGALA DAMODARAN

Tulika Books

Published by
Tulika Books
35 A/1 (ground floor), Shahpur Jat
New Delhi 110 049, India
www.tulikabooks.in

First edition (hardback) 2017

ISBN: 978-93-82381-92-1

Printed at Chaman Offset, Delhi 110 002

In memory of my grandfather
E.M.S. NAMBOODIRIPAD

Contents

Acknowledgements

My greatest debt of acknowledgment is to the wonderful artists and activists I met during the course of the work that finally led to this book. Sova Sen, Reba Roychowdhury, Priti Banerjee, Khaled Choudhury, Montu Ghosh and Sima Das in Kolkata; O.N.V. Kurup, Pattambi Madhavan, K.T. Mohammed, Medini and Anasuya in Kerala; A.K. Hangal and Javed Siddiqui in Mumbai; Swatantrata Prakash, Sheila Didi and Harshi Anand in Delhi – all shared their generosity and a deep sense that the stories needed to be told. They took out time despite frail health in most cases, and also shared with me whatever material they had in the form of recordings, songbooks or newspaper clippings.

To begin with, an independent fellowship from Sarai at the Centre for the Study of Developing Societies (CSDS), Delhi, enabled me to travel to Kolkata and Kerala a couple of times over a year, and this allowed me to frame the basic questions I was investigating. After that first year, I presented my work in different stages of its evolution at Sarai; to M.A. students at the School of Arts and Aesthetics at Jawaharlal Nehru University (JNU), New Delhi; at a conference at the Institute of Economic Growth, Delhi; at the Centre for Historical Studies, JNU, as part of the P.C. Joshi lecture series; at Lady Shri Ram College, New Delhi; at a seminar organized by Sahmat in New Delhi on the legacy of the progressive cultural movement in India; as the second Ila Dalmia Memorial Lecture, organized by the Ila Dalmia Foundation; at the Nehru Memorial Museum and Library (NMML), New Delhi; at the Centre for India Studies in Africa, Wits University, South Africa; and as a three-lecture series of the National University of Colombia at Bogota, Medellin and Cartagena. Many thanks to Vivek Narayanan, Suddhabrata Sengupta, Bishnupriya

Paul, Meenakshi Gopinath, Mahesh Rangarajan, Janaki Nair, Gargi Chakravartty, Veena Naregal, Rajen, Ram Rahman, Vidya Shivadas, Isabel Hofmeyr, Michelle Williams, Paolo Vignolo and Javier Saenz, who made it possible for me to test my ideas and also provided valuable feedback.

Several persons assisted generously in the archiving exercise. Kankan Bhattacharya, secretary, West Bengal IPTA, shared his collection of songs with me. In subsequent visits, Sima Das and Dr Samir Kumar Gupta introduced me to the world of Paresh Dhar's and Salil Chowdhury's lesser known music collections. Moinak Biswas generously shared his father Hemanga Biswas's writings and also recordings from the family's collection. I also thank Pratibha Agarwal of the Natyashodh Sansthan and Miley Mishey in Kolkata, and members of IPTA and the Awami Idara in Mumbai, for sharing photos and recordings. I benefited a great deal from discussions with Andalattu and Sreekumar in Kerala, Kankan Bhattacharya, Subodh More, Shaili Sathyu and Atul Tiwari in Bombay, and V. Ramakrishna and Volga Kutungar in Hyderabad.

Long discussions with Samik Bandopadhyay over the years helped me to gain a perspective on much of the material I collected in Kolkata, and open it up to questions that went far beyond the immediate contexts of its creation.

The idea of writing a book out of the material collected as part of the archiving–documentation exercise came from Indu Chandrasekhar of Tulika Books, who suggested that it might be important to assess the relevance of an old repertoire in contemporary times. Discussions with Indu were what initially made me expand the article written for the journal *Seminar*, in 2008, into a larger document that eventually culminated in this book. Many thanks to Indu for seeing this process through, and to Shad Naved who has painstakingly edited the book. Indu and Shad have also helped me work through my ideas and sequence the chapters carefully.

I joined Ambedkar University Delhi (AUD) in 2010, when the idea of writing this book had been with me for some time, but I was yet to get down to actually writing it. Being provided the opportunity to envision, set up and teach courses on music at the School of Culture and Creative Expressions in AUD proved to be catalytic in the writing of the book. I am deeply thankful to Shyam Menon, my colleagues and students at AUD, for nurturing and enabling an environment that, among many other things, made this book possible.

Many of the insights in this book have also come out of my own experience of performing the IPTA tradition's repertoire from 2008 onwards. Susmit Sen, Deepak Castelino, Pritam Ghosal, Harpreet, Tapan Mullick, Mark Aranha, Varun Gupta,

Anil Chawla, Anirbaan Ghosh and others have responded to the music with their instruments over the years, and contributed fundamentally to my understanding of what it means to sing and interpret a historical repertoire in contemporary times. Susmit Sen also produced the album 'Songs of Protest' that came out of my own singing of songs from my archive. Mark Aranha has done the song transcriptions that appear in the book.

There are innumerable friends and comrades with whom I have spent many years of my life and who have been key to my ideas taking shape as an academic, a political being and a performer, of whom I would like to mention some. Safdar Hashmi and Kajal Ghosh introduced me to the world of political theatre and music, and I have had several discussions with Sudhanva Deshpande and Moloyashree Hashmi, particularly over the last few years, on culture and politics. Madan Gopal Singh was instrumental in goading me on, and giving me the confidence that I could bring research and performance together, especially after long years of singing very little. His own work has been a great source of inspiration for how music and politics can seamlessly come together in performance. Ayesha Kidwai and I have shared with each other, through the process of the writing of this book and her own sensitive translation of Anis Kidwai's *In Freedom's Shade*, the excitement as well as the sense of responsibility that comes with working with material that involves history, memory and, most importantly, the unwritten and unsung people who shaped history.

Many thanks to Ameet Parameswaran and Smita Mitra for reading through drafts of the book and giving valuable suggestions.

In more recent years, my getting to know Ari Sitas as a colleague, friend and comrade influenced my thinking about aesthetics and politics in ways that I would not have imagined. What began as a specific enquiry into the IPTA's musical tradition turned into a much wider engagement with questions that could be addressed across diverse contexts as a result of intense discussions with him, especially given his own experience with the political cultural movement in South Africa. I have been very influenced by his essays in *The Flight of the Gwala Gwala Bird* series and have also been able to test ideas out in the course, Art and the Sociology of Popular Culture, that we co-teach in the Department of Sociology at the University of Cape Town. Discussions with Astrid von Kotze on culture and activism, and with Neo Muyanga, Sazi Dlamini and Jurgen Brauninger on music, have also shaped some of my arguments.

My parents have been my great support, especially through periods when I thought I did not have the ability to write a book in an area where I have no formal training or degrees, and it is their faith that has sustained me. They will be relieved that it is finally over.

I cannot adequately describe the role that Saumyajit has played in my forays into understanding the relationship between culture and politics, of which this book is a definitive output. He not only wholeheartedly participated in many parts of the fieldwork, saw my ideas taking shape and shared in the process and spirit of this book, but also painstakingly went through drafts with an incisive and critical eye. The book in its final shape owes a great deal to his careful reading and intense discussions over the years.

And finally, to my daughter Neelambari, who has been my friend, confidante and, in more recent years, co-performer, I want to say that the nuances of performance and its relationship to politics which we have discussed at length have found their way into this book in several ways. She has also put up with my absences and preoccupations patiently. It is the wonderful response of her generation of young people to the IPTA repertoire and its interpretation in contemporary times that has made this project really worthwhile.

New Delhi SUMANGALA DAMODARAN
December 2016

Glossary of Musical Terms

accent: an emphasis placed on a particular note or set of notes, either as a result of its context or specifically indicated by an accent mark

art song: a vocal music composition, usually written for one voice, with piano accompaniment, and usually in the classical art music tradition

atonal: avoidance of traditional musical tonality, organized without reference to a key

balalaika: a Russian stringed musical instrument with a characteristic triangular body and three strings

cantata: a work for voice or voices and instruments of the baroque era

chamber works: musical works that are composed for a small group of instruments, traditionally a group that could fit in a palace chamber or a large room.

chromatic scale: musical scale with twelve pitches, each a semitone above or below another

chromaticism: a compositional technique interspersing the primary pitches and chords with other pitches of the chromatic scale

contrafacta: the substitution of one text for another without substantial change to the music in vocal music

contrary motions: when two voices move in opposite directions

counterpoint: the technique of setting, writing or playing a melody or melodies in conjunction with another according to fixed rules

dissonance: a mingling of discordant musical notes, a lack of harmony

equal temperament: a system of tuning in which every pair of adjacent notes is separated by the same interval

formalism: the concept that a composition's meaning is entirely determined by its form and that meaning in music is primarily intellectual

forte: an indication or dynamic in music that means a particular part of a song is meant to be played strongly and louder. The other basic dynamic is 'piano', which refers to playing music softly and quietly

foxtrot: a ballroom dance having an uneven rhythm with alternative slow and quick steps

functional harmony: tonal harmony that provides a way of moving to and from a tonic note in an orderly fashion

harmony: the simultaneous sounding of three or more notes making up what are called chords, which reflect a sonic relationship with each other

homophonic: having one sound or line of melody at a time that is played by multiple instruments at the same time, or the movement of accompanying parts in the same rhythm as the melody

mode: a type of scale, coupled with a set of characteristic melodic behaviours

musical movement: a movement is a self-contained part of a musical composition or musical form. While individual or selected movements from a composition are sometimes performed separately, a performance of the complete work requires all the movements to be performed in succession

ostinato: a continually repeated musical phrase or rhythm

pentatonic scale: a musical scale with five notes per octave

strophic: the term applied to songs in which all verses or stanzas of the text are sung to the same music

syllabic text markings: where each syllable of a word is broken up and assigned to an individual note

symphony: an elaborate musical composition for a full orchestra with several movements

thumri: a light romantic and/or devotional form of Hindustani classical music

tone clusters: a musical chord comprising at least three adjacent tones in a scale

twelve tone scale: a scale where all twelve notes of the chromatic scale are sounded as often as one another in a piece of music while preventing the emphasis of any one note

Prologue

A young woman, Swatantrata, stands in front of a microphone facing a mass gathering of more than 80,000 peasants from the Punjab in Lahore, some time in 1943. She sings a *Heer*, a traditional ballad of northwestern India, which relates the story of a young girl from faraway Bengal who has lost her home and family to the ravages of a terrible famine. The lyrics of the *Heer*, written by Sheila Bhatia, a prominent songwriter of the left cultural movement in Lahore at the time, are as follows:

kinu phol dassan dukh dard saiyon
mera rog tan la ilaaj disse
kar kaat sain kannu chhutthe maittho
kyun sawaal ai bina jawaab disse

To whom can I tell my sad story?
Who can cure me of my malady?
I have lost my home and family:
Who can answer my innumerable questions?

Interestingly, this particular *Heer* did not recount a local story, as would appear from the customary description of the centuries-old love story of Heer–Ranjha. Instead it used a local, indigenous form to ask for solidarity from peasants in the Punjab towards peasants in Bengal. The *Heer*, an evocative lament for things lost, appealed for comradeship based on new solidarities between peasantries, between people across long distances who shared their opposition to colonialism.

The gathering had been organized by the All India Kisan Sabha (peasants' organization) that worked closely with the Communist Party of India (CPI) to generate awareness about the devastating Bengal famine. The programme on that day consisted of songs and speeches by communist and peasant leaders, many of whom were underground and appeared in public only briefly during the rally. Swatantrata's powerful singing was riveting and served a purpose: it drew attention away from the activity going on backstage – the arrival and departure of 'underground' speakers who ran the risk of being arrested, and who therefore become 'visible' only when they were ready to address the gathering. Many decades later Swatantrata recalled how the *Heer* had reduced large numbers in the audience to tears; in fact some of the peasants, thinking she had sung her own story, offered her food and shelter when they met her in the streets of Lahore the next day.[1] Sheila Bhatia, who later moved to Delhi and became a prominent theatre person, became well known for using the many forms of the indigenous *Heer* in her theatre productions.

Some time in the 1940s, the Bengali playwright and song collector Bijon Bhattacharya wrote a musical play, *Jeeyan Kanya*, in which he used a number of folk songs, all related to snake cults and snake-charming, that he had collected from different parts of Bengal. The songs were reproduced as they were and constituted an exercise in 'presenting' lost indigenous song traditions to wider audiences, but they were put together in a way that constituted the script and storyline of a play. The play told the story of two tribal clans at war with each other, and extensively used imagery from the snake-myth traditions of Bengal and neighbouring areas. Unfamiliar to those living in Calcutta, the collection of songs displayed a wide diversity of dialects, instrumentation and also modes of singing. In 1954, Hemanta Mukherjee, singer–composer and former cultural activist from Bengal, composed music for a Hindi film produced in Bombay titled *Nagin* (Snakewoman), which adapted tunes from *Jeeyan Kanya*. It was not only Hemanta Mukherjee who shot to fame with his compositions and his own singing for the film, but the film also went on, subsequently, to create some of the iconic snake-myth idioms of popular Indian cinema.[2]

hoi hoi hoi japan oi
aisho roheem ai rohomaan
aisho jogesh ai re poraan
gnaaye joto hindu musalmaan
toyyar raakho shob hothiyaar
chaaku laathi chora boksha
dhonuk boti shokto haathe
dhoro haathe dhoro hothiyaar

inquilab zindabad
bolo dushman ho barbaad
hoi hoi hoi japan oi

Come forth, Raheem and Rahman,
Come, o Jogesh and Poraan,
Come, all Hindus and Musalmans of the village,
Keep all your weapons ready:
Knives, lathis, daggers and boxes.
Hold the bow and the cutting knife in your strong hands,
Hold the weapons in your strong hands,
Long live the revolution!
Let the enemy be defeated!

Benoy Roy, a prolific songwriter from Bengal, wrote this anti-fascist song for a play in the early 1940s. Composed as a fast-paced marching song with hard drum-beats and strident singing, it symbolized the fear of Japan's imperialist motives in Asia and its alliance with fascism during the Second World War.

The futility of war and the contradiction of Indians fighting in what was termed an imperialist war, even as their country was ravaged by British colonialism, was described poignantly by Makhdoom Mohiuddin, Urdu poet and composer from Hyderabad:

jaane waale sipahi se poochho
woh kahaan ja raha hai

kaun dukhiya hai jo gaa rahi hai
bhookhe bachchon ko behla rahi hai
laash jalne ki boo aa rahi hai
zindagi hai ki chilla rahi hai

Ask the departing soldier,
Where is he headed, where is he going?

Who is that woman who cries,
Soothing her hungry children?
Can you hear life cry out amidst the stench of burnt bodies?

When liberation from British rule became a reality, Prem Dhawan, a songwriter–singer from Punjab who was living in Bombay at the time, wrote an exuberant song, '*Jhoom jhoom ke naacho aaj*', in celebration:

jhoom jhoom ke naacho aaj, naacho aaj
gao khushi ke geet
jhooth ki aakhir haar hui, haar hui
sach ki aakhir jeet

Swing and dance away today,
Sing a song of happiness.
Falsehood has finally been defeated.
Truth has prevailed after all.

The song's last verse, representing the hope that freedom would bring an end to hunger and unemployment, a hope that national liberation would bring forth a socialist future, runs as follows:

aaj se in sundar kheton mein
bhookh na ugne paaye
factoriyon mein mandaraaye na
bekari ke saaye
desh ka ye dhan daulat ye hai
saari qaum ki poonji
aaj kisi ke aage koi daaman na phailaye re

May hunger no longer sprout in these beautiful fields,
May there be no unemployment in these factories,
The wealth of this nation belongs to all,
May no one have to beg anyone else for anything.

The same Prem Dhawan, in lines written following the violence during the partition of British India, was to lament the kind of freedom that had been won:

basti basti maut ka dera
gali gali shamshaan
dharti lahu luhaan hai saari dharti lahu luhaan
arson bandookon ka pehra
sangeenon ka raaj
kaisa ye sauraj, kaisa ye sauraj
tum suno suno tum suno suno
suno hind ke rehne waalon
suno suno

Death stalks every locality,
Each street is a cemetery.
The earth is bloody, bloody is the earth.
We are surrounded by guns,
It is the rule of the bayonets.
What freedom have we got, what kind of freedom?
Listen, o countrymen,
Listen, all those who live in Hind.

Less than a decade later, in 1956, the Urdu poet Sahir Ludhianvi wrote '*Woh subah kabhi to aayegi*' ('That dawn will arrive some day'), when social transformation still appeared far away, when the post-independence state had shown itself to be repressive on several occasions and some part of the dream already had been shattered.

manhoos samaaji dhaanchon mein
jab zulm na paale jaayenge
jab haath na kaate jaayenge
jab sar na uchlaale jaayenge
jailon ke bina is duniya ki
sarkar chalaayi jaayegi
woh subah kabhi toh aayegi
woh subah kabhi toh aayegi

When society will no longer breed oppression,
When arms will no longer be cut off and no heads will roll,
When governments will no longer need prisons to rule,
That dawn surely will arrive one day.
That dawn surely will arrive one day.

The songs mentioned above were written and composed, as is evident from their description, between 1940 and 1960, two out of three crucial decades from the 1930s that marked a 'transitionary' period from colonialism to independence in Indian history. As the examples of the songs indicate, this transitionary period saw the cultural expression of a very wide range of political sentiments and positions concerning imperialism, fascism, nationalism and social transformation in India. Composed and performed in the tradition of the Indian People's Theatre Association (IPTA), a cultural organization aligned with the left political movement, these songs – along with hundreds of other songs written and performed in different parts of the country during this period – played a crucial role in articulating the role of culture, and specifically music, *in* and *as* politics in the country. Although formally set up as an organization in 1943, the IPTA's mandate and agenda were shaped from the 1930s onwards, when cultural and literary expression in politics took several forms – an important example was the Progressive Writers' Association (PWA), established in 1936.

The IPTA came into existence at a time when the left-wing strand of the political movement for national liberation from colonial rule, under the leadership of the CPI, had taken a position that set it apart in contrast from the mainstream nationalist movement. The gathering momentum towards decolonization needed to be accelerated, according to the assessment of the CPI, but within an understanding of class exploitation in India, and also recognizing the dangers from fascism and the need to arrest its growth. The possibilities for revolutionary transformation in India appeared immense and decolonization was just the precondition for that, even as there was a need for this to happen in an atmosphere of international solidarity of working-class movements.

The setting up of the IPTA and other such organizations was a response to a perceived need for new aesthetic forms that represented the people while distinguishing themselves from the cultural traditions of the mainstream nationalist movement, on the one hand, and commercial theatre, on the other. This 'people's art and theatre' attempted to reflect and respond to the travails of a colonized nation, as well as to the specifics of the multilayered oppression of the common people in the colonial and immediate post-colonial contexts. The IPTA aimed to assimilate and build upon spontaneous cultural responses to political events, to consciously bring aesthetics to bear on politics in theatre, music, dance, art and photography. The formation of the IPTA thus marked a formal adoption of the idea that music, dance, theatre and art would be used for conscious articulation of protest and resistance, and this was one of the early, if not the first, such attempts in India. It was the first attempt, also, to define a national-level movement which, in turn, would link up with anti-fascist and anti-imperialist movements on a world scale, along with the PWA.

Across the country, a large number of the best-known artists of the time became part of the IPTA, attempting to produce alternative aesthetic creations across diverse media.[3] The historical conjuncture of the transition from colonial to post-colonial regimes brought together a diverse range of artists quite spontaneously, even as the formal organizing, and the forging of resistances and alliances took place at the behest of the CPI. The conjuncture, seen as presenting an urgency that was perhaps unprecedented, was also full of possibilities: of freedom from colonial rule at the least, but also of social emancipation and transformation.

Regional and provincial branches of the IPTA were formed, all engaged in the creation of this alternative aesthetic. In some states, such as Andhra Pradesh and Kerala, other political cultural organizations – the Kerala People's Arts Club (KPAC) and the Praja Natya Mandali (PNM) – were formed, even if a few years later, which aligned themselves with the IPTA. While the PNM was formed in 1943, the same year as the IPTA, the KPAC came into existence only in 1951.

In all these formations, it was perhaps for the first time that large cultural squads consisting of dancers, musicians, actors, artists and photographers responded in diverse ways to political issues and events, the forms ranging from plays to dance-dramas to songs to dances to storytelling and much more. I refer to this set of organizations as the *IPTA tradition*, which includes the IPTA itself in its national and regional versions, as well as others like the PNM and the KPAC that aligned themselves with the IPTA.

Music constituted a significant aspect of the IPTA tradition's intervention, although this aspect was never studied or documented either by the left movement or by historians. In fact, work on the left cultural movement has been scanty and, where it exists, very specifically focused – becoming region-, language- or form-specific – not allowing for an overall or comprehensive view.[4] The left movement's, or, more specifically, the left cultural movement's, own documentation and analysis of the tradition have been sparse.[5] Further, within the available work on the IPTA, there is a complete absence of scholarship on music – what did get documented and analysed, even if only to a limited extent, were the theatre productions; these studies essentially looked at the IPTA, quite literally, as a theatre organization. As a result, hardly any evidence of the IPTA's vast musical repertoire is available publicly, let alone any analysis of the debates or processes that went into the creation of music in a most vibrant period that lasted from the few years preceding its formation until the late 1950s.

This book attempts to fill that gap in a limited way – it is about the IPTA tradition's music in a national as well as specific regional contexts, located within the overall cultural and political climate of the transitionary period in India, as well as in the context of the shaping of a radical imaginary in many parts of the world from the beginning of the twentieth century. It is the culmination of an archiving-cum-documentation project of the IPTA tradition's music that I undertook between 2006–07 and 2009.

It arose out of my own experience of singing protest songs as part of the group Parcham on a regular basis between 1983 and 1990, and sporadically later on. Formed in the post-Emergency period, along with the street theatre group Jana Natya Manch (Janam), Parcham's repertoire consisted of many IPTA songs, notably '*Tu zinda hai, tu zindagi ki jeet mein yaqin kar*' (You are alive, have faith in the victory of life), '*Aman ke hum rakhwaale*' (We are the keepers of the peace), '*Jaaga re jaaga re jaaga saara sansaar*' (The whole world has awakened), to name a few. Most of these songs were what I refer to as 'stereotypical' protest songs, which means they displayed a certain grammar, were rendered in a way that could be considered directly political with their lyrics as well as tunes being overtly mobilizational and exhortatory, and were typically collectively sung. One of the songs from Parcham's repertoire, sung from 1984 onwards, was '*Jaane waale sipaahi se poochho*' (Ask the departing soldier), written and composed by Makhdoom Mohiuddin, which defied the stereotype in that it had a lilting tune, it appealed strongly in emotional terms, it was more amenable to being sung primarily solo, and it did not display the grammar of a directly mobilizational political song. The song was written during the Second World War, when poor Indians were being conscripted into the British army, and it speaks of the miserable conditions at home while soldiers were being sent off to fight a foreign war.

Revived by Parcham during the days of violence perpetrated by leaders and members of the Congress party against the Sikh community following the assassination of Indira Gandhi, '*Jaane waale sipaahi se poochho*' revealed to me the cathartic power of an evocative song from an earlier period in history that questioned the meaningless violence inflicted by war in a poor country. Beginning with the peace campaigns in 1984, the song became very popular; and more than two decades later I set out in search of more songs that too, probably, had been forgotten over time.

I began the project of unearthing the IPTA tradition's musical repertoire and writing this book primarily led by my sensibilities and experiences as a performer. Having had no formal training in the methodologies or conceptual frameworks of history or cultural studies, which are the two disciplinary areas that this work trespasses into, it is bound to have flaws – for which I take full responsibility. I hope I have been able to put across some snippets of a momentous period in India's history and in the history of radical left-wing politics in the world, and to pay tribute to the creativity of some amazing artists and political activists of that period.

Notes

1 The description of the mass gathering, the number of people who attended it, its purpose and the structure of the programme are from my interviews of Swatantrata Prakash in 2007. Subsequently, following up on the evocative quality of the composition, it became apparent that this was no routine appeal for solidarity; underpinning the structure of the melody was a political appeal that went far beyond solidarity, reflecting the political relationship between colonial Punjab and Bengal in the last few years of colonial rule, and the role of the left in campaigning for the transfer of foodgrains from Punjab to Bengal. The *Heer*, a musical text that naturally conveyed anguish and appeal, was harnessed to convey the sense of helplessness of the situation.

2 Bijon Bhattacharya's *Jeeyan Kanya* was reportedly performed only once in 1946. Much later, some time in the 1960s, it was put together for another performance with different actors; it was then that the songs were recorded.

3 The list of eminent people from the cultural world who joined the IPTA, for long or short periods, is long. It is considered a significant fact of 'lineage' in popular cultural formations, in music, cinema and literature, in post-independent India.

4 For example, the works that are known and quoted are Bhattacharya (1971), Bharucha (1990), Bhatia (2004), Pradhan (1979; 1982; 1985). Of these, the first three are based on theatre, whereas the last three are the most comprehensive collection of documents available to date.

5 An exception to this has been the volumes by Sudhi Pradhan, which, as mentioned earlier, are a painstakingly put together collection of documents for the period 1935–64.

Introduction

The period from the mid-thirties to the end of the fifties of the twentieth century in India saw the cultural expression of a very wide range of political sentiments and positions around imperialism, fascism, nationalism and social transformation. It was a period that covered a crucial transitional phase, from colonialism to a post-colonial context.[1] This transitional period in India also coincided with a vibrant radical ethos in many other parts of the world where, among numerous political issues, the aesthetics–politics relationship came to be articulated and debated in unprecedented ways.[2] In India, although social issues had been addressed in writing and theatre through the nineteenth and early twentieth century,[3] expectations of the possibilities of transformation brought about a tremendous sense of urgency in artistic expression during the period of transition – and by the 1930s such spontaneous expression exploded, even before formal organization for such activity had begun.

The first two decades of the Indian People's Theatre Association (IPTA), the 1940s and 50s, thus have to be understood not only against the background of the vibrant 1930s, in terms of the internal conditions under British rule, the anti-colonial struggle and the factors governing the growth of the left movement within India during and after the colonial period, but also in the context of international developments within left movements, the characteristics and contradictions of nationalist anti-colonial struggles in other parts of the world, the threats from fascism and the conditions created by the two world wars. The reasons for and the manner of using culture for political mobilization were influenced, obviously, by all these factors.

The transition period in India pulsated with possibilities, situated as it was in the particular historical conjuncture that the early twentieth century presented;

and in the literary and cultural fields, a radical impulse came to shape the world of representation.[4] Fuelled by a leftward turn in politics and culture, it consisted of conceptualizing an alternative nationalism, and a unique and unprecedented internationalism, both of which were departures from mainstream anti-colonial political positions. In the literary and cultural fields this radicalization was prominent, even if the number of people involved were only a 'fraction'.[5] This fraction started emerging in different parts of the country from the late 1920s, sometimes initiating, sometimes responding to and sometimes actively participating in mass upsurges and agitations, around which the radical cultural turn was beginning to be imagined and expressed.

Echoing Priyamvada Gopal (2005), I argue that the period from the early 1930s to the years immediately after independence in India reflected the *perception* that radical endeavours and dreams were within the realm of the possible, and the literary and cultural fronts that were constituted – represented most prominently by the Progressive Writers' Association (PWA), the IPTA and their variants – made this dream central to their agenda.

This book is about the music produced as part of the IPTA tradition in the 1940s and 1950s, but it locates its ideological and creative dimensions on a continuum from the late 1920s to particularly the 1930s. It must be clarified that this is not an analysis of a complete archive of the IPTA tradition's music, as no such archive exists, nor is it a history of the music. Thus, although such a history needs to be written in its own right, this book examines specific questions that are relevant to understand the relationship between aesthetics and politics through this tradition of protest music. It also attempts to recover a critical part of the cultural history of the 1940s and 50s through an analysis of the contexts, circumstances and processes of creation of the music.

Protest Song

Apart from the historical relevance of the archive, such as the one this project is based on, and of a tradition such as the IPTA's, there are other compelling reasons for my interest in protest music *per se*. The first reason arises, as mentioned at the outset, against the stereotypes that have existed, certainly in more recent decades in India, about protest music having a typically standardized structure – for example, sounding agitational and mobilizational; conveying political messages stridently through lyrics, tunes and tempo; and mostly being sung by a collective – and perhaps for these reasons, not being good enough music. This stereotype has resulted, on the one hand, in activist musicians as well as political formations not considering songs as protest songs unless they conform to the standardized stereotype with respect to form and content, and, on the other hand, non-activist musicians dismissing protest music as 'mere sloganeering'. From a perusal of the IPTA tradition's music, it is possible to understand protest music as a highly varied and historically evolved kind of music, and to engage with the stereotypical protest song as being only a particular type within this larger genre. It is possible to argue for the legitimacy of protest music as music meriting analysis on its own terms, i.e. as music. This is a primary objective of this book.

The second reason for focusing on protest music comes from looking at music as social text, with the structure and grammar of music enabling us to draw inferences about the contexts of its creation. Especially in societies where music is not usually written down or notated formally, even when music is created with an explicit social purpose, like protest music, the objectives of creation and the nuances of particular forms that are used have to be understood from within the music itself. In this case, the available archive, incomplete as it is, has been compiled through a diverse array of modes and materials, such as interviews with artists, anecdotes, personal stories, old recordings and songbooks. The songs themselves, often reconstructed from incomplete or damaged recordings, have acted as a text from which it is possible, along with the recollections and anecdotes, to read back into historical events as well as into fascinating debates on culture and politics. In this sense the 'aural archive', especially in the absence of formal documentation, serves as a rich corpus of concepts that allow us to understand, in this case, the relationship between music and politics in a crucial period of India's history.

Third, analysing the IPTA tradition's music led me to try and understand it in the context of radical left-wing politics of the first half of the twentieth century, when the relationship between aesthetics and politics was debated vigorously in different parts of the world, both in Euro–America and closer home, for example, in East Asia and Southeast Asia. It became apparent that musicians of the IPTA tradition engaged with questions that were varied as well as fundamental issues of representation in the music–politics relationship, even if the debates and conceptualizations were not as well laid-out and documented as elsewhere in the world. More specifically, it became apparent that particular questions, even if their expression was through creative practice rather than in theory, highlighted the nuances of the role of music in societal change quite distinctly from the Euro–American cases, including that of the Soviet Union. By turning back to this distinctiveness, notably with respect to tradition, in the approaches to nationalism, modernism, the idea of the 'indigenous' and so on (shared, perhaps, with other colonized or less developed countries in Asia, Africa and Latin America), this book hopes to highlight that the radical project of the first half of the twentieth century was not only varied and geographically dispersed, but also that it threw up fundamental questions through these non-metropolitan experiences.[6] As Priyamvada Gopal has done in the case of the literature of the PWA, it is hoped that the analysis here of the musical repertoire in the IPTA tradition can help 'reconstellate key concerns' in the relationship between music and politics.[7]

Fourth, protest music in the period that we are addressing here had an interesting relationship with notions of 'popular culture', as the idea of the popular was played out in interesting ways in the context of early twentieth-century modernity and in the formative years of the Indian nation. Not only did the conception of what constituted protest music require an interrogation and explication of the music of the 'popular classes', in a Gramscian sense, but the IPTA tradition's musical forays and experiments significantly impacted the commercial arena, in this sense playing a role in shaping commercial mainstream culture too, even when standing in ideological opposition to it. This book, it is hoped, will highlight the ways in which the engagement with the idea of the popular happened as part of the radical imaginary through structures and processes of music-making, and, in this sense, will help reclaim the notion of 'popular music' from a mere focus on the market.

I use the idea of a *radical impulse* to describe the interplay of considerations that went into the crafting of a radical left-wing aesthetic in the first half of the twentieth century, and which may be seen to have informed the Indian experience substantially. The idea of a radical impulse and its role in shaping popular culture, as well as the conceptual framework for presenting *protest music as a certain kind of popular music*, are presented here. Through these two ideas, I interrogate the nuances of the relationship between music and politics.

The Popular

The shaping of what is referred to as 'popular culture' or the 'public sphere' in the contemporary world has taken place through many impulses, of which the *radical impulse* has been a critical one in many parts of the world. I use the term popular culture in a sense much wider than it has been used in recent times, employing the Gramscian idea of the culture of the 'popular classes' or 'the people', the production and consumption of which happens on a terrain that Stuart Hall referred to as 'the double movement of containment and resistance'.[8]

To elaborate, it has been customary in analyses of popular culture to attribute the adjective 'popular' to consumption by large numbers of people, i.e.

consumption mediated through technology and the commercial system. Popular cinema, thus, usually refers to mainstream commercial cinema, and popular music refers to commercial music.[9] In the wider connotation of popular culture that I am alluding to here, the range of what constitutes it encompasses the commonly used notion centering on the commercial aspect or a culture based on the mass market, and goes beyond it to encompass those cultural forms that 'have their roots in the social and material conditions of ordinary people'.[10] It thus allows for a focus not just on consumption by large numbers of people, but also on the production of cultural forms by ordinary people. Structures of power assert and establish hegemonic cultural forms through control and transformation in particular dominant forms, but these also contain elements of identification and recognition of forms that fall outside the sphere of the dominant and belong to the popular sphere. In this range, the cultural forms that are observed at any point of time reflect a continuous and uneven struggle by dominant culture to enclose and confine, with continuously emerging points of resistance to the attempts to dominate. The terrain of the popular, from this wide perspective, is not only a site where power is affirmed, but also a site of opposition. The actual practice of popular culture moves in the terrain of what Gramsci referred to as a 'compromise equilibrium'.[11]

This conception adds additional conceptual layers to a narrow understanding of the popular by emphasizing diversities in the systems that seek to establish control or where hegemonic power is affirmed and consolidated, and to understanding resistance not only as emerging spontaneously from but also as organized resistance through cultural movements representing the 'popular classes'. Thus, dominant and hegemonic structures themselves exhibit diversity and multiple influences, including those from 'the people'. Modes of opposition to these dominant structures, in turn, might happen through the non-organized expression or sheer existence of varied cultures of 'the people', or, in fact, might be formally organized through movements that represent 'the people'.

This conceptualization enables an understanding of the impact of organized cultural movements, through the creation of particular kinds of images, on extended 'popular audiences'. It also enables an understanding of processes of cooption of hitherto oppositional movements by dominant hegemonic constellations, such as in many post-colonial contexts, and the resistance to them, generating new kinds of oppositional cultures. It is in drawing out the nuances of the 'double movement of containment and resistance' that the radical impulse and its impact on popular culture can be understood.

Given such a notion of popular culture, I argue that a radical imaginary expressed through the arts was a crucial component that shaped popular culture from the beginning of the twentieth century. The importance of a cultural tradition such as the IPTA's has to be understood as part of a range of similar initiatives in different parts of the world that created this radical impulse.

The Radical Impulse

The rise of political movements and political upheavals have provoked artistic responses, making art a fundamental medium for expressing politics. Radical political movements, especially from the beginning of the twentieth century, provided the context within which artistic expression threw up what I characterize as a radical impulse, involving a combination of considerations, both purely aesthetic and political, that aimed to respond to and represent the times.[12] In doing so, the boundaries of artistic expression were consciously interrogated and pushed towards bringing out multiple interpretations of the idea of the 'radical'. While various elements of what might constitute a radical aesthetic can be found, over the ages, to arise in response to social and political movements, the conscious organization of such ideas into artistic or cultural movements has been reported only from the beginning of the twentieth century. The radical impulse that I define here is a historically specific one and does not allude to a 'universal' impulse, such as the 'utopian' impulse set out by Ernst Bloch.[13] However, even if defined in specific historical terms and circumscribed by particular historical circumstances, I try to draw out the nuances of processes that create a radical imaginary in the arts, which extend beyond the specificities of the historical period under consideration.

The radical impulse emerged in a particular historical conjuncture that the early twentieth century presented: the breaking out of the First World War and the Great Depression of the late 1920s and 30s, signalling a deep crisis in capitalism; the success of the Bolshevik Revolution and growing hopes from socialism; the growth of working-class movements and of an emancipatory socialist consciousness in different parts of the world; the radicalization of nationalist ideas in colonized countries and of the intelligentsia in different countries. The radical impulse, signified by a leftward turn in politics and culture, consisted in conceptualizing an alternative nationalism, and a unique and unprecedented internationalism, both of which were departures from mainstream nationalist positions, and which consisted in going beyond nationalism and towards substantial emancipation. It was also rooted in the need to establish the idea of 'the people' or 'the ordinary person' as a legitimate subject of history and art.

This impulse generated remarkable plurality as well as striking similarities of experience and responses in cultural terms. By making an emancipatory agenda possible after the revolution in the Soviet Union and through an alignment of such movements with the fight against colonialism, the radical turn brought about sweeping changes in the world of artistic expression which shaped anti-colonial movements, post-colonial cultural dispensations and critiques of such dispensations as well. It left a distinct mark on the mass media and on everyday forms of artistic expression, vital components of what constitutes popular culture.

Three sets of engagements characterized the radical impulse in cultural terms.

The idea of 'the people' as legitimate subjects of art

From the early decades of the twentieth century an iconography of 'the people' developed in various parts of the world, characterizing a radical imaginary that argued influentially for the legitimacy of a new subject, the ordinary person and his/her right to be accepted as a human being. The picture of the ordinary person was wide-ranging with artists and activists recovering oral histories and traditions; painters depicting scenes of everyday life; writers dabbling in realist literature; musicians recovering, composing and singing the music of the everyday; and photographers becoming preoccupied with capturing average citizens. This iconography of the 'people' was distinctive in the following respects: first, it was varied within and between locations in different parts of the world, even as there were threads that bound them together; second, it had to contend with different kinds of dominant iconographies and established structures; third, this diversity and oppositional positioning was to develop a peculiar, anxious relationship with mainstream culture in colonial countries. All these aspects were to influence popular culture substantially in the decades to come.

While this effort at creating a 'people's theatre', 'people's music' and 'people's art' originated in the 1920s, by the 1930s it had already become a kind of crusade. A wide variety may be seen in notions of the 'people' across different parts of the world: why and how they were to be represented and what 'people's art' was. For instance, there was a certain notion of the 'people' derived from the fact of colonialism and its destruction of indigenous cultures. So, from uncovering indigenous traditions, to the sharing of such traditions between different regions in creating a larger geographical imagination, to working with different regional traditions to create hybrids in the course of translocal solidarities, the radical artists sought to 'bring back' the culture of the people, which Denning refers to as the 'documentary aesthetic'.[14]

A critical engagement with the terrain of the 'nation'

The radical cultural project, especially in the colonies, had to contend with nationalism and the need to 'imagine communities', as Benedict Anderson was to argue influentially. This nationalism 'from below' often involved great discomfort with mainstream conceptualizations, even as the politics of anti-colonialism rendered the need to inhabit nationalism's cultural realm a real, albeit tense one. The discomfort, which was fuelled by a radical emancipatory politics, consisted of a self-critical and self-reflexive nationalism, something that did not necessarily project the 'glory' of cultures but in fact questioned mores and traditions in their own societies, even as it tried to construct an identity for the nation. Thus, extending from Japan, China, Korea and India in Asia, to Mexico and other Latin American countries, nationalist iconographies from below threw up images of exploitative conditions in colonial and feudal societies, and of the commonalities across such exploitative situations binding people together in imagining the nation.

This, in turn, resulted in foregrounding the idea of the 'radical' or a transformatory agenda within nationalism, and also in raising questions of 'nationality' inside the national territory. Further, as I have already mentioned, hitherto unexplored solidarities between the 'real, unrepresented and marginalized people' which went beyond local contexts necessitated the cultural representation of such 'horizontal comradeships' that also allowed for an imagining of the nation as a common identification in a way that departed from the norm. In the process of such horizontal collective identifications and imaginings, a variety of ways in which the indigenous traditions of 'the people' could be recovered, reproduced, transformed and represented in terms of form, space and kinds of audience became grounds for experimentation. This was buttressed by arguments for the need to recover and reconfigure traditions that had been distorted by colonialism and commercial theatre. This critique, in fact, led to the visualizing of several collectivities based on class (workers and peasants) or social categories (such as the indigenous people in Latin America, dalits and adivasis in India), on the one hand, and those that transcended physical boundaries of region and nation, on the other. Thus, nationalism from below went along with internationalisms based on social location as well as common histories of exploitation under colonialism. The latter factor, again, contradicted mainstream nationalist ideas based on territoriality and exclusivity, generating potential and actual tensions.

In imagining these multiple nationalisms from below, the radical discourse was investigating the notion of the 'national–popular', thus engaging critically with the 'usable past',[15] whether classical or indigenous. This is important to remember, because the notion of the 'usable' past was to become critical in creating genres of popular culture then as well as in more contemporary times. In the post-colonial period, some of these inclusive processes and experiments got appropriated as well as standardized, emerging as blueprints for the representation of multiple identities in the context of the nation and also as forms representing popular culture, mediated through state patronage and the market.

The urgency of the project for freedom, and of emancipation and social transformation

By bringing various notions of the 'people' to the forefront in cultural expression, and in extending the idea of the 'nation' to account for and represent cultural differences and also cross borders, the radical cultural project was setting out a transformatory agenda that called for emancipation from various kinds of exploitation, national freedom being only a beginning towards that. For national movements, it set up the task of creating post-colonial dispensations that would embody this comprehensive emancipatory agenda. It was this 'radical–popular' ethic that would urge the translation of a radical ethic into a concrete system of rights, which was to throw up images of 'false freedom', of repression and marginalization of radical expression, and of a betrayal of commitment to a radical agenda – images that were to significantly impact cultural expression.

Understanding the aesthetics of the radical impulse across different experiences in the period that concerns this book brings forth the following points. First, colonialism and underdevelopment, diversity and difference generate autonomous issues and questions to do with representation, voice and form, which the radical 'fraction' and artists within it have had to contend with. Historical and sociological similarities necessitate and describe aesthetic 'acuities' which generate patterns that connect cultures via the radical aesthetic. Aesthetic acuity is a combination of aesthetic sensibilities that accrue in a person by virtue of his/her occupying a particular or many aesthetic constellations, each of which is constituted by specific symbols, grammar and history, and which influence creativity and responses.[16] In other words, it refers to the formed and unformed elements and bits that constitute an artist's universe of creativity, which allow him/her to navigate their art or craft. An artist may be at the confluence of many such constellations.

Second, especially in ex-colonial countries, the post-colonial dispensations actively showcase and coopt the diversity of this radical aesthetic, often repressing the potential of the radical. Third, the 'radical impulse' also faces numerous challenges from within, having to do with rigidity of interpretation, organizational structures and artistic autonomy, which in turn often again repress the potential of the radical. Fourth, what is commonly perceived as popular culture, i.e. forms which are produced for and consumed by newly emerging and constantly changing audiences, is influenced strongly by the conceptions and contradictions thrown up by the radical imaginary, or the 'radical–popular'.

How did the radical impulse specifically play out in music? What were the musicians as well as the political movements they were a part of attempting to do through creating resistance/protest music? I argue below that a conscious process of intermediation between the processes of production and consumption of music was crucial following the political and cultural movements' need to represent 'the people', and protest music thus emerged as a form of *popular* music. This process of intermediation involved the creation of new audiences and shaping them, and through this process of 'popular-ization', the world of representation was shaped substantially too.

Protest Music as Popular Music

Despite the recognition of the social importance of music, and the knowledge that social structures and developments are reflected in varied ways in musical structures, music has not been given a fair hearing in the social sciences. If there has been little systematic investigation of the relationship of music to culture or society as a whole, even less effort has been expended on a systematic investigation of the interrelations between music and politics or, more specifically, music and protest. The category of protest music, thus, has been subjected to only limited analysis as a musical category alone, despite there being a whole range of work on particular kinds of music that have embodied protest, consciously or unconsciously, in different parts of the world.

The lack of a systematic analysis of protest music is reflective of pre-set hierarchies assumed between 'high' and 'low' or *popular* music, where such categories are employed to judge whether particular kinds of music may be considered seriously or worthy of analysis. It has been highlighted by scholars in the field of popular music studies that the little attention given to and in fact the denigration of popular music have been important features of conventional musical scholarship from the west.[17] Largely coming from the European art music tradition, dating to the early part of the nineteenth century, the embeddedness of music in social processes is itself actively denied because it is seen to distort the tonal qualities of 'good' music and interfere with the ability of music to appeal to 'higher' human sensibilities.[18] In the dominant western musicological framework, therefore, the tendency to associate structured and superior listening with the autonomy of musical processes from history or society gets reflected in the need to attribute the labels of 'high' and 'low' to different kinds of music. In fact, even a scholar like Adorno, who argued that all music should be viewed as a distinct field of activity that can only be understood within larger social processes, uses a framework rooted in the discourse of 'high culture' to critique popular music.[19] Many forms of popular music, such as jazz, rock, rap and so on, which have contained within their history and practice strong elements of protest, have been dismissed as inferior music and as often dangerous from such a perspective, using ostensibly objective criteria of structure, style, skills and techniques. This music is often belittled as not worthy to be considered music 'on its own terms'.

Further, as stated earlier, there is a stereotyping of what protest music is from the point of view of critics as well as political activists, with the 'typical' protest song ostensibly containing features such as easy reproducibility, collective forms of rendering, and easily recognizable mobilizational and agitational formats. In practice, however, protest through music historically has seen the adoption of extremely diverse forms across cultures, and the actual range and depth of this category of music is extensive. It is difficult, therefore, to arrive at a simple set of principles that constitute the category of protest music.

The work that does exist, even if it is remarkably scanty in comparison to actual practice and experience, has two characteristics. First, the conceptual analysis is based on Euro–American experiences with protest genres, both as part of and outside formal political movements. Second, the focus of scholarly work has to a large extent been on individual genres and their use in politics.[20] While the insights from all such work are valuable in locating the emergence of or engagement with specific genres of music in expressing political positions or locating their politics historically, a conceptual framework that encompasses the diversity of experience and yet specifies the basic principles around which the relationship between music and protest can be understood, is yet to be worked out.

I present here an analytical framework for understanding protest music as popular music through the social and political processes that its creation reflects and impacts, keeping in mind diverse contexts, but also accommodating the particularities of societies such as India where oral, aural and other non-written transmissions play a major role in the dissemination of music.

It has been customary in standard analyses of musical forms to talk about categories or genres such as folk, art, popular, traditional and modern. Often, these kinds of classifications tend to be ethnocentric and based on 'socioeconomic and cultural arrogance',[21] with serious value judgements about the superiority of music from familiar contexts and where, by implication, 'other' contexts of musics are described as inferior.[22] Further, notions of 'high' and 'low' music, internal to specific social contexts, have often carried similar subjectivities and otherings that tend to be more about power than aesthetics.[23]

However, even with attempts to move away from judgement about the superiority or inferiority of specific kinds of music, almost all such classifications are accepted to suffer from imprecision. Despite this, I adopt a classificatory system here that serves a useful purpose and that, to some extent, can help to identify sociomusical phenomena.[24] It is underpinned by a distinct position that music is a manifestation of social life and experiences, and that the musical and sociological aspects are inseparable. While being concerned with 'objective' principles of musicality, the external manifestations of music as revealed, historically and anthropologically, in varieties of social activities, in work and in play, the analysis simultaneously engages with the social processes that generate and create changes in musical practices. It is concerned, in the analysis of social processes that underpin different types of music, with transmission mechanisms that allow for the reproduction and transfer (whether oral or written, whether explicitly taught or transmitted through non-musical activity, whether employing particular technologies for transmission) across generations. The classification of genres includes folk music, classical or art music, and popular music.

In this sort of framework, folk music (often referred to as indigenous music of agrarian, forest-, mountain- or desert-dwelling or other communities) is music practised in groups, that meets the approval of (i.e. is understood and valued by) the group, and is maintainable by the group without training or extensive specialization. Often folk music is not taught as music, it is not even consciously considered music, but in practice is coterminous with ritual or other activities that are non-musical, relating to subsistence provision and regular existence of the communities, resulting in it sometimes being termed 'functional'. The relationship with non-musical activities also results in it not being transmitted as music, but as ritual or a necessary component on occasions that denote or celebrate functions and activities in regular life. While folk or indigenous music is often quite complex, it is usually complex in predictable patterns, and the complexity is acquired through group performance or in very specific and consistent ways rather than through solo virtuosity that allows for a great deal of elaboration or improvisation. The grammar of a folk music tradition typically exhibits little intentional variability from performance to performance. Further, although in a lot of communities the performers are/were a specific group of people within the community, in the stereotypical folk song there is hardly any distinction between the performers and audience, to the extent that the actual performance can have a great deal of call-and-response-type structures or a grammar which requires repetition of the lead parts in a collective voice, indicating extensive participation by a large number of people of the community. For these reasons, it is often argued that folk music comes as close to spontaneous expression as possible.

In comparison, art or classical music is characterized by structural complexity, strict rules, theoretical frameworks involving grammar and modes of rendering, variation and elaboration. Even as such music comes with given grammatical structures, it tends to stretch grammatical boundaries with personal innovation, and 'extended, formal performances that frequently focus on an individual's creativity are an important feature of art music traditions. The musicians in an art music system are professionals, the products of intensive (and intentional) training over a period of many years.'[25] Art music often historically emerges from indigenous or folk forms of specific regions, and, typically, art music systems use forms from folk systems and imbue them with elaborations based on the rigours and complexities of the art music of the region. Because of the need for conscious teaching and instruction through apprenticeship or family ties, and the art musician being a specialist, there is a clear divide between performers and audiences in art music systems, although they would typically be acquainted with each other through systems of patronage that are often based on social hierarchy.

Popular music is distinguished by the coming into existence of audiences that are larger than the first two, and involves 'indirect' patronage by a mass audience,

> in turn dependent on some technological means of either physically collecting an audience in a single space or of disseminating the music performance (either through broadcast media or recorded media) . . . a unique feature of pop music systems is the presence of at least one individual who controls the merchandising of the performance (the concert hall owner, the promoter, etc.) or who controls the music-recording technology and markets the artifacts created. These individuals, as well as the musicians, must respond to the tastes and attitudes of their mass audience if the music they are creating or marketing is to survive.[26]

To be accessible across diverse segments of the mass audience, this music (in its content and format) needs to be matched to the convenience and availability of time with the potential audience, resulting in a fairly consistent use of short musical structures and high levels of repetition of the forms used. Traditionally available genres that can either match up more easily to these requirements, such as relatively simpler and repetitive folk forms or forms that can be easily rendered in 'song' formats with standardizable structures, become more amenable to 'popularization' than complex art music that, even as it becomes commercialized, needs to rely on a niche audience even when transmitted across large distances. And even then, it has been documented in the case of India that compact formats, limited time availability for rendering it and relative standardization became prerequisites for successful merchandizing of art music through recording technologies, often leading to debates around 'showmanship versus substance' in art music.[27]

When samples of folk music are marketed as popular music, the seamless and reciprocal relationship between performers and audience gets split into specific relationships between performers, audiences and merchants or intermediaries as separate entities. For example, the blues, which developed into a popular music system in the 1920s, developed from the rural folk music of the southern United States. The 'folk music' revival of the 1960s embodied all the characteristics of a popular music system with its professional composer/performers, its marketed recorded artefacts (sound recordings and sheet music), its numerous performance venues and its audience that became widespread globally.

Given the characteristics of different genres of music, and the transformations that occur from relatively more localized and perhaps pristine formats into popular music, we can say that consciously political (or protest or resistance) music may be considered a specific type of popular music – although it might come into existence to counteract some typical manifestations or outcomes of specific kinds of popular music prevalent in particular regions. Here I am referring to the anti-commercial music stance of radical music in its stated objective of creating and performing music of 'the people'.

Despite this specific and strong positioning against particular kinds of popular music and their ideologies of production and dissemination, the reasons for my labelling of protest music within the genre of popular music are the following. First, it comes into existence consciously with the desire to expand music's influence to a larger audience than that which customarily/traditionally listens to or practises that music. It attempts to gather audiences and employ technologies that can disseminate the music widely. The political entity, in this case, the political organizational structures that employ culture to spread a political message, plays the crucial role of the intermediary that emerges only with popular music.

Second, in this process of conscious intermediation, crucial changes occur, consciously and unconsciously, in the way in which different existing forms of music relate to audiences, a feature typical of popular music. The changes in folk music forms, typically, are in terms of delinking from ritual as practised in conventional ways, changes in texts to project a particular politics, and adoption of formats that are amenable to listening by larger audiences. When art music was used it typically employed its grammar (producing *raga*-based songs, say, in India, or writing western classical music-based compositions in 1930s' United States), but was adapted to performance formats involving text with political content or performance in public gatherings – at factory gates, mass rallies and processions, and the like.

Third, the repertoire that emerges reflects the representation of a large number of existing forms and genres from across many regions and traditions simultaneously, being performed in a vast multiplicity of contexts quite separate from their origins, within the overall constraints of qualifying as 'music of the people' and as expressions of politics. Popular music, as noted earlier, allows for a wide range, unconstrained perhaps by custom but constrained, in turn, by the objectives of performance, like in the case of political music analysed in this book. The IPTA and the related organizations in its tradition, I will argue, played the role of a mediator that attempted to respond to new audiences and also to shape those audiences fundamentally, to expose them to a new and alternative aesthetic.

Often, when political mobilization involves music, whether as part of a composite performance or on its own, the former stems essentially from the multiple and divergent roles that music plays in people's lives. A cultural political movement typically responds to diverse circumstances, and assesses at different points how art and, in this case, music can be used for political mobilization. It is seen that the intervention/intermediation of politics or of the political intermediary, then, does not have unilinear effects, i.e. the transformations mentioned above do not undercut dynamism or creativity. This is important to mention here because from the standpoint of the stereotypes that prevailed later on about the protest song, or judgements about protest music as not being serious enough as music, the 'politicization' of traditionally available musical formats has often been seen to curb creativity and destroy authenticity, charges that have also been levelled against popular music. While these arguments will be taken up in later chapters, here I focus on the transformations in general.

The effects of 'popular-ization', for example, are the 'typical' effects and manifestations of folk music, where the 'uses' or purposes of music creation veer away from 'expression on its own' without a target audience necessary for 'performed expression', where the performance depends upon the kind of audience and vice versa. For instance, regions have a corpus of traditional tunes or formats which are 'use-specific', meant for rituals or different stages of social life (wedding songs, funeral songs, harvest songs, boatmen's songs) that possess a specific grammar and are usually codified (which occasion demands what kind of music, what other performance happens alongside, etc.). These kinds of music, which are the indigenous or folk music of specific regions or communities, may be considered examples of spontaneous expression, where the demarcation between performer and audience might not be possible except through social divisions and codes. Even if removed from the context of ritual or specific occasions, these music forms express and reproduce the known codes of expression familiar to a large number of people and reproducible by almost anybody in the community. The transition from pure expression to performed expression, where there is a separation between the performer and the audience even if there is a reciprocal relationship between them, occurs with the mediation of a patron or an interpreter of the expression. This patronage or interpretation results in assessments of the value of the performed expression, of its showcase ability or its purposiveness, and with all of this, the creation of the performer. The transition in this case is from pure expression to expression for particular purposes, to enhance the specific effects of performance through the emergence of the conscious performer. Popular-ization in the political sense outlined here, i.e. the creation and shaping of wider audiences in response to the needs of political mobilization, involves the forging of new collectivities or 'horizontal solidarities' based on political identities, and the representation of this through performance throws up interesting aspects of the nature of political collectives, especially in non-western contexts, particularly because of their engagement with indigenous collective forms and their harnessing for political mobilization.

Transformations also occur in the popular-ization of other genres of music, from within local contexts as well as from elsewhere. The employment of different genres and forms from one's own as well as outside contexts for political mobilization, thus, involves deviations from 'original' contexts, and in fact raises questions of representation about who, why and how particular forms are used. Through these questions, as well as the creative responses to them, the process of popular-ization itself allows us to understand the relationship between music and politics. The analysis of the IPTA tradition's protest music repertoire presented in this book is an attempt to understand *this* process of popular-ization.

Methodology

This book is the culmination of an archiving-cum-documentation project of the IPTA tradition's music that I undertook between 2006–07 and 2009. Ever since I was part of the protest song movement in Delhi as a member of the group

Parcham in the 1980s and the early 1990s, with the group's repertoire consisting of a large number of songs handed down from the IPTA, I was interested in finding out what might have been lost from what, by all accounts, was a vibrant musical tradition. Most of the songs that were remembered over the years, however, fit into the stereotype of the protest song mentioned above. The experience of singing the song '*Jaane waale sipahi se poochho*' with the group, which defied the stereotype in many ways, and the remarkable impact it had, suggested to me that that there might have been many more similarly emotionally evocative and lilting songs that had been created around major historical events of the transitionary period. '*Jaane waale sipahi se poochho*' is a Hindustani song, written and composed during the Second World War by the Hyderabadi poet Makhdoom Mohiuddin, about the futility of war and the abject conditions of existence of the people who were conscripted into the British Army as well as their families. It was written to be sung primarily by a solo voice with a chorus, and is an example of a powerfully evocative song that appeals to the emotions of the audience. In this sense, it defies the stereotypical protest song format and might not qualify for being directly mobilizational. The song, which was revived by Parcham in December 1984 after the carnage against the Sikh community in the aftermath of the assassination of Indira Gandhi in Delhi, and its subsequent popularity in various campaigns against communalism and war, brought forth the cathartic power of such songs.

Many years later, in 2007, I was fortunate to be introduced to the eminent actress and activist from Calcutta, Sova Sen, by her daughter Bishnupriya Paul, who in turn put me in touch with the remarkable Reba Roychowdhury, singer, dancer and actor of the IPTA from the 1940s onwards. Reba-di, who was in her late seventies by then, was quite immobile with a fractured hip and suffering from cancer. Her severe debilities notwithstanding, she spoke emotionally and eloquently about her days in the IPTA in Bombay and Calcutta. Two long interview sessions with her made it clear to me that here was a goldmine of wonderful music waiting to be recovered and archived which, even if only some people remembered it, was still available, albeit in limited circulation. Along with the songs, many of which Reba-di sang beautifully even at that age, there were dozens of anecdotes about people and events which described the crucial historical period in ways that no formal history seems to have recorded. Reba-di's recollections and her passionate singing decades after she had been active in the IPTA allowed me to frame a whole set of questions around music and politics, apart from the documentation exercise itself. In Calcutta I subsequently met and interviewed Priti Banerjee (Priti Sarkar when she was in the IPTA), Khaled Chowdhury and Montu Ghosh, who had been active members in the

1940s. Priti-di, whom Ravi Shankar is reported to have named as one of India's best singers in the years he was with IPTA, spoke about his contribution to the IPTA's musical idiom and about the creative process in the IPTA's Bombay Central Squad.

Kerala's left-wing music has been preserved largely as the tradition of the Kerala People's Arts Club (KPAC) songs from the 1950s, a dozen or so of which became an integral part of the popular music repertoire in the state. However, the history of the music produced before the KPAC's formal inauguration in 1951, or that which came up spontaneously from the peasant or trade union movements, is scarce, as is an understanding of the debates that characterized the left cultural movement in the state. Interviews with Pattambi Madhavan, Andalattu and O.N.V. Kurup, and the collections of old songbooks of work songs from Andalattu revealed the range as well as debates around '*viplava gaanangal*' (revolutionary songs) along with numerous stories and anecdotes around the songs. A meeting with two octogenarian women, Medini and Anasuya, from Alappuzha yielded again a valuable collection of forgotten songs and anecdotes from the trade union movement around the coir factories of Alappuzha in the 1940s. Like Reba-di, they sang the songs lustily and Medini-chechi, I discovered, was the singer, in the 1940s, of the wonderful song '*Pachhapanamtatte*' (O green parakeet) whose tune I was trying to find.

One of the most memorable and touching encounters in this project was with Swatantrata Prakash, artist, singer and veteran of the handicrafts revival movement in the country. Swatantrata-ji, who lived in Delhi, was attempting in 2008 to write her memoirs which would have a chapter on her involvement with the IPTA in Lahore in the few years before independence. She contacted me through the person who was helping her write her memoirs and wanted help in identifying some of the songs she had in her notebook, preserved from the 1940s. Meeting and interviewing her provided valuable insights into the musical ethos in Lahore in the mid-1940s, and into the role played by her, Sheila Bhatia, Sneh Sanyal and others in creating and performing progressive theatre and music there. The most valuable song that I came across in my interaction with Swatantrata-ji, which is also a key example of the reconstruction that this project has involved, is the *Heer* written in Punjabi by Sheila Bhatia on the Bengal famine and performed in Lahore during the early 1940s.

Mumbai was another valuable place where I was lucky to meet different sets of people who put me in touch with facets of the city's and Maharashtra's contribution to the left cultural movement of the first half of the twentieth century. That history, interestingly, is remembered in a fractured way, with a clear demarcation between the Urdu/Hindustani and the Marathi segments, even though it was not so in the 1940s. The present members of the very active Bombay IPTA shared a lot of material and stories with me, and through them I also met the inimitable A.K. Hangal, who was bedridden and very debilitated but who retained vibrant memories of his IPTA days. Subodh More, trade unionist and literary activist, proved to be the bridge that helped me make sense of both the powerful *Shahir* tradition and the *Taraqqi Pasandi* tradition of the IPTA in Maharashtra in general and Mumbai in particular. Subodh shared songbooks, recordings and written material about the music that came out of the trade union movement, particularly in Mumbai's mill area. The source of one of the songs I went in search of, which has been important in the methodology used in this project, '*Par na jhanda yeh neeche jhukaana*', was obtained from Subodh More.

The songs '*Kino phol dassan dukh dard saiyon*' in Punjabi, '*Par na jhanda yeh neeche jhukaana*' in Hindustani and '*Pachhapanamtatte*' in Malayalam, through their trajectories and the anecdotes around them as well as my own discovery of them, have been key to the methodology I have engaged with in understanding the creative processes underlying the making of protest music, as well as in pointing to historical events that have otherwise gone unrecorded in the writing of history.[28]

I have also been able to collect songbooks and published material from the Telugu-speaking regions through V. Ramakrishna and P.V. Madhusudan Rao in Hyderabad. Access to actual recordings in Telugu has, however, been limited, largely due to my inability to travel extensively. For songs in Telugu, therefore, I have worked with the songbooks, interviews with activists of the Praja Natya Mandali in Hyderabad and secondary literature. Similarly, for the repertoire from Assam, I have relied on the detailed memoirs of Hemanga Biswas and the work done by Prachee Dewri for her doctoral dissertation which she has generously shared with me.

I have used recordings, song lyrics and anecdotes as material from which it is possible to unravel aspects of creative processes that are mediated by politics. I have also read critically and between the lines into the major arguments and disagreements that emerged within the IPTA tradition in the 1940s and 50s. The method that I have used to read music as a social text, and move from its grammar and emotional content backwards into historical events, will emerge in later chapters, when the music itself is discussed. I argue that the diversity of the tradition and the debates around it, while India-specific, reveal dimensions that are relevant to a wider discussion on the relation between art and politics, and, more specifically, the variety of ways in which music can have a bearing on politics and vice versa. This is because it is not just the variety of forms that is obvious in a country as varied as India, but the complexities of aesthetic production in contexts of various influences and where such production had multiple objectives, often working against one another.

Through all these encounters, I have found a huge repertoire of songs from different parts of the country, straddling an amazing array of styles, forms and lyrics.[29] The process of collecting these, from people's often fading memories, old notebooks, memoirs and poor-quality recordings, has been exciting on its own, because it often involved reconstruction and authentication, leading to interesting connections between people and from people to events. Discovering and recording an unrecorded history of the period through its music thus, however incomplete or partial, is enchanting on its own. What is perhaps even more fascinating is that through this it is also possible to unravel the creative processes that went into making music that was overtly political, processes that possibly have relevance much beyond local contexts, even as they get created with firm moorings in the local. In other words, what is fascinating about the repertoire I have unearthed is, on the one hand, the aesthetic quality of the music itself, and on the other, the vignettes of what goes into creating an 'international of the imagination'[30] as revealed by the repertoire and the process of its creation. This book is an attempt to understand those vignettes through a deeper look at this musical repertoire.

Music and Politics: Key Issues in Understanding the Relationship

In this section, I go on to key concerns that arise in the relationship between music and politics as they emerge from analysing the IPTA tradition's music as social text. The questions are organized around what I consider to be the important debates in the relationship.

Either by conscious initiation in the formally organized cultural movement, or through the actual experiences of creating music (whether formally organized or not) and the responses that it generated, several debates were sparked off, which commented on interesting issues around the relationship between music and resistance in the IPTA tradition. These debates were sometimes consciously initiated as such or very often were reactions to creative output, as aesthetic responses themselves. Thus, both the published and unpublished, though well-known debates, as well as the music itself formulate interesting questions and issues that, I believe, go beyond the specific context of India or the regions within it.

Chapter 1 discusses the history of the IPTA from its formation in 1943 until its formal disbanding as a national organization in 1957, in the context of the unfolding of the 'radical impulse' or left-wing aesthetic in different parts of the world in the first half of the twentieth century. It lays out the context in which the national and international terrains were engaged by radical writers and artists in different parts of the world, which formed the background against which the PWA and the IPTA came into existence.

Much has been discussed about the problems the IPTA faced as an organization, with the first split occurring as early as 1946. Artists bickered furiously with each other; those who broke away often got depoliticized; many got involved in alternative cultural and political formations. In music within the IPTA tradition, there was an explosion of forms and creativity throughout the 1940s and 50s, even as there were allegations from musicians and other creative people about the movement suppressing creativity. Often these questions became salient when controversies emerged over disagreements between musicians, sometimes complicated by organizational interventions that would favour one position over another. Many times, because of the unpleasantness created, the points of the debate got obscured and epitaphs were written which focused primarily on the personality clashes, and the need to establish 'right' and 'wrong' points of view. These debates, even when they were specifically about music, often reflected positions on cultural expression taken as a whole, because the IPTA and its tradition did not necessarily distinguish between different aspects of cultural production. These concerns, broadly classified into four sets as below, straddle a whole range of issues to do with representation in and through music in cultural movements of the left, and also bring forth two important tropes that have been deployed to establish the legitimacy of the representation: *authenticity* and the *collective*. These two tropes are developed in conceptual terms in Chapter 1, and are then taken up along with actual experiences of music-making in subsequent chapters.

The first set of concerns that emerges from the repertoire has to do with the notion of 'people's music'. Is it the myriad traditional or indigenous musical forms, the folk music of hundreds of social groups, the tribes, the itinerant wandering singers? How can the existing corpus of 'old' or traditional music be interpreted, used or rejected in terms of its ability to reflect the lives of ordinary people and represent their problems? How should the long-standing classical music tradition be assessed/considered as a benchmark? How may 'modern' or 'western' forms of music be used to represent the people and depict or articulate resistance? Underlying this set of questions, there was the anxiety of the rural versus urban audience, and the middle class versus 'working-class or peasant' musician. This set of questions, as well as those laid out below, are taken up in Chapter 2 in the international context and in Chapter 3 for India, with both chapters looking at the variety in analysing, interpreting and (re)inventing traditions in the definition of people's music.

Second, given the above range, should people's music be spontaneous and faithfully represented or deliberately crafted out of whatever forms are considered appropriate and through newer forms? When spontaneous music emerges that reflects the lives of ordinary people, how should it be assessed?

Third, what is the distinction between progressive and reactionary music – is it about lyrics or form? Is experimentation with the grammar of music part of the articulation of protest, i.e. what are the innovations with the nature of the sounds produced, the use of voice, pitch, harmony, orchestration, instruments and so on? In other words, to what extent does the range of music reflect the physical content of the music itself and the politics that it seeks to convey?

Fourth, what is the relationship between the individual and the collective in a cultural political movement, and how does it get reflected in music? Specifically, whether solo songs are more important or 'group songs', whether individual talent should be projected or resisted. Within the idea of the collective, what should be the relationship between the 'mass song' and the 'composition'? Linked with this is the idea that collective music should have a simple grammar that can be sung by anyone, in turn getting linked to the question of whether music should appeal because of its own aesthetic or due to the role it plays or the story it tells, or the way it tells the story, and so on.

An important dimension of the debate on the collective, which spills over possibly from theatre, is the idea of authorship: about who owns the progressive song. This becomes important when musical production takes place in a commune or collective, with the lead being taken by one or other member but with contributions by others. In such a case, when eminent musicians, in taking the lead, create music that leaves a clear imprint of their style, should it be attributed to them or to the collective? Further, if musicians 'use' each other's tunes on later occasions, where would authorship lie?

A third dimension relates to the individual in the collective, especially the role of the cultural activist: whether the cultural activist can afford to focus exclusively on cultural expression; how he/she relates to the rest of the political movement and to the commercial world; and how/whether these are important determinants in the assessment of the activist's work. Some related issues arise also in terms of the classification of 'progressive' and 'reactionary' music: whether an explicit political message is contained in it, whether political music needs to have lyrics that versify political slogans and so on. This hierarchical classification is also manifest in the idea of culture, especially music, as the 'entertainment department' in the left political movement, resulting in strong resentment among musicians.

Chapter 4 formally analyses the music of the IPTA tradition in terms of folk-based, classical music-based and western music-based sub-genres, and situates it within the world of popular music as well as the wider aesthetic that emerged in the late colonial and immediately post-colonial period in many parts of the world:

an aesthetic that grappled with complex issues of nationhood, nationality, language and class. Chapter 5, the last chapter of the book, takes up the trope of authenticity in order to engage with specific questions that have been raised with regard to left cultural practice, both from within the left movement and outside it.

Notes

1 The importance of this 'transitional period', covering a couple of decades before and a decade-and-a-half or so after independence, in understanding cultural impulses that shaped the Indian nation has been underscored in Gopal (2005), a study of the radical literary movement in India during that period. The possibilities that transitional periods present for cultural expression and the dynamics of that expression are key aspects that I seek to bring forth with respect to music in this book.

2 Studies of the radical ethos in the arts from the late 1960s have looked at the emergence of cultural movements in specific countries, but those focused on the larger aesthetic or political dimensions that went beyond studies of specific countries emerged mostly from the 1990s.

3 Numerous social reform movements for the abolition of 'abuses in social life' (Sarkar and Sarkar 2008) used the print media, literature and theatre from the nineteenth century, this happening with a progressive enlargement of the public sphere, creating fractured domains and the posing of difficult questions involving caste and gender.

4 As the title suggests, the idea of the 'radical impulse' is one that is going to be used and unpacked for its nuances in aesthetic terms throughout this book. It is a term that Priyamvada Gopal has used in her book, and I have developed it into a conceptual category.

5 Priyamvada Gopal's study (2005) of the radical literary movement in India uses the Gramscian idea of 'fraction' to convey the power to influence thinking that a particular group, even if small, might have in important periods in history.

6 I have argued elsewhere (Damodaran 2014) that often the 'foundational concerns' of the relationship between art and politics are assumed to come out of metropolitan experiences, whereas when such diverse experiences are considered, the foundational concerns themselves become far wider-ranging.

7 Gopal (2005): 3.

8 Hall (1981): 228.

9 Storey (2009).

10 Hall (1981): 228.

11 Gramsci (1971): 161.

12 I am referring to the cultural movements initiated by political movements of left and democratic persuasion, spurred by ideologies of emancipation and class struggle, as radical cultural movements. I have used the same idea in other work that I have done (Damodaran 2014).

13 Ernst Bloch, in his *Principle of Hope* (1954), lays out the utopian impulses present in art, literature and other forms of cultural expression across the centuries, in the pursuit of utopian dreams and desires for perfection.

14 Denning (1996a).

15 Denning (1996a) uses this concept to refer to the investigation of 'folk' traditions in the music of the Popular Front in the United States from the 1930s.

16 Aesthetic 'acuity' and 'constellations' are two ideas that have been developed in collaborative

work with Ari Sitas in the teaching of a course on 'Art and the Sociology of Popular Culture' in the Department of Sociology, University of Cape Town, since 2012.

17 Middleton (1990); Frith (2007).

18 An understanding such as this reflects an ideology of 'superior' listening that is associated with the ability to undertake a formalistic and cognitive analysis of musical work, which makes music structurally autonomous of social processes.

19 Bennett *et al.* (2005): 2; Middleton (1990): 34–62.

20 For example, Bennett *et al.* (2005) present a critique of the method of using 'high' and 'low' categories to understand any music through a detailed collection of essays on the rock tradition in Europe and North America. Barker (2015a; 2015b), who reviews conceptual issues that have arisen in the analysis of protest music, bases his own research on the American counterculture; and Drott (2011) describes ways in which rock, jazz and contemporary music, all responded to the events of 1968 in France, often in contradictory ways. Aadnani (2006) is a survey of protest music and poetry in North Africa in the contemporary period, discussed in the context of the *rai* musical tradition. There are numerous studies of the Nueva canción movement in Latin America (Elliott 2011; Gasporotto 2011, for instance), of Rebetiko in Greece (Tragaki 2007), and of the anti-apartheid movement (Olwage 2008; Ballantine 1984).

21 Booth and Kuhn (1990).

22 This declaration of 'other' music contexts as inferior comes from a framework rooted in the history of western classical music, particularly from the nineteenth century. Among sociological understandings of music, Max Weber's famous analysis of 'rationality' in western classical music and denunciation of the rest as the 'unorganized conglomeration of non-rational tone successions' (Weber 1969), in *The Rational and Social Foundations of Music*, is a prominent example of the arrogance being underlined here.

23 While the idea of superiority or inferiority of particular kinds of music can be historically located to the development of music academe in the west from the early nineteenth century, as pointed out earlier, it has also characterized countries with strong classical music traditions such as India, and has also been noted for Indonesia, Thailand and Turkey.

24 Following Booth and Kuhn (1990) and Frith (1989).

25 Booth and Kuhn (1990): 148.

26 Ibid.: 419.

27 For example, Subramanian (2006) for south Indian and Weidman (2006) for north Indian classical music.

28 The specific details of each of these have been provided in shaded boxes in Chapter 3.

29 In all, I have a collection of about 200 songs in my archive.

30 I have borrowed this term from Sitas (2007) who has used it in *The Ethic of Reconciliation* to refer to a consequence of art production, whereby publics and audiences develop sensibilities and dispositions that are necessary for the creation of an ethic of reconciliation in societies that have seen inordinate violence.

1

IPTA: Formation and Debates

The Indian People's Theatre Association (IPTA) came into existence in 1943 as an organization to respond to the political contingencies of fascism and the Bengal famine, and to coordinate and consolidate the cultural responses they spawned in different parts of the country. The progressive cultural movement in India had come into its own in a decisive way in the literary sphere first with the setting up of the Progressive Writers' Association (PWA) seven years earlier, in 1936, and also as a series of initiatives in theatre, dance and music in different parts of the country before the formal setting up of the IPTA. The formal inauguration of the IPTA took place at the All India People's Theatre Conference held in Bombay on 26 May 1943.

The first bulletin of the IPTA is headed by the epigraph: 'People's theatre stars the people', and it resolved to build a theatre not only of the people but also by them, to build

> not a movement which is built from above but which has its roots deep down in the cultural awakening of the masses of India . . . which seeks to revive the lost in that heritage by interpreting, adopting and integrating it with the most significant facts of our people's lives and aspirations in the present epoch.

Further, it added, 'It is the task of the Indian People's Theatre Movement at present to portray vividly and memorably through the medium of the stage and other traditional arts the human details of the important facts of our people's rights and enlighten them about their rights.'[1] Hiren Mukherjee, whose famous speech on the occasion laid out some of the early ideas, called upon 'the drama which has during the last half century and more in our country, touched some of the lowest depths of degeneration', to 'pre-eminently help in developing a real people's art. Dramas are collective performances: writer, actor, producer, audience, all together create the play.'[2]

The name 'People's Theatre' was suggested for the Indian context by the scientist Homi Jehangir Bhabha, who also reportedly involved himself with Marxist ideas along with a whole host of progressive people of the time. The first General Secretary of the IPTA was Anil de Silva, a vibrant artist from Sri Lanka and the trade unionist N.M. Joshi was its first President. Benoy Roy, K.T. Chandy, Mama Varerkar, K.A. Abbas, Garikapati Raja Rao, Makhdoom Mohiuddin, Rashid Jahan, S.A. Dange, Shambhu Mitra, Bishnu Dey and Rajendra Raghuvanshi were among those who were elected to the executive and as office bearers of the Association.

The leading spirit behind the setting up of the IPTA was the Communist Party of India's (CPI's) General Secretary, P.C. Joshi. Numerous memoirs written by prominent artists who became part of the IPTA, including those who left it later, talk about the role played by Joshi in conceptualizing the idea of a cultural front in India. By the time the IPTA was formed as a national organization, its activists came from several regional traditions, using forms and cultural traditions that were local, and a history of prior interpretations of how culture can be used in political mobilization at the local and regional levels.

The constitution of the IPTA at the national level immediately saw regional responses: in Bengal, Andhra, Assam and Kashmir, to name only a few. The Praja Natya Mandali was set up in the Telugu-speaking regions of Andhra, Rayalaseema and Telangana in the same year. Bengal already had a group called Voice of Bengal, which used music and theatre extensively to create awareness about the famine, and the IPTA's formation consolidated this further. In Assam and Kashmir, the IPTA was formally constituted a few years later; and in Kerala in 1951, with the formation of the Kerala People's Arts Club (KPAC).

The formation of the Progressive Writers' Association (PWA) in 1936 marked a definitive stage, a crystallization of the radicalizing tendencies and events that had begun in the early 1930s in India; the IPTA's formation took the project forward by extending the radical project consciously and organizationally beyond literature, to the arts. The PWA had put forward a new radical agenda for progressive, anti-colonial writers, of reflexive self-criticism, of interrogating social contexts along with critiquing colonialism, of placing the writer at the centre of this interrogative process.[3] An alternative vision for the social responsibility of writers in society, a different view of the writer's role in social transformation, was beginning to take shape in a deliberated manner. The PWA's manifesto announced the need for liberating both literature and the arts from the trappings of elitism and colonial neglect, by truly representing the aspirations of ordinary people:

> It is the object of our Association to rescue literature and other arts from the conservative classes in whose hands they have been degenerating so long, to bring the arts into the closest touch with the people and to make them the vital organs which will register the actualities of life, as well as lead us to the future we envisage. While claiming to be the inheritors of the best traditions of Indian civilization, we shall criticize, in all its aspects, the spirit of reaction in our country, and we shall foster through interpretative and creative work (with both Indian and foreign resources) – everything that will lead our country to the new life for which it is striving. We believe that the new literature of India must deal with the basic problems of our existence today – problems of hunger and poverty, social backwardness and political subjection. All that drags us down to passivity, inaction and unreason we reject as reactionary. All that arouses in us the critical spirit, which examines institutions and customs in the light of reason, which helps us to act, to organize ourselves, to transform, we accept as progressive.[4]

Against the background of the PWA's interventions in literature and the accompanying cultural movement that had erupted in several parts of the country, when the IPTA's first bulletin announced that 'People's theatre stars the people', the organization was setting out several agendas or challenges for itself. The first challenge was to conceptually develop the idea of people's art, people whose 'struggles for freedom, economic justice and a democratic culture' were found to be major characteristics of the period from the First World War. Organizationally, in the regional movements, it already had concrete links between cultural activists and the common people and a wide variety in cultural exploration as well as interpretations of what people's art could be. Bhattacharya argues that Romain Rolland's notion of a people's theatre as an alternative to bourgeois theatre might have served as an inspiration behind the inception of the IPTA;[5] but, while the development of European capitalism and the low incidence of indigenous forms in Europe might have allowed him to visualize it as theatre *for* the people, in India, because of the existence and vibrancy of countless indigenous forms, this meant theatre *of* and *by* the people as well.

The second challenge was to figure out how all the regional strands could be brought together organizationally as a movement and conceptually in envisioning a 'national' culture, even while preserving the regional or the local. As part of this, a serious assessment of the heritage, of classical and indigenous forms, was considered necessary.

Third, it needed to understand commercial art and performance, and the need to wean audiences away from them, even as it would create a non-commercial but professional theatre. Hiren Mukherjee's famous speech at the 1943 IPTA conference openly declared war against the commercialization of the performing arts, especially as a late-colonial 'distortion'. The critique of commercialization was a major one as it attempted to point out the need for an unhindered flowering of artistic expression or a cultural awakening. This objective, which was essentially setting out a socialist utopian vision, was to be expressed again in a different way in 1957. By then, the IPTA saw this flowering as being possible through the state institutions for culture, institutions that were set up as part of the Nehruvian framework; this position, in turn, was critiqued heavily for 'revisionism' and 'class compromise'. More will be said on this later in the book.

Fourth, the need for innovation and experimentation in establishing the new vision was expressed right at the beginning, through cross-cultural interaction across different parts of the country as well as, wherever possible, with other countries.

By articulating all of the above separately and clearly, the IPTA was doing three significant things. One, it was, for the first time in India and possibly without too many precedents in a non-socialist context elsewhere, giving concrete expression and legitimacy to the idea that the culture of the 'people' *is* the culture of the nation. As Dharwadker notes, 'the movement's historical role in defining the culture of the people as the basis of theatre in the new nation remains unassailable'.[6] In the post-colonial context, it was not possible for the Indian state to disregard this imperative, even if only in a populist way. Further, the IPTA was perhaps, with the benefit of some experience in the regional movements, anticipating the fact that this task would need to grapple with several possible contradictions, even while hoping that what would emerge would be fresh, new and at the same time popular. Simultaneously, given IPTA's connection with the Communist Party of India, it was formally setting in place a culture within left political mobilization where cultural intervention would become an obvious form of that politics. According to Bhattacharya,

> it spearheaded a movement which created such a demand among audiences . . . it was a great achievement to give dramatic form to what was emerging as a new political reality . . . it might have served as the first step towards building a mass organization which would establish cultural links even in those areas where little other political work had been done.[7]

The historical conjuncture in which the radical aesthetic was being explored saw an interplay between the need to oppose imperialism, confront fascism, and focus on retrograde practices and exploitative conditions within the country. Further, there were many multiple, coexisting genres of public performance and media of representation in the country, such as: (i) the whole range of religious, secular, folk performance forms all over the countryside; (ii) the modern medium of film and recording studios that had an audience in urban and semi-urban areas; (iii) theatre and music that represented self-conscious and expressive modernisms as in the modern nationalist stage tradition; and (iv) the colonial tradition in music and theatre. By the time the IPTA was set up, therefore, a complex corpus of performance traditions, continuously changing, diverse and vibrant, was available to it, which it would need to work through in the effort to craft an alternative aesthetic.

In an assessment of the progressive cultural movement in India fifty years after the formation of the PWA, the communist veteran E.M.S. Namboodiripad noted that it took place at a time when three trends were seen in the national movement: first, the Indian National Congress's 'move to the left', symbolized by Jawaharlal Nehru's address to its Lucknow conference in 1936, where he held that 'some people in the Congress, and they are a growing number, want to change the land system, and the capitalist system', and also that there was a need for 'ending private property, except in a restricted sense';[8] second, the emergence of an organized central leadership for the CPI which unified all the scattered communist groups working throughout the country; and third, the formation of the Congress Socialist Party (CSP), the breakaway left-wing group of the Congress party, its members ranging from avowed Marxists like Jayaprakash Narayan and Narendra Dev to supporters of the British Labour Party like Minoo Masani. At the time of the PWA's formation, therefore, left-wing ideas were not alien even in the mainstream of the nationalist movement, and this was to get reflected in the kind of aesthetic questions that were raised by those from the left around nationalism. In many parts of the country the communists and the CSP worked together, with the boundaries seeming fluid.

The decade of the 1940s saw, along with the Second World War, the devastation brought about by the Bengal famine, which provided the impetus for the progressive cultural project to take shape beyond writing, in dance, theatre, music and art. It also saw the beginnings of contradictions posed by the change in the ideological line, from opposing war to supporting a 'People's War' led by the Soviet Union along with its ally, Britain, following the attack on Stalingrad by Nazi Germany. The CPI, in line with the Comintern position, treated the war as an inter-imperialist war, having been preceded by the Munich Pact in 1938 and the Soviet response to it through its non-aggression pact with Germany in 1939. Within a few days of the declaration of war, the CPI decided to call for a general strike, an anti-war protest strike, in which more than 90,000 workers participated, making it the first anti-war strike in the whole international labour movement.[9] The communists were the first to start protesting against the war burden imposed on the people, and their campaigns, along with the proliferation of writing and cultural expression, were extensive. The German attack on Stalingrad found most of the Indian communist leaders imprisoned, for their anti-war activities and their demand for immediate national independence, at the Deoli detention camp, where they had been detained with the Socialists, who also had been actively opposing the war.

In 1941, the 'Jail Document' signalling the adoption of the 'People's War' line of the CPI was drafted at the Deoli camp. The shift in the characterization of the war caused deep confusion among the members of the CPI and especially the cultural movement because, politically, this meant a tempering of its anti-British stance and in fact a reversal of the anti-war stance. With culture constituting an important basis for anti-war campaigns, the sudden change of line was interpreted by artists as an infringement on artistic freedom and many felt unable to abandon earlier creative work in terms of its content.

While the Bengal famine and its devastation shook the conscience of artists committed to the progressive cause, also unleashing enormous creativity, it brought forth the need to condemn and fight British colonialism aggressively for creating the conditions for the famine, even while supporting the war. With the CPI's shift from an imperialist war to a people's war line of action in characterizing the Second World War, one of several anxieties that came to characterize the aesthetics–politics relationship in the radical cultural movement in India had surfaced. However, the movement was also growing exponentially in size and creativity in this period, forming the basis for the formal establishment of the IPTA in 1943. Habib notes that while the communists opposed both the Congress's decision to launch non-cooperation against the British and the British government's provocative policy of repression, these were political positions, and 'in practice the communists avoided open cooperation with British officialdom, built up trade unions and Kisan Sabhas, and fought in a restrained manner for the people's day-to-day demands and relief. In the situation they became practically the sole legal spokesmen for the common man.' Despite an overt political position that British colonialism would not directly be attacked, campaigns were organized against hoarders and for proper food distribution; 'grow more food' campaigns, appealing directly to peasants, and relief activities were also organized.[10]

Against the background of these historical developments, the left-wing cultural movement had taken root by the beginning of the 1940s, and poetry, dance, theatre and music had become a part of political mobilization. Despite inter- and intra-regional differences among the cultural movements – whether they were peasant or working-class-based, rural or urban-based, and so on – what they had in common was the need to define 'people's culture' in different ways, to bring out the conditions of life under colonialism and local exploitation, and at the same time forge an internationalism for socialism and against fascism. The creation of the IPTA took this cultural project forward, to concretely address questions of national culture, people's culture and the forms that artistic expression must take with such deliberate adoption of cultural means for political mobilization.

Many of the ideas put forward formally by the PWA and the IPTA were not new. Non-English literatures had begun to highlight strong nationalist feelings in the years before the First World War in India, and important developments took place in different genres of writing reflecting mainstream nationalist sentiments as well as beginning to lay the groundwork for alternative nationalist visions. For example, in Urdu the short story came into existence as a genre, pioneered by Premchand, and ordinary people became the subjects of storytelling, marking a unique feature in representational modes. In Telugu, from 1870, social reform themes that questioned retrograde social practices used literature extensively. Political literature with nationalist themes came into existence from 1920 onwards. In the early 1920s, a novel banned by the colonial government (titled *Malapalli* by Unnava Laxminarayana) talked about socialist principles of economic and social equality, and a play (*Ryotu Bidda* – Son of a Peasant – by Sabnavis Rama Rao) was written on the problems faced by the peasantry. Similarly, in Urdu, a young poet, Akhtar Husain Raipuri, published an article titled '*Adab aur zindagi*' (Literature and Life) where he argued that fiction and poetry that did not depict everyday lives of the common people were irrelevant.

In Bengal, along with the coming into existence of journals that published working-class literature, like *Langol* and *Ganabani*, left-wing, progressive writers who wrote for these also established links with avant-garde writers who were raising questions of sex and morality, attacking the conservatism of Indian society and proposing drastic political alternatives. These self-critiques were to influence the depiction of ordinary people in the literature of the PWA and, later, in the art of the IPTA.

Thus, by the mid-to-late 1930s, a consciously political cultural project was beginning to be manifested in India: one that sought to self-consciously define the writer's role in social transformation, in self-reflexive interrogation of traditions, and in lending the necessary creative dimensions to the radical and nationalist agenda of the left. The organizational impetus provided by the setting up of the PWA helped crystallize a lot of the spontaneous cultural mobilization happening in different parts of the country.

Internationally, there had been a boom in progressive art and literature from the late 1920s, inspired by political developments of a decade earlier, which was characterized by tremendous social change and organizations that were set up to deal with that change. In analysing the genesis of such a 'novelists' international', Denning writes:

> Three initiatives were particularly influential. The first was the formation of the first international writers' association, Clarté, in 1919 by Henri Barbusse . . . which led to a series of international writers' congresses. The second was the emergence of a proletarian culture movement in revolutionary Russia, a loose federation of clubs, education societies, and workers' theaters . . . which soon became known by the abbreviation 'Proletcult'. The Proletcult movement reached its peak in the Soviet Union in the early 1920s, spawning workshops, journals, and rival groups, and its example resonated around the world. . . . The third initiative was the Baku conference of 1920, which marked the turn by the Communist inheritors of European socialism to the anticolonial movements in Asia and Africa, generating the powerful alliance of Communism and anticolonialism that was to shape the global decolonization struggles of the twentieth century.[11]

This last point is important to remember because it was to give rise to an internationalism that was unique, with the recognition among left-wing activists in the advanced capitalist countries, including imperial countries like Britain, that freedom from colonial rule was an important objective for a genuine and representative radical agenda. In countries like India, the dialectic between nationalist and internationalist in the cultural movement was to unfold in complex ways, with the international influences themselves being varied and uneven. The cultural movement was to reflect this dialectic by absorbing influences from diverse contexts, but at the same time responding in strongly local, rooted ways.

Among the known influences on the PWA and the IPTA, the idea of 'Popular Frontism', originating from an alliance of the communist and socialist parties with the bourgeois parties to fight fascism, is one. The idea of 'popularizing culture' through organizing had gained currency in 1930s' France of the Popular Front; influential cultural fronts were also being formed in the United States in the post-Depression era of the Works Progress Administration. The term 'cultural front' was increasingly used by those on the left, with full support from the Comintern and the Soviet Union, to 'connote their insistence on culture as one arm, or front, of a widening campaign for social, political, and racial equality'.[12]

While the Soviet and European influences are known and have been well acknowledged, developments close by, in East Asia and Southeast Asia, were also to influence the progressive cultural movement in India, as this book seeks to emphasize.[13]

This dimension of internationalism for artists, based on a broadly socialist, anti-imperialist agenda, before the Soviet or Euro–American anti-fascist initiative of the 1930s, has been relatively obscured in cultural histories of progressivism of the twentieth century until recently. It is also seldom considered that the debates on modernism and tradition as they were reflected in the arts and literature in the context of colonialism nearby, for example in Southeast Asia, might have found strong echoes in a country like India, defining the contours of a radical impulse in that country from the 1930s onwards. As a result, there has been a tendency to understand the progressive movement in India almost as a derivative discourse, fashioned entirely by the possibilities, challenges and constraints of the Soviet Union, on the one hand, or the progressive movements in Britain, continental Europe and the USA, on the other.

What is perhaps not as well acknowledged in the literature is how the conditions of colonialism and the specific social contexts of the colonies, for example, in East Asia and Southeast Asia, influenced the aesthetic and literary forms that were generated, quite distinct from the ways in which things unfolded in Europe, the Soviet Union and the United States. It is mainly from the 1990s that research about the radical cultural history of specific regions and countries, for example, Southeast Asia and Japan, has brought out particular dimensions of the radical interventions in literature and the arts.[14]

One of the themes that preoccupied progressive artists in these countries, even before the Soviet-inspired anti-fascist writers' fronts were formed, was that of imperialist expansion in Asia by Japan. Resistance to Japanese imperialism in Korea, Taiwan and China was given organized support from proletarian organizations originating in those countries, as well as in the Soviet Union and in Japan, and writers and artists formed a very important part of this resistance. The idea of imperialism encompassing the perceived threat from Japanese aggression, apart from British colonialism, resulted in complex aesthetic responses that cannot be understood if the possibility of influences from East Asia and Southeast Asia are not considered. In music, particularly, this anxiety was expressed again and again, as will become clear in later chapters.

The insights provided by historical evidence on the development of radical culture in Southeast Asia and Japan from the 1920s, I believe, are crucial to emphasize for two reasons. First, because it allows for an understanding of the early-to-mid twentieth-century radical impulse as being far more widespread and diverse than is commonly held: in other words, as extending over geographies where substantial internal diversity and variations in cultural practice necessitated highly plural aesthetic expressions of this radical impulse. Second, because it helps locate some of the specific concerns that were expressed by Indian writers and artists in the period, possibly confronted with the same kinds of issues as, say, by those in Shanghai or Tokyo.

It was thus the interesting interplay between the need to oppose imperialism, confront fascism, understand and take the side of specific anti-colonial struggles in different parts of the world, and, at the same time, confront retrograde attitudes within their own cultural contexts, that characterized the objectives of progressive writers and artists in the first half of the twentieth century – and this was seen in India as well. The contradictions that could emerge within and between these distinct yet interconnected political imperatives played themselves out in the cultural field in interesting ways, and India was a country where this happened extensively.

Representation: Realism, Modernism, Self-critique

It is clear that the PWA and the IPTA set out with the objectives of crafting a new aesthetic and creating a space where 'diverse issues pertinent to regenerating nation and national culture could be discussed'[15] – where the contours and desires of social change could be explored, and new identities and collectivities imagined, through aesthetic means. In both the IPTA tradition and the PWA, the question of form, i.e. how to represent 'the people', was key to how the cultural politics would emerge; and realism was considered the appropriate representational mode, although the actual connotations of realism were to be hotly debated.

One connotation of realism as a formal technique arose out of the understanding that a critique of others (in this case British colonialism) could happen only when a comprehensive and multifaceted self-critique took place, involving a critique of class structures, family ideologies, bodies and sexualities, absences and silences in social life. Ghosh notes that in art, the debate on realism had been initiated by Nandalal Bose in the late 1920s, when he moved away from painting Hindu gods and goddesses towards relatively realist portrayals of landscapes around Santiniketan and scenes from the lives of adivasis who lived there.[16] In 1938 Samar Sen, an active member from Bengal who was part of what came to be termed the 'Calcutta Group', argued in his paper, 'In Defence of Decadence', that reality as a whole including its decadent elements ought to find reflection in art, which was contested by another artist, Saroj Dutta, who argued that only progressive and 'positive' elements should be sieved out of reality and represented by artists – a precursor to more such debates that were to occur subsequently. The question of the depiction of filth and decadence, the precoccupation with gender issues, sexual mores and sexuality in writers like Ismat Chughtai, Miraji and Rashid Jahan in Urdu, or other 'narrations of discomfort' under colonialism were important dimensions of the debate around realism, and not merely the realist depiction of heroic peasants and workers, as a later interpretation under the credo of 'socialist realism' would seem to suggest.[17] The quest to 'narrate discomfort' and stretch realism's limits as a representational technique were also important in putting forth the idea that colonialism involved very specific erasures and exclusions. The task of radical representation, therefore, was to begin a process of reorganizing the aesthetic order and consciousness in colonized countries by bringing back what had been excluded or erased. Woodcut and linocut artists, therefore, created prints with peasants, beggars, prisoners, rickshaw pullers, boat trackers, famine victims, war refugees, industrial workers and political protestors, with aesthetic representation aiming to give visibility and voice to groups whose presence and demands had been ignored.

Further, the 'Progressives', as the PWA writers and IPTAs artists came to be known, also engaged extensively with issues of tradition, even as realist portrayals were given more prominence. In an editorial in the inaugural issue of *Naya Adab* (New Literature), the journal of the PWA, the writers clearly stated that progressive literature did not claim to break off relations with old or even ancient literature; on the contrary, this literature could be the 'most trustworthy guardian and heir of ancient literature'.[18] The IPTA too devoted a substantial part of its conscious deliberations[19] as well as actual practice to evaluating both classical traditions and engaging with folk traditions from different parts of the country.

Through considering questions of realism, tradition and modernism, the interventions in literature and the arts were thus engaging with ideas of nationalism and defence of the national culture of India by means of critical self-reflection, and they were not to echo the standard nationalist rhetoric. In Gopal's words:

> It would not be enough, however, simply to posit an originary national culture in response to fascism and colonialism for, on these native grounds, 'narrow nation-

> alists' and 'revivalists' waged their own war against the people at large. The most meaningful strategy in this minefield of contradictions and ambiguities would be to create spaces and institutions that would enable writers to 'popularize' culture and enable the understanding of multiple contradictions in social existence under British rule.

Thus the radical writers and artists stubbornly inhabited the terrain of the national, even as it was a tense existence, generating an alternative nationalism.

The parallels between South Asia, and East Asia and Southeast Asia, around questions of realism and tradition are noteworthy. The issues addressed by the proletarian literary and cultural movements that came out of Southeast Asia and Japan were about the relationship between modernism and tradition, between the east and the west, and about what realism meant in terms of representation.

By the 1920s, with Shanghai emerging as a major centre of progressive art and literature,[20] modernist artists from different countries in the region had found it to be an ideal, novelistic landscape for 'representing the anxieties of industrialism, capitalism, nationalism and selfhood'.[21] Writing scathingly about conditions of living in a colonial metropolis, about squalor and degradation of life, descriptions of filth and mobs, of decrepit landscapes and degraded lives became synonymous with realism in literature.

Radical literary activists such as Lu Xun and Tian Han represented varying ideas of modernism and tradition in the creation of a proletarian consciousness. Tian Han, a representative of the Chinese avant-garde, a feminist, and a nationalist proletarian writer who wrote twenty-seven traditional operas, sixty-three spoken dramas, two western-style operas and more than a thousand poems, argued, as early as 1920, that proletarian art needed to synthesize feminist principles, thus making a unique contribution at the time to what has been termed 'proletarian modernism'. He also saw proletarian art as embodying western modernist principles along with those of traditional Chinese opera, in contrast to Lu Xun, who wrote satirical pieces about the feudal decadence of traditional opera, ideas that Mao Tse-tung was to formally endorse later in his writings. Another feature that distinguished Tian Han from Lu Xun and other fierce modernists was his understanding of proletarian art, and of the poet as fulfilling both spiritual and material needs.[22] The contrast between the strongly materialist philosophy of Lu Xun and the combination of spiritual and materialist philosophies in Tian Han offers interesting insights into plural interpretations of proletarian art and literature. Similarly, conversations between left-wing writers and the avant-garde, who were strongly influenced by left politics in Japan and Southeast Asia, reveal the kind of relationship between the two categories of artists that was also seen in India during the same period.

Thus we can see that the colonial context in Asia threw up particularities that generated aesthetic responses that were articulated through alternative nationalisms and internationalisms, which in turn generated further representational questions and impulses. What is important and interesting to note is that the multiplicity of considerations that went into the imagination of what constitutes the 'radical' – ranging from realism and its various dimensions, the relationship between the spiritual and the material in understanding tradition or the relationship between modernism and tradition in representing the 'ordinary person' – reflects not only the dynamics of creative processes when a transformatory social vision is being explored, but also demonstrates how societies might connect with each other *through* these processes. It is not known whether artists in India learnt concretely about debates in, say, Shanghai in the 1930s, but it is true that news about political developments travelled and generated interest in an internationalist milieu, spurring creative processes and reflecting the radical impulse that this book focuses on.

However, the subsequent emergence of hardline views on culture from within the left movement and the relatively mechanical interpretations of what radical culture should be like have also resulted in a limited historical view of how international influences were reflected in the IPTA's creative output. These, in turn, have also been interpreted by those who question the left's cultural project in India as being derivative and inauthentic. I move on now to the debates and contradictions that emerged between the distinct yet interconnected political imperatives, and how they played themselves out in the cultural field between the 1940s and late 1950s.

From Formation to Disbanding

Eight major conferences of the IPTA were held in the period 1943 to the late 1950s, before it was formally disbanded as a national organization. Over this period, like the PWA, several contentious issues arose that reflected diverse points of view, backgrounds and political developments. The deliberations and manifestos of the eight IPTA conferences and other documents provide insights into changing perspectives on the art–left politics relationship as seen through the IPTA experience.

One of the issues that came up, reflecting serious ideological positioning around the relationship between art and politics, was a contradiction between the 'cultural section' and the 'political section' of the literary movement, to begin with, and later, of the cultural movement. Writings by Mir and Mir, Ahmed Ali and Rashed, and Geeta Patel bring out some of the tensions and contradictions that arose within the PWA around this time.[23] As early as 1939, Ahmed Ali, one of the writers of the *Angaarey* collection, stated that he felt pressurized to refuse to publish material that did not directly talk of workers and peasants.[24] This position was elaborated in a 1949 document of the PWA that laid out several principles of progressive writing, and also resulted in censure and criticism of writers who wrote about sex and sexuality, such as Ismat Chughtai, Miraji and Saadat Hasan Manto, those who did not explicitly write on political themes, like Rajinder Singh Bedi, and those who were 'ambiguous', like Faiz Ahmed Faiz.[25] The PWA document adopted a strong resolution drafted by Ali Sardar Jafri – in what came closest to a socialist realist credo expressed as firm principles – which stated that progressive writing should be about the 'sorrows of the world' and not 'sorrows of the heart', that it should be direct and explicit (avoiding metaphors and similes), and optimistic and positive.

In the same year, an important annual conference of the IPTA adopted a report that stated the organization's clear anti-government stance, post-independence:

> The Allahabad Conference was a landmark in the history of the People's Theatre movement, because this conference worked out the correct ideological stance of the People's Theatre movement in the current political situation and the correct organizational structure necessary to implement its programme. The Allahabad conference will remain memorable in the history of the People's Theatre movement for its bold declaration of struggle and its rejection of the path of compromise that was being followed so long.[26]

It was argued that this strident position became necessary for two reasons: that internally, the IPTA had adopted a policy of 'compromise' at independence, in 1947, a euphoric, over-inclusive stance that failed; and that the post-independence state had proved to be repressive and anti-people. Specifically, the murder of two IPTA activists by Congressmen in a case known as the 'Dixon Lane murder', and severe repression, torture and arrest of cultural activists in 1948 and 1949, necessitated, according to the 1949 conference, serious reorganization within the IPTA as also a transformed view of people's culture.

For the IPTA, reorganization involved reduced autonomy, even if it was an independent organization constituted primarily by people from other mass movements, where every member would become 'both a soldier of the cultural front and of the greater struggle'.[27] The job of the members of the cultural front would be to train members of the mass organizations, and the instructor-members were not to be the 'few middle-class artistes (who) have gathered around the IPTA' even after 'seven years of the movement'.[28] The incapability of many middle-class artists to build

The Bengal IPTA singing squad performs on an open truck:
All India IPTA Conference, Ahmedabad, 1948

up the organization or 'change their outlook', despite their best intentions, resulted in the Association not becoming a mass movement, according to the assessment reflected in the report.

Further, clear positions were taken against the independence of drama or music squads that were not intrinsically connected with other mass organizations, and also that the cultural movement was not to be built up only by cultural workers but by members deputed by mass organizations to work on the cultural front.

The Central Squad performs on stage at the All India IPTA Conference, Allahabad, 1949: (second from left onwards) Usha Dutt, Salil Chowdhury, Hemanga Biswas, Bhupati

It is crucial to note that for the first time the idea of the *artist–organizer*, as someone who did not need to be an artist himself, was being articulated, and this was based on severe anxiety regarding the role middle-class artists had been playing in the IPTA. This anxiety was to play itself out again and again over the years, as will be seen below and in the next chapter. The 1949 conference at Allahabad consciously elected the working-class poet Annabhau Sathe as the President of the organization, and this was seen as symbolic of the push against middle-class domination of IPTA.

This hardening of stance and closing of ranks reflected the emergence of hardline cultural positions in the international communist movement between 1947 and 1954, a move from 'culture as representation' or 'culture as expression' of and by 'the people' to 'culture as weapon'. It coincided with the adoption in the Communist Party of the Soviet Union (CPSU) of resolutions against the infiltration of 'western decadence' in literature, drama and films, and with the Garaudy–Aragon debate in France about the nature of 'communist aesthetics' and the degree to which communist parties need to have control over cultural fronts. Sudhi Pradhan records that Mao's epoch-making Yunan lecture, which laid the foundations of the Cultural Revolution in China, influenced the ideological line that was adopted.[29] The CPSU's line reflected the hardline position of Zhdanov, who was elected as head of agitprop in 1947, and who, in the early 1930s, had argued that socialist realism, which depicted the life of workers and peasants, needed to project 'positive heroes' that would inspire the people.[30] Further, artists in the cultural front also needed to serve the party and its mass organizations like other members, according to the Zhdanovist credo. This line was to influence communist parties in different parts of the world who adopted it formally in the late 1940s. In France, the imposition of the Soviet line led to severe disagreements between intellectuals in the French Communist Party (PCF), encapsulated in the Garaudy–Aragon debate. Roger Garaudy, who was in charge of the intellectual wing, wrote in an article titled 'There is No Communist Aesthetic' that communist artists should be given a certain level of freedom, that socialist realism should not be imposed as a credo, and that the Party should not interfere in cultural affairs. He was challenged by a group of orthodox people led by Louis Aragon who counter-argued that the task of the cultural front was 'to espouse all the ideological and political positions of the working class, to defend in all circumstances, the positions of the Party . . . to cultivate in ourselves the love of the Party and the spirit of the Party in its most conscious form' – a position that was adopted formally by the PCF in 1947.[31] Influenced strongly by the PCF, the Communist Party of Italy (PCI) too adopted the Zhdanovian credo in 1947.

Politically, in India, 1949 was part of the period when the CPI was considering armed struggle against the post-independence state; its position on independence was that it was fictitious and this involved a closing of ranks in the face of severe repression. It was the period of the Telengana armed struggle and the arrest, in 1948, of hundreds of communists – including of several PWA and IPTA activists all over the country – by the Nehru government in response to their call for armed struggle. Organizationally, the need to close ranks was interpreted in terms of the need to limit the middle-class influence, counter what might be seen as decadent and bourgeois tendencies in art, and also to curb the indulgence shown towards artists and their art, in turn subsuming cultural activity to the political aims of the mass organizations and the Party. There was a clear change of stance from the 'openness' that characterized the 'Joshi period' (1943–49) to the rigidity associated with the 'Ranadive' line, once B.T. Ranadive was elected as the the General Secretary of the CPI.

What were the perceived 'distortions' of the Joshi period that the 1949 conference sought to correct? First, the underplaying, in cultural productions, of class conflict in the country, based on an understanding of class unity against fascism and colonialism. These productions, it was argued, represented the postponement of a mass cultural movement, and the 'central ballet troupe formed in Bombay and the drama troupe formed in Calcutta respectively under the Central Committee and the State Committee of the party, paved the way for the formation of commercial art groups with a small number of initiates'.[32] What was being referred to here was the imagining and the performance of the 'popular', the experiments with forms that would become acceptable to varied audiences across diverse contexts all over the country, even while conveying radical messages. Second, the autonomy that was given to music and theatre squads in the initial years of the IPTA. Cultural work was given the status of full-time Party work, with artists living in the Party communes being paid a monthly stipend like any other full-time Party worker and running the cultural squads like professional companies, without the commercial aspect. The 'exclusivity' granted to cultural work thus was brought into question, as seen above. Third, this in turn also got linked up to the substantial presence of 'middle-class artists' and those with an urban bias, with 'petty bourgeois revolutionism' as its theme, reflecting a 'capitulation to the big bourgeoisie'.[33]

Four years later, the relatively stringent stance adopted in 1949 was almost completely reversed and the IPTA was called upon to forge a wider solidarity between artists across diverse fields, ranging from theatre, music, dance, art and film. Politically, this reflected the unfolding of the Peace Movement worldwide and the involvement of the left in it.

> Today the forces of peace are far stronger than the forces of war. . . . In India we witness today a stupendous growth of united mass movements for bread, peace, democracy and national sovereignty. Along with that is taking place a spontaneous cultural upsurge throughout our country, breaking down all artificial barriers between art and the people.[34]

In order to harness the spontaneous cultural expression, it was deemed equally necessary to bring in 'fighting elements from the working class and peasantry', on the one hand, and on the other, set up organic links with professional artists as in the film world. In fact, stalwarts from the film world were also elected as all-India office-bearers of the IPTA.

This shift from the stance of the 1949 conference to a more open engagement that centred primarily on cultural aspects was closer to the 1930s' and early 1940s' stance of the cultural movement. It also happened in an ethos where the post-independence state was seen to be less overtly repressive, and the progressive movement felt it necessary to engage with popular culture and entertainment forms that were emerging in a newly independent country.

A significant feature that marked the 1953 IPTA conference was the setting up of three commissions (for music, dance and film) to research existing cultural forms, assess the classical and folk heritage, and debate the idea of the alternative aesthetic. Across the commissions, the following resolutions were adopted: that the classical and folk heritages would form a valuable basis for the development of the new aesthetic; that cultural activity of an alternative type also required substantial investments; that rigour in the practice of the arts and a strong focus on developing technical aspects, such as stagecraft, lighting and cinematography, could not be dispensed with in creating people's art. For example, the Drama Commission's report presented to the conference stated that '. . . dramatic art cannot be confined to one kind of play. It has room for tragedy as well as comedy, for tears as well as laughter' – probably negating a tendency towards the stereotypical 'positive' socialist hero of Zhdanovist socialist realism.

Various other resolutions that were adopted urged the government to withdraw censorship against artists, to repeal the highly repressive Dramatic Performances Act (passed in 1876, invoked in 1946, and which remained unrevoked in 1949), to provide subsidies and spaces for cultural activity, to provide basic living emoluments to theatre and cultural workers, and to devote 20 per cent of the national budget towards education and culture.

In 1957, the last conference of the IPTA, before it was disbanded as a national organization, endorsed the culture-building project of the Indian state, symbolized by the setting up of academies for literature (the Sahitya Akademi), for music and theatre (the Sangeet Natak Akademi) and for art (the Lalit Kala Akademi). It underscored the need for developing a 'healthy sense of national pride', and to understand what was 'new' in the urges and aspirations of the people, represented by autonomous interests of the people to understand their heritage and folk culture. It was appreciative of the state for responding to the people's urges by setting up the three Akademis, the organization of drama and folk-dance festivals, and providing

unity

FOR A PEOPLE'S CULTURE

In This Issue :

THE ALL-INDIA PEACE CONVENTION

NEW FORMS IN THE INDIAN THEATRE, An Interview with Dr. Mulk Raj Anand

THE CLASSICAL CHINESE THEATRE IS CHANGING, *by P. C. Yu*

I SHALL NOT SING, Poem *by D. N. Nadim*

BARBADYA KANJARI, Short Story *by Anna Bhau Sathe*

Price : Six Annas

ART - LITERATURE - DRAMA - CRITICISM

JUNE 1951

Unity, cover of June 1951 issue

The Rebel

by Anna Bhau Sathe

THE Inamdar held Tatya's nose tight between his teeth, and Tatya pulled hard at the Inamdar's earring, with the finger through the ring—just as a dervish pulls a bear by his nozzle. A big scuffle was on, and both of them went for each other.

The trouble started because Appa Mang's son Tatya had turned rebel. In fact, Tatya was forced to be rebel overnight.

Twenty or twenty-five houses stood at the outskirts of the village. They looked desolate. Everyone was busy with rope making. The sun was about to set, and darkness was beginning to envelope the *Mang* houses. Everything looked gloomy. After searching for food all day, birds had returned to their nests. On a lone lime tree, sparrows were still chirping and their young ones still danced with joy. In the *Mangwada* (*Mang* residential area) the work was reaching a high pitch. Glancing at the setting sun, the *mangs* twisted the jute ropes feverishly. Their only thought was to finish as much work as possible before the sun set. Moving their toy rings, the children turned homewards. Some of them were still eager to continue the game and fidgeted around. Nobody spoke to anyone else.

At the far end of the *Mangwada* stood a lonely hut. Appa Mang, with his one hand held before his eye, sat near the door making a rope. He had nothing on his body. He was trying to do as much work as possible with his one eye. The rays of the setting sun shone brightly over his clean-shaven head. From far off one could see the white bristle of his beard round his very dark face. The sun went beyond the horizon and Appa went inside the hut.

Inside, Appa's sister Changuna was busy preparing the evening meal. Ever since her husband died, she looked after her brother's home. And when Appa's wife left this world she became his companion. She had spent most of her life at her brother's home.

Short story by Annabhau Sathe, published in *Unity*, September 1951 issue financial assistance to artists. The understanding on which such an assessment was based was that colonialism had destroyed the soul of the traditional and folk arts and resulted in a numbing of aesthetic sensibilities in the mass of the people, something that independence and the commitment to a 'Nehruvian socialism' consciously tried to resist. However, a statement questioning the extent to which the government took this job seriously – reflected, for example, in the scanty attention given to culture in the Second Five Year Plan of 1956 – was also adopted at the 1957 conference.

To summarize, even a quick scanning of the political positions adopted by IPTA as a formal organization, between its formation in 1943 and its disbanding as a national organization in 1957, brings out the extensive scope of the issues that arose, ranging from the relationship between the CPI and cultural fronts, the autonomy of cultural activity within the political movement, and the class positions and backgrounds of cultural activists. These years also saw the formal adoption of positions that represented extremes: extremely liberal on the one hand, and intensely narrow on the other.

How can we understand the different positions that have been summarized above in terms of the radical impulse? Two crucial tropes around which left cultural practice saw contradictions unfold, and in terms of which many of the debates can be understood, are of the *collective* and *authenticity*. Around these two tropes, the

The IPTA emblem, designed by Chittaprosad

nuances of which will be unpacked in conceptual terms below, were centred a large part of the arguments around the legitimacy or genuineness of left cultural practice from within the left movement, as the brief description of the IPTA's positions above reveal, as well as from outside it.

The Collective

The theories and ideas of the collective in left-wing art and cultural movements need to be assessed from several distinct yet interrelated aspects that were explicitly debated as well as expressed through anxieties and positions adopted by organizations and movements in different parts of the world. In the Indian case, especially in the music of the IPTA tradition, very little material exists that addresses the notion of the collective and its aesthetic dimensions, despite political movements defining and organizing new collectivities or 'horizontal solidarities'. In other words, even as the need for a cultural dimension to activities of the Communist Party was met with the setting up of the IPTA and its vigorous functioning in the first two decades, there were no explicit deliberations involving the aesthetic ideas around the collective. This, however, is not true about the left-wing music traditions in, say, the United States, Germany, the Soviet Union or China. In India, these issues came up often through intense personal disagreements between people, censure and isolation of specific individuals, assertion and negation of particular positions in documents and conferences of organizations such as the IPTA, as described in the previous section. I have attempted to read much of this as constituted by fundamental ideas around the collective, and this is presented below.

I, We, Them and Us: The Collective in Left-wing Cultural Practice

The following issues around the collective can be isolated from the arguments made at various points in the left cultural movement in India and elsewhere.

First, the role of the individual in collective mass movements, the latter representing the larger sites of mobilization under which culture is subsumed. In the specific case of culture, this is considered more crucial because often it is artists whose expressions of autonomy in interpretation and functioning typically spark off discussions on the role of the individual, on the one hand, and the autonomy of cultural activity within left-wing political formations, on the other. Second, various ideas of the collective that is being mobilized, i.e. 'the masses': who can represent them and what kinds of forms are effective for them. Third, the nature of the idealized and, at the same time, inclusive new collectivities, new solidarities – and what aesthetic forms are appropriate to represent these.

I lay out below what might be considered clusters of 'positionings' on the above issues. The cluster does not imply that all the positionings always went together; it only implies the possibilities of relative compatibility between the different positionings within each cluster.

Cluster A

1. The cultural movement is only one part of the larger mass movement of workers and peasants against exploitation and against imperialism/colonialism. The issues taken up by the cultural movement must reflect the specific positions adopted by the larger mass movements which, in turn, are aligned to the Communist Party. Even if the autonomy of the cultural movement is recognized as valid, the degree of such autonomy has to be strictly circumscribed by the Party's view on various issues. From this viewpoint, the cultural worker is foremost a worker of the Party with Party work being the primary responsibility, and such a worker should be 'thrown up' from the ranks of the masses.
2. It is the job of the movement to represent the masses in the above sense, and at the same time be there 'for' the masses by converting political analysis into easily comprehensible aesthetic formats.
3. It is necessary to understand the culture of the masses but at the same time break out of 'known' aesthetic forms in order to be able to put across dreams of a new world and forge new solidarities that would often break away from old collectivities. This requires the laying down of strict aesthetic principles to convey these 'new' emotions.

Cluster B

4. While the cultural movement is part of the larger mass movement, cultural work has to function autonomously of the movement and the Party. The cultural worker or activist has to focus exclusively or mostly on his/her craft in a collective with other such workers, and that activity is as legitimately political as other mobilizational or organizational activities. Here the responsibility of the artist is to the collective of artist–activists.
5. The aesthetic principles that determine the effectiveness of this politics is determined also by the demands of the craft itself, to do with innovations, experimentation, quality and training. To this extent, the cultural worker has to be a good artist, irrespective of where he or she gets 'thrown up' from.
6. There can be multiple ways of interpreting what 'of the masses' can be used

for this politics and what is appropriate for the masses in the project of fighting for or moving towards a new world. The aesthetic principles that express new collectivities and aim to build a new society are not rule-bound or limited in terms of expression or form.

The multiplicity of actual positions that may be generated out of the above is obvious, and the twentieth century is replete with diverse examples that incorporated one or more of these positionings. These positionings, in turn, resulted in some of the most commonly experienced splits and conflicts in cultural movements of the left, and thus constitute some of the critical debates in the aesthetics–politics relationship.

Given these, we can see that the IPTA tradition's engagements with the various dimensions and self-positionings of the collective were primarily about the artist–activist and the autonomy of cultural work. This, in turn, also connected with questions of authenticity of those who represented the collective, which I take up conceptually later.

With the oft-quoted Allahabad conference of the IPTA adopting resolutions that laid down the basic principles of the role of cultural activists in mass movements of the left, reflecting crucial ideas of the individual within the collective, collectives in this case were identified as 'larger movements of peasants, workers and the toiling masses of the country', in turn organized and led by a vanguard Communist Party. Following the Second Congress of the CPI in February 1948, which adopted a 'left sectarian line', the IPTA conference held subsequently adopted positions on art and culture in keeping with this line – what were termed as its 'bold declaration of struggle and its rejection of the path of compromise which was being followed so long'.[35] 'This association will be building up the People's Theatre movement on behalf of the revolutionary masses as a part of them . . . from within this democratic revolution will emerge a cultural army, class-conscious artistes and a democratic art', stated the major resolution adopted at the conference. A review report prepared after the conference explained:

> The People's movement should be consciously built through the struggles of the different sections of the people and through day to day movements for democracy . . . it should emerge principally through different mass movements . . . it should have an independent organization on the basis of these movements and an able and conscious leadership . . . it should supply the mass movements with cultural weapons . . . we should clearly define the role of the organizers who will be deputed to the different organizations . . . every member shall become both a soldier of the cultural front and of the larger struggle . . . the work of building up the People's

> Theatre movement should not rest solely on the people's theatre workers but shall naturally grow up also under the leadership of organized mass fronts . . . the present state is that after seven years of the movement, a few middle-class artistes and talents have gathered around IPTA . . . many of them are incapable of building up the organization . . . only able and leading workers of IPTA should go into the mass movements, the rest of the members will conduct middle-class squads as local branches, but not as independent drama or music squad . . . regional branches grown out of middle-class squads will not be the major part of the theatre movement.[36]

The clear subordination of the artistic role of the artist–activist to the larger collective also meant that the cultural movement would be 'organized' by what Ritwik Ghatak later referred to as the 'art-organizer', who most often would not be an artist but a Party worker who was deputed to 'organize' cultural activity:

> There is no such thing as an Art-Organizer, it is a monstrous tautology. No such job exists. The nature of the task indicates that only artists can handle the job. . . . This way of thinking is shallow and a dangerously wrong approach to organization building. All the tasks are to be executed by the artistes themselves, because Communist artistes are the organizers.[37]

He stated this in a document titled 'On the Cultural Front' that was submitted to the CPI in 1954, which argued for the creation of an Academy for Histrionic Arts and a Conservatory for Music for the creation of collective art and music, and which reflected the objection to the idea that the organization and disciplining of art and artists in the Communist Party needed to be in the hands of people who might themselves not be artists.

Apart from responding to the repression of cultural activity, the Allahabad conference also took a clear position against the IPTA ethos of the 'Joshi period', as noted earlier. P.C. Joshi's idea behind forming the Bombay Central Squad of the IPTA was to bring together artists who were sympathetic to left-wing politics, and to generate the conditions for collective development of their craft on principles and issues animating the politics of the CPI. Ghatak's document was an affirmation, in the early 1950s, of the 'Joshi position' that characterized the early IPTA years, where artistic production happened in collectives located in communes in some parts of the country. The communes were managed on rigorous principles of frugality, living and eating together irrespective of class and ethnic backgrounds, strict discipline, and rigorous debate and training. It was a pre-given principle that the cultural worker had to be a good artist irrespective of where he or she had got 'thrown up' from.

The strident position adopted by the Allahabad conference of the IPTA in 1949 was in a sense a negation of the idea that the artist's primary responsibility was to the creation of collective art. Again, Ghatak's document was one of a few pieces of writing that spelt out what could be considered the 'Joshi position' with respect to proletarian or progressive art, and its relationship to traditional and other art forms prevalent in the country. In arguing for the setting up of a Federation for Collective Arts, it stated:

> Artistes are specialists who search for content and assume a special way of looking at things. It comes to them as a result of prolonged effort . . . the content and form of their creations come to them as a result of sustained effort. They 'utter' and become distinctive. Then starts the process – this 'agony', this 'suffering', is understood in its 'collectivity' in order to be uttered.[38]

> Different groups and collectives of artists, from their own organizations, will join in such a federation. Each of these collective organizations will hold the right to secede. . . . Within the framework of a minimum programme, their distinctive characteristics might and will be widely divergent. . . . They might move on a strictly professional basis or may be a group of art-enthusiasts, of a *Mahalla* who come together once a year to appear on stage. In fact, they will be as heterogeneous as possible. . . . We can win over the common artists first . . . the real common artists, who have the integrity of artists as well as the integrity of human beings. . . . We must reach out and bring them into our fold. . . . Remember, the Party is interested in ideologically guiding them; the Party gets no benefit from bullying them into set forms in the organization.[39]

During the formative years of the IPTA, with both the Second World War and the Bengal famine being events that led to massive political mobilization, the issue sometimes arose, in artistic production, of spontaneity versus adherence to the Party's ideological line. While the IPTA's formation itself was stimulated by the need to respond to both these tragedies and there was a profusion of artistic production around both, at the ground level activists often felt constrained by the Party's line which at certain points emphasized an anti-fascist position over an anti-British one. The 'people's war' line adopted by the Party after the Soviet Union joined the war meant that fascism had to be fought against, creating the impression of being soft on anti-British mobilization. In music this tension was felt strongly, as is evident from the musician Hemanga Biswas's memoirs, for example, where he chronicles how, in a day-to-day sense, what the singer–activist saw was the death and misery caused by the famine, but how he needed to underplay the British role in creating these as compared to the encouragement received to write and perform anti-fascist songs. The efficacy of the position was enhanced in the Indian case by the fact of Japan's aggression towards the British empire, with Japanese air forces bombing Chittagong, a far eastern district of Bengal.

So, while Party positions were adopted in response to specific political contingencies which possibly required a hierarchization of the objectives of the political struggle, a mechanical application of such political priorities to artistic production resulted in deep fissures and hardline positions which, I would argue, were completely against the spirit of creativity that the radical impulse implied.

The deliberations and decisions put forward at the Allahabad conference and the anxieties expressed in Biswas's memoirs reflect the first positioning in cluster A above. In practical terms, it meant that mechanical interpretations created the demand for songs or plays on each political position taken by the mass organizations as the collective struggle 'had to be represented' in cultural terms. The consequence could either be tremendously creative responses or very poor-quality products in the garb of a cultural-ideological arsenal. What is significant is that often positions 1 and 2 went together, which, when applied ahistorically and in the form of well-established, non-debatable aesthetic principles of representing the collective, resulted in mechanical ideas about progressive or left-wing art.

This combination of positionings was not a response to developments within the cultural movement in India alone, but also represented the influence of powerful debates happening within the left culture in France, Italy, the Soviet Union and elsewhere, as noted earlier. First of all, the credo of socialist realism, coined by Zhdanov in 1934 and adopted as the unequivocal principle for left-wing art in the Soviet Union in 1945, was interpreted as necessitating organizational rigidity and surveillance – and hence the importance of the art-organizer. In France, Italy and the United States, what came to be known as 'Popular Frontism' between the mid-1930s and the mid-1940s, and resulted in a more plural interpretation of what collective art could be, was replaced by relatively rigid positions for the creation of socialist art. Second, the Garaudy–Aragon debate in France, referred to earlier in this chapter, with Aragon's conservative position prevailing in the debate, found an echo in India in the form of the rejection of the 'Joshi position' on culture. Laurent Casanova, who was appointed as the PCF activist in charge of intellectuals and culture in 1947, summarized the role of communist intellectuals thus: 'To espouse all the ideological and political positions of the working class, to defend in all circumstances, and with the utmost determination, all the positions of the party . . . to give the proletariat any additional arguments that you can'.[40] Third, the proletariat collective needed to be represented in optimistic, heroic terms, through collective images across different forms of cultural representation.

Apart from the political issues raised by questions around the collective, crucial aesthetic–representational issues also lay at the base of the debates. These positions were also about authenticity of representation, i.e. *who* would represent the marginalized and the oppressed in whose interests the movement had been launched, and *what* of tradition would be represented and *how*. These were seen as debates within the IPTA in India, with Ritwik Ghatak, Shambhu Mitra, Utpal Dutt and many others coming up with explicit positions centring on the creative process itself and on issues of authenticity in representation. From the 1960s onwards there were alternative movements in India that questioned those aspects of tradition engaged with the authenticity of representations of the indigenous, and also of those who represented the indigenous (especially if these were seen to represent privileged sections of society). This also resulted in questioning the effectiveness of the politics of representation as such.

Below, I turn to this second question, that of authenticity, around which many debates within the literary and cultural movements can be classified.

Issues of Authenticity in Left-wing Cultural Practice

Questions of authenticity in cultural representation involve both anthropological enquiry or exercises in cultural archaeology in pursuit of little-known forms from various cultures, on the one hand, and the representation of the *indigenous* and of *tradition* in social discourses, on the other. While the former mode accompanied developments in the field of ethnomusicology, for example, this section engages with the discovery of forms from primarily non-western cultures, i.e. with issues of authenticity as they arose within movements as well as assessments of such movements, in this case specifically of the left. Notions of authenticity in music, for example, have ranged from those about historical continuity or 'age-old traditions', autonomy from commercial imperatives, belonging to and being performed by the people it represents, and about transformations that occur in the modes of representation. Thus, from the use of what came to be characterized as elitist classical traditions to marginalized indigenous ones, as well as the identity of the performers, political legitimacy or illegitimacy has drawn on questions of authenticity. In turn, these questions also link up with more contemporary debates on the nation, nationalism and nationalities, and their representation. In the context of contemporary discourses on identity creation and the compatibility of left-wing engagements with identity issues, this section also explores questions of authenticity with respect to 'horizontal comradeships'. In other words, it addresses the broad contours of the debates around one of the foundational concerns of the relationship between art and politics: the representation of new identities as a part of left political practice, *in* politics and *as* politics.

I begin with the question of how to represent 'new' identities, for example, based on class. Questions of representation around the idea of the 'proletarian', an identity that was being shaped in the early decades of the twentieth century in Europe and the United States, dominated left-wing artistic production significantly. Proletarian art and literature were key pivots around which radical politics turned in Southeast Asia, South Asia and Latin America as well in the 1930s and later, and working-class cultural mobilizations continued well into the second half of the twentieth century. The idea of the proletarian was not received and applied mechanically in different parts of the world, even if a lot of received wisdom perceived it as such. In colonial and less developed contexts such as India, where the call for independence from colonialism was also linked up with anti-fascist solidarity, emancipation from class-based exploitation was crucially tied to freedom from foreign rule. Therefore, diverse segments of the population, not merely the proletariat, became the focus of mobilization and hence representation. Radical cultural intervention, thus, was about 'the people', 'the peasantry', 'the lower castes' and 'adivasis'. Major aesthetic debates foregrounded this idea through establishing the legitimacy of, and then figuring out ways to represent, the 'ordinary person' or 'ordinary people'.[41] The proletarian, or a person with a distinct working-class identity, which is what most of the European and American cultural movements were focusing on, was only one kind of person who was being represented or mobilized.[42]

Thus, even a new, 'constructed' class identity such as the proletariat resulted in a wide variety of interpretations, informed and necessitated by local contexts. In fact, some of the most fascinating debates about the role of middle-class artists in cultural movements of the left happened in the context of such debates on representation.

A crucial dimension of the authenticity debate in India, as mentioned earlier, had to do with this question, of *who* is involved with the revival, preservation and showcasing efforts; in other words, whether they are authentic bearers of tradition, especially the folk. In the case of the IPTA, this anxiety was repeatedly reflected in assessments conducted in conferences about the role of middle-class artists, as this chapter has described in detail. Further, it has also involved doubts being raised about whether a class-based identity such as that of a 'worker' is inauthentic and forced, driven by the imperatives of political mobilization of the left, in turn obscuring 'real ethnicity or identity'.

When the IPTA conference held in 1949 stated, with alarm, that a 'few middle-class artistes have gathered around the IPTA' and this resulted in the IPTA not becoming a mass movement, the inauthenticity of the middle-class artist was attributed to such a person's ineffectiveness stemming from his/her class background which, it was argued, is delinked from 'the people'.[43] This kind of assessment has been frequent in the left movement as well as from critics outside, and is often linked to an urban–rural divide and a necessary equation between the rural and 'the people'. This notion of the inauthentic artist relates to the class they belong to.

The twentieth-century discourse on authenticity involved not only indigenous forms and folk culture, but also the so-called classical traditions or those that operated under patronage systems of the ruling elite. Both indigenous and marginalized cultures of the dominated people as well as traditions, often considered 'classical' and under patronage, were transformed under colonialism, and were often drawn into discourses on cultural nationalism as part of the anti-colonial struggle. The idea of the nation and authentic national culture were central to how the tradition was conceived, and this became a pivot around which authenticity issues arose – beginning with critiques of cultural nationalism, and going on to critiques of left-wing identity politics and culturalist interventions. This will be taken up in detail in the last chapter.

The critique of the left project as being inauthentic can be summarized as an attempt to create large identities, akin to that of a hegemonic nationalist project, resulting in an artificial and forced homogenization and obscuring of differences based on sub-nationalisms or 'other' identities.[44] This critique, based on an ideology of sub-national, sub-regional, ethnic identity, extends in three directions. (i) It results in a questioning of identity locations such as class within left ideology, arguing that class-based identities, on the one hand, and internationalist and nationalist politics, on the other, are overarching and artificially constructed; in fact, that class-based politics, by underplaying identities of origin such as caste, reasserts dominant non-class hierarchies and inequalities. (ii) In terms of cultural interventions, it introduces the idea of the inauthentic artist, the 'middle-class' or 'upper-caste' artist–activist who reproduces the ideology of his origins, and the authentic marginalized or lower-caste artist–activist who is uncomfortable with the suppression of subaltern or caste identities.[45] (iii) It questions the authenticity of the aesthetic creations and conflates this critique with the critique of a homogenizing nationalism. Clearly, the notion of authenticity encompasses identity, people and cultural products.

In later periods, the non-authenticity critiques of cultural movements of the left hinged on questioning the genuineness and the transformatory potential of this politics that allegedly ignored identities such as caste or ethnicity.[46] Questions of whether the people involved in specific interventions were eligible to do so, primarily due to their origins in terms of caste, class or location, have also been significant in debating issues of authenticity. The question of legitimacy, in turn, has spilled over into questioning and establishing the genuineness of such people's intentions to represent the indigenous, where the distance between them and such sources of the indigenous is considered to be obvious and apparent. Further, it has also spilled over into questioning the legitimacy of the politics that they represented, with such political movements being accused of, in effect, encouraging practices that discriminate against the genuine practitioners of the indigenous forms, thus at best serving a reformist and paternalistic agenda.

In assessing such strident critiques that assail the inauthenticity of representation as well as the politics that such representation attempted to convey, based on the subject-positions of the people concerned, the following points are importent to note. First, they bring out aspects of the construction of the radical aesthetic that concerned itself with class, nation and ethnicity, and the factors that influence their multiple cultural imaginings. Second, the cultural energies that are unleashed in radical moments, as occurred during the 1940s and 1950s that this book is about, result in multiple interpretations and explorations, often contradictory to each other, and need to be understood as such, not just in terms of deterministic conclusions. The critiques, both internal to the IPTA that hinge on class as well as the identity-based critiques, I argue later in this book, tend to be deterministic, in the process denouncing or caricaturing the political legitimacy of particular people or politics. Third, it is the multiplicity of interpretations of how a radical political agenda can be carried through the arts that marks the impulse as truly radical. To interpret political positions mechanically in terms of how artistic practice should unfold and, in fact, to come up with codified rules for creative expression limit the possibilities of art *as* politics and relegate it to either mechanical practice or sheer entertainment.

Notes

1 Pradhan (1982): 131.

2 Ibid.: 135.

3 The highly quoted landmark that spurred the formal setting up of the PWA was the publication of a controversial short story collection titled *Angaarey* (Embers) in 1932. Consisting of stories and a play written by three men, Sajjad Zaheer, Ahmed Ali and Mahmuduzzafar, and a woman, Rashid Jahan, it was a critique of familial and sexual mores, of conservative and hypocritical social life, and the 'absence of circumspection' in north Indian Muslim society of the time. Scathingly attacked by many in the Muslim community as being obscene

and blasphemous, and the writers being overtly Europeanized, it was also condemned by organizations like the All India Shia Conference.

4 Pradhan (1982): 57.

5 Bhattacharya (1971).

6 Dharwadker (2008): 313.

7 Ibid. (2008): 8.

8 Namboodiripad (1986).

9 Habib (1998): 23.

10 Ibid.

11 Denning (2004): 57.

12 Denning (2004). In France, the Communist Party played a pivotal role in this process, sponsoring the formation of the Association of Revolutionary Artists and Writers (AEAR) in 1932, 'with the aim of gathering together, under the vague aegis of the party, all intellectuals opposed to fascism' (Gopal 2005). Maxim Gorky, Romain Rolland, André Malraux, Thomas Mann, Waldo Frank and others organized the World Congress of Writers for the Defence of Culture in Paris in 1933, which proved to be very influential in India.

13 Gopal (2005); Mir and Mir (2006), for example, on the PWA.

14 Examples of such studies are Bowen Struyk (2006) and Denning (2004).

15 Gopal (2005): 17.

16 Ghosh (2002).

17 Patel (2002).

18 Mir and Mir (2006): 23.

19 This is seen in several documents published in Pradhan (1979; 1982; 1985).

20 Shanghai was a city where Japanese radicals met up with Comintern representatives to found the Japanese Communist Party in the early 1920s, as well as where the Chinese Communist Party was founded in 1921. Being a large and bustling industrial city, it had a prominent working class and more than 500 labour unions in the 1920s. In the backdrop of Chiang Kai-shek's taking control in China in 1927, a large-scale revolutionary literary movement was launched in Shanghai, with the League of Leftwing Writers (established in 1930) and League of Leftwing Dramatists (established in January 1931) promoting proletarian literature and theatre in the city, which had strong links with similar organizations in Japan. With international proletarianism offering an alternative imagined community, during the 1930s, Japanese, Korean, Taiwanese and Chinese writers and activists jointly opposed Japanese imperialism and the Pacific War (Bowen-Struyk 2006).

21 Bowen-Struyk (2006).

22 In an article titled 'The Poet and the Question of Labour' written in 1920, Tian Han argued that the poet and the worker both fulfilled such needs, and that the endeavour in creating a socialist world should be to create a 'holy world' where soul and flesh coalesce, and where workers and other oppressed people could work equally with writers and intellectuals, and where women would be part of the socialist order (Chen 2006).

23 Mir and Mir (2006); Ali and Rashed (1977–78); Geeta Patel (2002).

24 According to Patel (2002: 90), Ahmed Ali marks a Village Poets' Convention held in May 1938 as beginning this shift from the 'literary' to the 'political' faction. Ali subsequently resigned from the PWA, and Mir and Mir (2006) argue that a large corpus of the PWA's work consisted of didactic content that was explicitly 'socialist', laying out the contours of a realism that focused on content and less on form.

25 Geeta Patel notes that the moral high ground and outrage that was expressed against the

Angaarey collection by critics, terming the writings 'obscene, morally depraved, base, filthy and foul, trash' (Patel 2002: 102), foreshadows the fervour and tone with which writings by many of the PWA's own writers on sex and sexuality were characterized, and the 'movement's own evolving strategies of exclusion resembled the format of the responses to the first major collection of writing attributed to the newly forming progressive movement' (ibid.: 103).

26 Pradhan (1982): 49.

27 Ibid.: 57.

28 Ibid.: 58.

29 Ibid.: 10.

30 Guiat (2003): 59.

31 Ibid.

32 Pradhan (1982): 9.

33 Ibid.

34 Ibid.: 148.

35 Ibid.: 49.

36 Ibid: 51. These positions, it may be recalled, were asserted as a result of assessments that the cultural movement had gone astray from stated principles and needed to be reined in. The specific incident known as the Dixon Road murder, where an IPTA member and another person were shot dead by Congress party miscreants at a cultural function organized by the Bengal IPTA, and generalized arrests and repression of left activists, including IPTA activists, by the state in newly independent India, were stated as reasons why a strong line needed to be adopted . This position reflected the repression that was unleashed by the post-independence Indian state on left activists all over the country. Several IPTA activists were jailed in this period.

37 Ghatak (1954): 32.

38 Ibid.

39 Pradhan (1982): 43.

40 Quoted in Guiat (2003): 60.

41 Mitra (1980).

42 Even within Europe, documentation of the guerrilla theatre during the Greek resistance, for example, in the 1930s shows that the resistance consisted of a broad front composed of alliances across political groups, classes and nationalities whose only affinity was based on anti-fascist sentiment; the resistence, hence, was like a 'negative unity in diversity' rather than a monolithic entity. The target of representation, like in the Indian case, was a widely defined category of 'the people'. In cases such as these, diversity was perhaps underwritten into the structures that evolved as well as in terms of the targets of representation (Myrsiades and Myrsiades 1999).

43 Pradhan (1982): 58.

44 Menon (2007); Naregal (2008).

45 Ibid.

46 Ibid.

2

People's Music and the Radical Impulse

From its second decade, the twentieth century saw the need for a people's art – a need to represent, unearth, popularize and express through forms that emerged from and belonged to 'the people'. We have seen that this radical impulse in art was fuelled by events of the unique historical conjuncture of the first half of the twentieth century, and the varied iconography that emerged from the early years of that century to represent 'the people' in art and literature. In fact, the actual experience of colonialism fashioned responses in, for example, the Southeast Asian and East Asian countries, quite distinctly from the Euro–American contexts. Notable within this experience was the engagement with tradition and indigenous forms, as also the distinctive engagement with the classical tradition.

This chapter is about distinct and, at the same time, diverse notions of 'people's music' that emerged in radical left-wing movements from the early years of the twentieth century. It attempts to weave the story of how a plethora of ideas and experiments on what people's music is, should be and can be emerged in different parts of the world, fuelled by the need to craft an alternative aesthetic. The next chapter will focus on people's music in India within this tapestry, but will also attempt to highlight the distinctive nature of Indian experiments with radical music, primarily its intertwining with other performative traditions and its experience with colonialism. In other words, I attempt to bring out the variety of ideas that constituted the 'radical–popular' in music in the first half of the twentieth century in these two chapters.

Early Twentieth-Century Ideas

The international left movement's conscious deliberations on music for the sake of emancipation started by the mid-to-late 1920s with the success of the Russian Revolution, economic uncertainties and social upheaval in the prelude to the Great Depression in the advanced capitalist world, and the fight against colonialism in different parts of the world. In Germany and Italy, the deliberations had to deal with extremely strong and orthodox notions of music nationalism in the wake of fascism. In the United States, the experience of the International Workers of the World (commonly referred to as the Wobblies) with creating a spontaneous body of music along with the growth of the union movement in the 1910s provided a backdrop for subsequent experiments from the late 1920s. The Wobblies, a union formed by socialists, anarchists and radical trade unionists in 1905, sought to mobilize the working class as a whole in the United States (as against craft unionism that had been in existence until then),[1] and was also well known for using music as part of its activities. In China and Japan, by the 1920s, there had been major debates about proletarian literature, with writers like Tian Han engaging creatively with the idea of 'tradition' and the Chinese classical heritage, on the one hand, and the question of 'western influences' on proletarian literature, on the other. These questions, of tradition, heritage and modernism, were to resurface much later, during the Cultural Revolution in China, as part of a distinct notion of people's music.[2] A critique of 'western' as embodying 'imperialist', 'bourgeois', 'commercial' and 'decadent' tendencies would influence developments in Brazilian radical music much later, by the 1960s, but similar considerations were important for discussions on people's music in India as well.[3]

The following section consists of a broad sweep of the considerations that were important in discussions on people's music in the cases of the United States, Germany, France, the Soviet Union and China until the end of the 1930s. Briefly, the following issues are common to the diverse experiences. First, a constant negotiation between simplicity and accessibility, on the one hand, and modernism or the idea of the avant-garde, on the other. Questions of simplicity encompass the directness or otherwise of lyrics and the presence or otherwise of musical accompaniment, and extend into a complex musical grammar involving types of harmonies, the relationship between the mood of the lyrics and the music that went with it. Second, the issues of representation that are debated are, who represents the people, interpretation (how the music is put across, whether it can be 'changed' through interpretation) and authorship (whose composition it is eventually), as fundamental in constituting the relationship between music and politics. Third, questions about the nation and how it is imagined are debated through music, where the radical intervention creates a substantial plurality.

From Proletkult to Socialist Realism: People's Music after the October Revolution

The revolutionary music movement in the Soviet Union in the period from the early years after the Russian Revolution until the Second World War consisted of three distinct phases: (i) from the revolution until the end of the 1920s, when, along with debates on the definition and implementation of an ideologically correct musical agenda, there was a substantially plural ethos of musical creation; (ii) the 1930s, which retained some of the pluralism, even as stances about 'correct' revolutionary music started hardening; (iii) the late 1930s onwards, when the socialist realism credo, even if plurally interpreted, began to be rigidly applied in organizational terms. While the revolutionary musical ethos of the 1920s was diverse and consisted of various explorations of varying ideas of 'genuine people's music', the 1930s were to bring in more definitional and 'correct' notions of music for the people. Through the 1920s, composers sought to convey the ideas of the Russian Revolution through music, to create music that would appeal to the largest number of people who previously had hardly any access to it and, at the same time, in fact as part of it, experimented extensively with modernism in classical music. The engagement with modernism, its relationship with tradition and the question of 'formalism', however, were to become contentious issues by the mid-1930s, when socialist realism was defined and declared as the appropriate mode of representation in socialist art.

In less than a year after the revolution, the various music conservatories in the Soviet Union were nationalized and brought under Narkompros (the Commissariat for Higher Education), an influential organization that was to play a significant role in Soviet cultural policy. Muzo, the music department of the Narkompros, was set up to coordinate musical activities. Narkompros was headed by Alexander Lunacharsky, whose attitude towards the role of artistic creation in the new society was open, recognizing the need for creative freedom and individuality of expression. Asked in 1918 by a group of composers about the conservatories' relationship with Narkompros, Lunacharsky expressed firm support for complete autonomy in musical life, and also for the value of musical specialists to the cause of the revolution. As a Bolshevik intellectual, he encouraged artists to pursue 'revolutionary inspiration' in their art, but also defended pre-revolutionary cultural achievements as the legitimate inheritance of the proletariat and sought to elicit cooperation from highly skilled, politically independent professionals. By then, an experiment called the 'Proletkult' had already taken shape, bringing forth a highly varied agenda for the 'new people's music'. The period from 1918 until the mid-1930s, especially until the end of the 1920s, was thus characterized by multiple interpretations of how the musical and political revolutions might fuel each other. In Nelson's words,

> Images of cultural life . . . include a frenzy of cultural iconoclasm as well as the joyous mass celebrations of the overthrow of the old order . . . [there was] an even stronger urge to democratize music and the arts and thus break down barriers between educated Russians and the common people . . . signalling the beginning of a quest for an inclusive art.[4]

We review the major trends here.

First, the organizational and theoretical efforts of Muzo resulted in engagement with a range of idioms, from the radical avant-garde to the heritage–classical. Headed by the maverick futurist composer Arthur Lourie, who was handpicked by Lunacharsky, Muzo's initial phase saw a reflection of the ideology of the 'equation of revolutionary chaos with the spirit of music'.[5] For Lourie, the revolution itself was music. Soon enough, control moved away from him to a set of people who got involved with expanding Muzo and initiating a spate of organizational changes. One of the key developments under the expanded Muzo was the institutionalization of music theory and musicology, involving definitions and methodologies of 'musical science' in Ak Muzo, the academic sub-section of Muzo. Highly theoretical in orientation, a group of composers (Mikhail Ivanov-Boretskii, Leonid Sabaneev, Nikolai Garbuzov and Nadezhda Briusova) worked on aspects such as 'ultrachromaticism', an alternative, fifty-step to the twelve-tone scale, and the acoustic basis of harmony.

Second, was the Proletkult movement. The Proletkult (an acronym for *Proletarskie Kul'turno Prosvetel'nye Organisatsii*, or Proletarian Cultural Organizations), an organization formed a few days after the revolution, which held its first organizing conference soon after its formation, took shape as a loose coalition of clubs, factory committees, workers' theatres and educational societies, and expanded by 1918 to define a unique political culture for a new society. It was inspired by the ideas of Alexander Bogdanov, or the *Vpered* (Forward) circle in Russian Bolshevism, and believed that an autonomous working-class intelligentia, a proletarian vanguard, needed to take charge of post-revolutionary culture. Frolova-Walker and Walker (2012) note that while the obvious inspiration came from Bogdanov's strident positions on this, the plurality reflected Lenin's and Lunacharsky's positions as well: their appreciation of Russia's musical heritage; their interest in preserving it on the one hand, and their fascination with the innovative and the avant-garde, on the other.

The Proletkult sought to redefine the relationship between an intelligentsia that had cultural skills and access to education, and the working class. Its membership and objectives were wide-ranging, from radical egalitarians who aimed to create an intelligentsia-less society to those who wanted to transmit the art and culture of pre-revolutionary Russia to the working classes, to give a chance to the intelligentia to pay off a 'centuries-old debt' to the working classes by opening the doors of art to them.[6]

The Proletkult was autonomous of the Communist Party of the Soviet Union (CPSU), even if many of its members were also CPSU members. There were furious debates over whether the new culture would be made 'from above' or 'from below' by the workers. Many of Russia's finest artists taught in Proletkult's programmes, notably Stanislavski in theatre, Andrei Beluga and Nicolai Gumilev in literature, and also Alexander Kastalskii, Reinhold Glière and Dmitri Vasilev-Buglai. It functioned with considerable state support and artistic freedom to exercise multiple understandings of political culture. For example, in Moscow, the music department was run by people who believed that folk music should form the basis of proletarian music, as a result of which the Moscow Proletkult had a large folk section and classes for instruments like the balalaika. In contrast, in Petrograd, Ia. Uzolin, who was in charge of the music division, believed that the organization should create revolutionary songs. In Kologriv, where Maria Shipova, a conservatory graduate was in charge of the music division, piano, violin and songs by Russian classical composers were taught.

Third, three sets of people who symbolized musical life in the 1920s, presented in Nelson's work, consisting of the militant Revolutionary Association of Proletarian Musicians (RAPM), the Organization of Revolutionary Composers (ORK) and Prokoll, a collective organization of conservatory students. These three sets of people have been put together within the larger classification because they were relatively minor in importance in terms of size, unlike Muzo and the Proletkult, but at the same time signified important tendencies in the understanding of revolutionary music. Within these, the RAPM constituted an extreme application of Marxist aesthetics and principles to music and Nelson (2000) points out that most scholarship, by focusing on the extreme views of the RAPM, overlooks the musical diversity of the left-wing in the Soviet Union in the 1920s.

The rise of the RAPM in 1923 happened in an effort to 'redress the backwardness in the musical scene', as a balance between 'elite music' propagated by some people and the 'degenerate and light' genre promoted by those who published, disseminated and publicized foxtrots, popular songs and the like. The RAPM consisted largely of amateur musicians – in fact, those who were merely activists and not musicians. An assessment of the heritage and musical legacy consisted of categorizing folk music as that of the masses, and art music as revolutionary only if it represented ascending classes within the bourgeoisie which overthrew the older feudal order, such as Beethoven's music written during the French Revolution. Art music, in the RAPM's assessment, as it existed in the Soviet Union in the 1920s, reflected the decadence of an 'ascending class in decline', as did urban popular music or western dance music. The RAPM's composers also worked with ideas of appropriate musical structure. For example, Aleksandr Kastalskii worked extensively to set folk melodies to choral music. Nelson notes that his most significant work, the 'Agricultural Symphony', used traditional folk songs and dance tunes to score for a full symphony orchestra, a choir as well as for two soloists.[7] The RAPM was, in organizational terms, fanatical and a terror, causing it to be disbanded as an organization. The ORK, the second group of musicians in the 1920s, composed music around romantic revolutionary themes, using poetry from Vladimir Mayakovsky, Demian Beduyi and others.

The term 'socialist realism' is said to have been coined in the year 1929 by Ivan Gronsky, with the formation of the New Union of Writers. It was also used at an October 1932 meeting in Maxim Gorky's apartment which Stalin attended, where the idea that – '[a]n artist must above all portray life truthfully. And if he shows our life truthfully, on its way to socialism, that will be socialist realism' – was to be included in an address to the writers soon.[8] One strand of research into Soviet aesthetics, especially on socialist realism, argues that it could be reduced to demands for accessibility, tunefulness, stylistic traditionalism and folk-inspired qualities in art,[9] whereas more recent work argues that socialist realism was, to begin with, only visualized in terms of how art forms 'would reflect the new life of the proletariat, it would be a truthful reflection of the progressive, revolutionary aspirations of the toiling masses building communism' in the early 1930s.[10] This aspiration for a socialist art was shared by a range of Soviet artists across diverse art forms, but got established as a credo and was interpreted in more strict organizational terms only subsequently. To illustrate, Gorky published an essay titled 'On Socialist Realism' in the beginning of 1933 which provided a definition for the term, followed by a further definition from Stalin – 'cultures, national in form and Socialist in substance' – as well as the statement in 1934 by Andrei Zhdanov, the CPSU's representative to the first All-Union Congress of Soviet Writers, defining socialist realism as 'depicting reality in its revolutionary development'.[11] Subsequently, its interpretation in organizational terms meant that socialist art:

> should exhibit three elements. It should have an 'ideological content' (*ideinost*) meaning that it should express a core idea of communism. It should also exhibit

> a 'Party' (*partiinost*) element, meaning an active or militant aspect illustrating the human dynamic effort aimed at achieving the better future. Finally it should display a spirit of national popularism (*narodnost*) by its referencing the whole population rather than just a limited section as in bourgeois art.[12]

Further, the socialist realist idiom in music was expected to focus on particular forms such as cantatas and symphonies, and use musical materials from folk melodies (especially of the non-Russian nationalities). What this meant was that works of art would be appraised mechanically for containing these elements and critiqued if they did not.

What is not as apparent is whether the 'doctrine' of socialist realism, as understood by the CPSU as well as musicians working for the revolution, necessarily denounced experimentation and modernism in music. Following from material published from the 1970s onwards about socialist realism being an outright rejection of modernism, with the two ideas being polar opposites, more recent work on the relationship between modernism and socialist art argues that this was an extreme view, 'encouraged by historians who illustrated a split throughout the twenties between the modernists and proletarian factions, with the proletarian factions "winning" in the end'.[13] A key example in the argument about the split has been that of the composer Dmitri Shostakovich where it has been suggested that he was either an uncritical loyalist or a disillusioned dissident whose music, dismissed as being 'formalist', went against the idioms of socialist realism. It had been argued, for example, by Solomon Volkov's highly influential book, *Testimony* (1979), that Shostakovich, in his early years, was an ardent modernist, who was forced by the government to change into a socialist realist and who then encoded anti-government messages in music.[14] His 'Symphony no. 5 op. 47', in particular, has been quoted as the example of a work that the composer was forced to write by the Soviet government against his creative desires, which he converted into a veiled protest against the government. However, other studies argue that composers who were modernist in the 1920s 'willingly turned to socialist realism by the early 1930s, overturning the previous idea that composers had fallen prey to the aesthetic and that all music composed in the thirties was of poor quality'.[15] In fact, as in the United States, modernism provided the background from which artists were influenced by and then engaged with radical politics, bringing in modernist ideas into visualizing socialist art in the Soviet Union.[16] The analysis of works of composers such as Shostakovich shows their deep engagement with questions of how socialist realism could incorporate modernism, and also demonstrates how the composer himself brought changes in his style and use of idioms over time; in fact particularly after one of his operas, 'Lady Macbeth of Mtsensk' (1936), was critiqued by the Party newspaper *Pravda* as being shallow in its construction and lacking emotional depth. What was being objected to, according to Pearson, was the open portrayal of a woman's sexuality, as well as her characterization as defying 'family values' that were being upheld in the Soviet Union at the time, and specifically the so-called dissociation of 'form from content', i.e. formalism.[17] Shostakovich's next piece of work, his 'Symphony no. 4, op. 43', showed a marked change in structure, followed by a 'Fifth Symphony' which reflected his own changed perception and engagement with modernism as a style, a monumental work that was met with critical acclaim in the late 1930s. Pearson argues that:

> Shostakovich could have easily played it safe in response to *Pravda*'s criticisms and composed a socialist cantata or something based on folk tunes. He instead composed a symphony based on his own material, tonal yet full of dissonance, using elements he had been criticized for (such as the satirical tone of the second movement), yet refining them and fitting them organically to the symphony as a whole, and throughout rising to the challenge of creating his best symphony yet. . . . he . . . seems to have taken *Pravda*'s criticisms seriously, if critically. In this respect he did not betray his artistic integrity and creative development while also continuing to adhere to the socialist realist aesthetic.[18]

What seems to be apparent from a balanced view of available evidence about the post-1934 period is that the dominant musical expression of socialist realism conformed to the norms set, but musical expression and different interpretations of socialist principles continued with composers like Shostakovich and Rachmaninov, albeit under strict scrutiny and fear of censure and exile.

From 'Being a Phonograph' to the Cultural Revolution: People's Music in China

As early as in 1928, in an essay titled 'The Echo of the Phonograph', the prominent writer and critic Guo Moro urged leftist cultural workers to 'be a phonograph'. Cultural realism here was being refracted through the lens of emergent media technologies symbolized by the phonograph.[19] This aesthetic of 'phonographic realism' was an important component of left-wing mass music produced in China in the 1930s, which 'recorded' the struggles and aspirations of the proletariat and subsequently played them back to society as a means of social mobilization.[20] However, the image of the phonograph, read as representing the commercial aspect of music, could also be used to draw out the imperatives of left-wing musical production. A brief review of the cultural scene in China in the first three decades of the twentieth century is provided here to illustrate this.

Shanghai in the 1920s and 1930s was a bustling, multicultural city with a significant audience for 'westernized' music, a prominent gramophone industry and, in fact, a keen jazz culture. It was in this context, combined with the predominantly rural and peasant economy-based society, that various notions of 'people's music' unfolded in China. A young trumpet player, Buck Clayton, who arrived in Shanghai in 1935 for a long engagement at a ballroom and later became famous as a member of the Count Basie orchestra, stated that he spent the happiest two years of his life in Shanghai.[21] Shanghai became famous as the jazz appreciation centre of Asia and also gave rise to a genre referred to as the Chinese 'modern song' (*shidai qu*), a hybrid genre of American jazz, Hollywood and Chinese folk music. This new genre, dismissed as 'yellow' or 'pornographic' music by critics on the left, became a reference point against which alternative left-wing mass music positioned itself in the inter-war years, 'in which yellow music and anti-colonial mass music rub sonic shoulders and contend for a measure of dominance within a newly constituted media marketplace'.[22]

The emergence of the left alternative also occurred in the backdrop of a widespread movement for modernization of Chinese music, a critical evaluation of tradition that followed in the wake of the May Fourth movement in 1919 and the harnessing of music for 'nation building'. A new generation of Chinese musicians who were exposed to western music, such as Xiao Youmei (President of the Shanghai National Conservatory of Music) and Wang Guangqi, argued that Chinese music was outmoded and stagnant, a tradition at a standstill, and characterized by a lack of a tempered scale, functional harmony, counterpoint, orchestration, standardized notation and the technical sophistication of an instrument like the piano. Modernizing music was considered an absolute necessity, and there were major initiatives to popularize western musical techniques, set standards for musical performance and practice, and also institutionalize music education.[23] Similar to what happened in many countries where nationalism was the driving force for politics, this 'sonic regime', supported strongly by the Kuomintang Nationalist Government, was emphasized as a 'distinctly Chinese' musical idiom. This was something that was taken up as a mission by left-wing artists as well before the Chinese Revolution and also in the post-revolutionary period, as deliberations on revolutionary music took place. Musicologist Helen Young, in categorizing 'socialist realist' music in China, classifies it as a sonic regime.[24]

Urbanization and the accompanying process of commercialization in the arts had resulted in folk forms moving to urban theatres, as happened in India by the 1920s. Jones records:

> With the growth of mass media like gramophone records and wireless broadcasting, urbanites were able to listen to recordings of *tanci*, *pingju* and *shenqu* . . . resulted in a certain degree of cross-pollination of musical forms. . . . Cantonese musicians began to incorporate guitars, banjos and saxophones into their regional music. Popular musicians set pentatonic melodies drawn from urban folk traditions into jazzy harmonies.[25]

This popular idiom was soon to be criticized by 'serious' musicians as well as those on the left, as 'degraded' and 'vulgar' hybrid forms in opposition to rural folk traditions.[26] Created mainly by a well-known and then controversial musician, Li Jinhui, this kind of music came into being in the late 1920s and was denounced as 'decadent sounds' by Nie Er, the iconic left-wing musician (about whom more will be said below) – the decadence being characterized ostensibly by the use of 'bad forms of Western music' such as jazz which, it was feared, would degrade the nation's culture.

The 1930s created some of the iconic left-wing musical traditions that came from China. Nie Er, a young musician then, initiated the creation of 'mass music', marking itself as distinct from European art music traditions, from 1932, through the eight-year-long war with Japan. He composed a large number of 'realist' songs of dockworkers, newspaper sellers, sing-song girls and others whose lives he had 'recorded', the kind of music that would 'cry out on behalf of the masses', according to him.[27] Among his famous compositions was the 'March of the Volunteers' (adopted as China's national anthem in 1949), the 'Song of the Road' and the 'Vanguards'.

In 1933, the artists Tian Han, An Er, Ren Guang, Zhang Shu and Lü Ji formed the Soviet Friends Society in order to study Soviet mass music and composition. The next year they set up another group, the Music Unit of the Left-wing Dramatists Union, to integrate more musicians into the production of music and films for the revolutionary cause.

By the end of 1935 over a hundred choirs and singing societies had been founded across Shanghai, also involving the development of new commercial media and the 'cacophony of a colonized metropolis of more than three million inhabitants, in which above sixty radio stations operated by the mid-1930s.'[28] These societies gathered regularly to sing patriotic songs in the hope of boosting the morale of the Chinese people and the army.

In the rural areas, the communists had been using music for political mobilization from the early 1920s. In January 1921, members of the Marxist Research

Society at Beijing University were urged to go out into the countryside, and recover and use folk tunes to compose songs for peasant mobilization. The working class was also soon to be mobilized, with music playing a major role, from 1921 onwards. By the end of 1929, calls were once again made 'for more extensive use of oral and visual forms of literature and art in the Red Army's political work', and by the early 1930s, the fusion of revolutionary content with popular artistic forms was widespread.[29]

After the revolution, the kinds of music that were officially seen to be revolutionary and truly representative of the people were the following: the genre of the mass song; large-scale compositions and cantatas that could easily carry political messages; symphonies and symphonic poems with revolutionary titles, and 'modernized' traditional Chinese music with emphasis on its proletarian roots rather than its feudal and imperial past. Art songs and chamber works declined dramatically as these genres were considered to be elitist, and contemporary western compositional techniques, which were considered modernist or formalist, were banned. Extreme interpretations of what constituted 'decadent' or 'bourgeois' music and the consequences for those who produced such music happened from the late 1960s onwards, with the Cultural Revolution. But as with the case of the Soviet Union, the evidence on actual music produced in China, even during the Cultural Revolution where fear of torture or censure prevailed, shows considerable nuance in interpretation. For example, Mittler demonstrates that revolutionary operas, eight of which were performed officially across China hundreds of times as the exemplars of progressive art, in fact constituted a high point in the development of Chinese operatic art in the twentieth century, in their addressing of tradition and progress.[30] Often accused of having destroyed, through politicization, the subtleties of the Peking Opera, it is held in more contemporary work that in politicizing it, the continuous change that characterized the Peking Opera across the centuries was taken to a new level, where some of its symbolic and musical intricacies were explored further and taken to a much larger number of people than ever before.[31]

Reds, Blues and Songs of Protest: From the Discovery of the Folk to Folk Revival

The idea of creating 'music with a conscience' took shape in concrete terms in the United States from the Great Depression, around three sets of people. The first set comprised members of the Communist Party USA (CPUSA), who expressed the need for a different music. They were influenced by cultural aspects of the left movement that came out of the trade union movement of the 1910s, particularly the use of song in the organizing of the Wobblies.[32] CPUSA leaders Michael Gold and V.J. Jerome began to write radical lyrics on topical themes, and also translated songs from across the ocean in an effort to create a musical repertoire for the times. The Party's national cultural organization, the John Reed Club, formed a subsidiary Music Committee in May 1931 christened the Workers' Music League, which was intended to focus and consolidate all the music activity of the CPUSA, but also to 'formulate a systematic theoretical approach to proletarian music'.[33] The League included divisions for composers committed to creating communist music, performing musicians and also music publishers. It also produced its own periodical, *The Worker Musician*. In 1932, with the death of Pierre DeGeyter, the composer of the 'Internationale', the John Reed Club was renamed in his honour.

Political music originating from the working-class movement had already become popular in the United States, and was, until this period, largely spontaneous. For example, towards the end of the nineteenth century, political songs such as 'Coal Creek Rebellion' were produced in prominent strikes and labour battles, where mine owners in Tennessee used convicts as forced labour in the mines. The first national strike of the United Mine workers in 1897 gave rise to the well-known song, 'Miner's Lifeguard'.[34]

The second set of people consisted of professional composers like Elie Siegmeister, Marc Blitzstein and Aaron Copland, among others, who were beginning to question and break away from what they perceived as the bourgeois and elitist trappings of classical music in the European, particularly French, tradition as it existed in the United States at the time. They were keen to imbue classical music with 'modernist' idioms and create socially responsive music. They worked closely with CPUSA activists and lyric writers.

Siegmeister was a Harlem-born composer who, like many budding classical musicians of the 1920s, trained initially in the United States and then moved to Paris for a few years. He studied under Nadia Boulanger, a famous Parisian teacher of the time, whose influence made him perfect his technique, but at the same time made him conscious of elitism and conservatism in classical traditions of the time. His two articles titled 'Social Influences in Modern Music' and 'The Class Spirit in Modern Music' in a leftist journal, *Modern Monthly*, in 1932, and his composition, 'The Strange Funeral in Haddock', according to Oja, epitomized his social commitment in music.[35] It was based on a proletarian chant by Michael Gold of the CPUSA. The chant and recitation related the story of a worker who was scalded at work by an avalanche of molten steel and whose co-workers responded by plans of retribution at his grave. Siegmeister's musical response to the text was 'harsh and hard-hitting', where 'the vocal line is angular, with frequent disjunct leaps, and the accompaniment is filled with clusters, ostinatos and jolting accents'.[36] The harshness was also reflected in the vocal delivery with the requirement that the singing be 'harsh, nasal and nasal-mocking'.[37] Siegmeister's composition reflected the influence of proletarian chants in public meetings and also the radical music language of the 1920s, symbolized by 'percussive ostinatos and strident yet tonic-centred harmonies'.[38]

In this same spirit, in 1932, members of the Workers' Music League, particularly the leaders of a Composers' Collective that was part of it, in an effort to teach some of the more accessible songs of the new revolutionary material to others, published *The Red Songbook*. The songs in it ranged from contemporary works at the time to standard ones such as 'The Internationale' and 'Hold the Fort', 'The Preacher and the Slave' by Joe Hill, 'The Soup Song' by Maurice Sugar, to 'The Comintern' by Hanns Eisler and V.J. Jerome, and the 'I.L.D. Song' by songwriter Ella Mae Wiggins, an organizer of the National Textile Workers' Union from Gastonia, North Carolina. The *Songbook* contained 'Notes for Teaching Mass Songs', where clear hints for successful group singing were provided so that each song could be performed clearly and its words understood by all. These selections, it was clear, had a specific purpose, and were not intended 'to be performed in idle settings'.[39]

The third set of people consisted of folklorists, those who had set out to discover an 'authentic' music of the people. The conditions in the country after 1929 prompted many intellectual, cultural, social and political leaders to turn to the people to find their 'usable' past.[40] Some of them had fled the United States in the previous decade, returned home in the 1930s and attempted to reconnect with American society by incorporating images of ordinary people at work. Throughout the decade, which resulted in an iconography of the *people*, where scholars 'conducted oral histories, painters depicted scenes of everyday life, writers dabbled in realist literature, and photographers became preoccupied with photographing average citizens',[41] the folk revival in music happened as an essential element of cataloguing the people's experiences and cultural traditions. In a recent review of the folk revival, Donaldson notes that while this effort originated in the 1920s, by the 1930s it had become a crusade.[42] The revivalists focused on the ethnic, racial and geographic diversity of the United States, and aimed to discover an authentic national heritage that contained traditions to which Americans could turn in order to re-establish a 'stable communal identity' during an era of social, cultural and economic transformation and turmoil. While discovering and showcasing music that was diverse, by the end of the decade, the revivalists had crafted a notion of nationalism that consolidated the notion of democracy based in cultural pluralism and cosmopolitanism, together with an interest in securing political and economic rights for all citizens. Crucial to this folk revival was the idea that African–American music was as American as that of rural, white, settled communities. For example, in the music manual for the New Deal Resettlement Administration, Charles Seeger wrote, 'The African strain, probably the largest and most powerful of the racial minorities, is thought by many to constitute a separate category.'[43] This, however, was a false distinction, for, as Seeger argued, '[African–American] folk music has been so modified as to have become part and parcel of the American traditional idiom.'[44] Furthermore, Seeger dismissed the categorization of black music as different from the Europe-derived white folk music:

> [A] large proportion of the negro population and of the negro musicians of the United States have as much European as African ancestry. The current vogue of the term "negro" music is, therefore, to be deplored. If white music did not have a racial label affixed to it, then neither should black music.[45]

John and Alan Lomax, Carl Sandburg, Charles Seeger and Benjamin Botkin were key figures in the 1930s revival, followed later by Pete Seeger. From the mid-1930s, there was an acceleration of the folk revival movement as left-wing politics in the United States moved to its Popular Front phase, where connecting with the larger democratic impulses in the country and discovering the country's national identity became a stated priority.[46] Denning and Donaldson argue that the folk revivalists' message and their music, coming as they did from a left-wing tradition, also fit in well with the pluralist, democratic populism of the Roosevelt administration, both interested in creating the image of a resurgent, authentic and democratic 'Americanism.'[47]

The three sets of people worked together in different ways with multiple objectives: depicting the life of ordinary Americans, representing their struggles in workplaces, and innovating with musical styles and idioms. Siegmeister's early compositions reflected the influence of the Young Composers' Group, consisting of well-known musicians like Aaron Copland, Charles Ives, Arthur Berger and Bernard Hermann. Their interactions were intense and they created different kinds of music. In a letter to Copland in December 1932, Siegmeister wrote, 'The best thing about our bunch is nobody likes anybody else's music – wouldn't touch it with a ten-foot pole. Exceptions are me and Irwin, I like both his and my stuff and he says he thinks we're both terrible.'[48] Further, as composers they were trying to find ways to break out of the 'uppity elegance' and 'Frenchy-frenchy tiddlywinks music', referring to the French influence on American composers. For them challenging received trends, in this case bougeois French compositional styles, and looking for a homegrown, independent and compassionate musical idiom became the way to producing 'music for the people'.

Another group, the Composers' Collective, which functioned between 1932 and 1936, was affiliated to the CPUSA's Workers' Music League. As part of it, composers such as Marc Blitzstein, Charles Seeger and Aaron Copland held weekly meetings to deliberate on the social role of music, conducted worker choruses, organized seminars to analyse factors that went into the composition of workers' songs, and brought out songbooks. A major aim was to bring music out of the concert hall into workers' organizations, a democratization that was to be a significant element of conceptualizing people's music. In 1934 and 1935, two workers' songbooks (*Worker's Songbook I* and *Worker's Songbook II*) were brought out, consisting of mass, choral and solo songs. The mandate that the Composers' Collective imposed upon itself was hard – to be collective, to appeal to the working folk, and, at the same time, to satisfy composers and the professional music world; the introduction to the first songbook declared, 'The Composers' Collective is a group where conservative and radical musical thought and taste meet in free and vigorous clash upon the question of a definition of a musical style "national in form, proletarian in content".'[49]

There were also varied opinions on how dramatic or accessible the music should be. 'One group felt that the music should be extremely simple in the so-called mass song; another wanted the music to be revolutionary because the movement was revolutionary.'[50] In fact simplicity, often considered necessary for accessibility, was often pitched against modernism involving revolutionary content, for example, through bichordal harmonies. What is interesting here is that the issues of simplicity or modernity were fundamentally related to musical grammar, i.e. something that went beyond the lyrics or the message and engaged with the musical structure. This was also reflected in avant-garde experiments with modernism in music, with the use of atonal sounds depicting industrialism, challenging substantially the grammar of the European art music tradition.

This was also the beginning of an engagement with 'the people's own music', a precursor to the folk revival in American radical music. With the CPUSA moving into its Popular Front phase, the Composers' Collective adopted folk music as 'true people's art'. However, even within this, there were varied interpretations that represented significantly different attitudes to folk music. Some, like Charles Seeger, were committed to 'the authentic', and did fieldwork, collected and documented songs, whereas others, such as Earl Robinson, sang these songs and wrote their own folk songs as well. People like Siegmeister worked on these songs to create something new, 'performing artfully constructed arrangements and interpolating into their symphonic statements tunes from oral traditions.'[51] Alan Lomax published an anthology of folk songs that consisted of melodies with no accompaniments, where 'being authentic and evoking native surroundings' was the overriding concern. Lomax, whose idea was opposite to Siegmeister's, as seen above, responded to the latter through an appreciation of the tunes that he used, but criticized his use of accompaniment as well as his interpretation of tunes through the use of accompaniment.

Siegmeister, in fact, took his complex project further; even while writing a large number of work songs, he moved to 'a new stage of writing in his career where his musical keenness and social concerns would unite further through the interpolation of folk song with musical writing.' In an article titled 'Of and For the People' from 1944, he wrote:

> We here in America could learn a lot from the old composers, who never looked at what kind of haircut a musician had, but borrowed impartially from long-hairs and short-hairs, as long as their product had vitality and meaning for the people . . . and just to show that there is no fundamental difference between folk music and symphonic music, some of our best composers have turned to the people and begun to use our song treasury in symphonic and other serious works . . . have started on the pathway that I believe is leading to the true and original music of America.[52]

The Composers' Collective was also important for the development of the idea of the collective in music. By 1932–33, it had intensely debated the idea of the 'mass song' as a response to the rise of workers' and peoples' choruses all over factories in New York, and faced with the need to put tunes to proletarian chants and recitations that were being heard.[53] It was considered necessary to produce more and more music for the revolutionary cause and what existed in the American tradition was mostly in the form of 'contrafacta to folk tunes religious hymns', so the new mass song needed to emerge, collectively produced and with specific characteristics that marked it out as revolutionary. The traits of that style, Oja notes, include 'primacy of the words and their message, syllabic text markings, homophonic, hymn-like texture, frequent open octaves and fifths in the bass and forte as the preferred dynamic marking.'[54] In addition, Copland and Blitzstein opened their songs with rhythmic fanfare, contrary motions (at phrases like 'Shake the Midtown Towers'), sudden changes of mood (for 'Come With a Storm of Banners'), and so on. What distinguished this kind of composition from a lot of the other workers' choruses and songs was that they believed that the best of the old harmonic and melodic traditions needed to be preserved, though 'injected with a new life' so that they could attract even an unsophisticated singer. Blitzstein's initial proletarian compositions were characterized by an intense sobriety, which also constituted a distinctive trait of a lot of such music, ostensibly because it predominantly conveyed the grimness and difficulties of working life under capitalism. This changed later in Blitzstein's case, when his compositions distinctly turned lighter and more infectious.

A multitude of musical idioms, old and new, were thus created and worked with in the left-wing cultural movement of the United States in the first four decades of the twentieth century. The formalization of organizational structures for cultural work under the CPUSA sat quite comfortably with the exploration of a variety of ideas about appropriate music, even if the impetus for inclusiveness might have transformed into relatively homogenized notions of 'Americanism'.

Gestic Music as People's Music: The Brechtian Contribution

In Germany, questions of what constituted a genuine people's music was explored through the theatre of Bertolt Brecht, practised from the 1920s onwards and theorized later in the 1930s. Brecht's idea of music for progressive theatre, epitomized by his 'epic theatre', involved a notion of 'gestic music'. This was a certain kind of music that would allow the actors on stage to exhibit 'social gests' or socially didactic gestures that were not merely expression, but expression that would portray and vividly explain the emotion that was expected or being enacted.[55] The use of theatre music in accordance with the required 'new point of view' meant a break with the Aristotelian conventions in theatre, a striking innovation involving the strict separation of music from other forms of entertainment on stage. It also meant not just musical background scores or compositions, but the singing of 'songs'. In Brecht's words, when he described a performance of *The Threepenny Opera* in 1928:

> Even superficially this [the separation] was evident from the fact that the small orchestra was installed on stage. For the singing of the songs a special change of lighting was arranged; the orchestra was lit up; the titles of the various numbers were projected on the screens at the back, for instance 'Song Concerning the Insufficiency of Human Endeavour' or 'A Short Song Allows Miss Polly Peachum to Confess to Her Horrified Parents that She is Wedded to the Murderer Macheath'; and the actors changed their positions before the numbers began. There were duets, trios, solos and small choruses. The musical items, which had the immediacy of a ballad, were of a reflective and moralizing nature.[56]

The songs that were performed, further, needed to 'become an active collaborator in the stripping bare of the middle-class corpus of ideas . . . so to speak, a muck-raker, an informer, a nark'.[57] For Kurt Weill, who composed the music for many of

Brecht's plays, it meant, according to Brecht, a transition from 'relatively complicated music of a mainly psychological sort' and a break with the prejudices which the bulk of the composers held. This application of modern music to the *song* was held to be novel and superior for the purposes of showing that the human situation was socially determined but also alterable. This kind of music also positioned itself against music which stuck to lyricism and cultivated expression 'for its own sake'. It also needed to avoid 'narcotic' effects, where audiences got carried away by the emotions expressed, and in turn be didactic and induce a critical approach in the spectator. Brecht wrote:

> Most advanced music nowadays is still written for the concert hall. A single glance at the audiences who attend concerts is enough to show how impossible it is to make any political or philosophical use of music that produces such effects. We see entire rows of human beings being transported to a particular doped state, wholly passive, sunk without trace, seemingly in the grip of a severe poisoning attack. . . . Such music has nothing but purely culinary ambitions left. It seduces the listener into an enervating, unproductive act of enjoyment.[58]

It was easy for Brecht's 'anti-narcotic' stance to be interpreted as an anti-emotion one, even though he was at pains to dispel any such implication. However, Hanns Eisler, who also composed music for many of Brecht's plays, took a hardline view of 'music for the people'. He rejected purely orchestral music as not being suitable for a workers' music repertoire and advocated the creation of simple, direct songs. In writing about the importance and role of the workers' music movement, he argued:

> [A]ll music forms and techniques must be developed to suit the express purpose, that is the class struggle. In practice that will not result in what the bourgeoisie calls style . . . in the workers' music movement we do not aspire to style but to new methods of musical technique, which will make it possible to use music in the class struggle better and more intensively.[59]

The workers' music movement needed to produce mass fighting songs that are 'quickly taken in, easily understood and accurate in attitude'.[60] Further, Eisler argued that workers' orchestras should never perform only orchestral works, as these were 'not right for a proletarian audience'. Clearly, the Brechtian didactic and 'muck-raking' musical idiom, designed for the stage, was being extended into an ideology dictating the 'correctness' of point of view.

Apart from composing music for the revolutionary theatre, including Brecht's, Eisler had also established firm principles for the workers' music orchestras.

Music without words or orchestral works alone, according to him, would be 'not right' for a proletarian audience, because 'such symphonic music . . . is not accessible to workers either materially or ideologically . . . the problem of symphonic orchestral music of a proletarian character is just as insoluble as the attempt to change a dress suit into overalls by painting it red'.[61] More appropriate would be programmes that consist of fighting songs and orchestral music with choruses practised with the public, a 'new revolutionary style of music [which] enables novel and original compositions to be so contrived that they can also be executed by untrained amateurs'. Further, in combination with agit-prop theatre groups, such workers' orchestras can 'prepare the technical conditions for large-scale meetings where political subjects furthering the revolution bring the message to the masses of people in an original and artistically effective manner'.[62] Eisler's views were very influential in the United States in the 1930s, when the workers' choruses operating under the CPUSA were deliberating on appropriate music.

What were the elements of the radical aesthetic in music that can be seen from the experiences described above? First, the ideologies that constituted the left-wing politics of the time, notably nationalism, anti-fascism and an emancipatory socialism, were expressed musically in different ways, revealing interesting similarities and contrasts. If tradition had to be engaged with, it ranged from classical traditions to indigenous ones, and it needed to contend with varied conceptualizations of nationalism. The musical expressions of nationalism had already involved experiments with classical and indigenous music in different parts of the world that were about the 'people' who constituted the nation. In engaging with national identities and colonialism, the radical musicians were also germinating musical ideas in an emancipatory socialism.

Second, in doing so, questions of tradition, heritage and the 'people' were articulated around ideas of modernism and realism, with the Euro–American experiences (exemplified by the American, German or Soviet cases) being distinct from, say, the Chinese case. As in literature, the actual conditions of life under colonialism and the spectre of Japanese imperialism were to influence the musical idioms that depicted the 'usable past', and drew on realism and modernism.

If the allusion to modernity had to involve challenges to the western classical tradition through atonality and the sounds of industrialism in Euro–America, it had to be through the adoption of western musical formats in non-western musical cultures. If, in the 1930s, the United States 'discovered' the music of the countryside and constructed a folk idiom, the Chinese were more deeply exploring an already existing engagement with the 'indigenous'. If radical representation had to be about 'the people', it had to sometimes be a 'phonograph' or at other times play an interpretative role. While a 'documentary aesthetic' of recording the music of the people and playing it back to them was significant and extended across contexts, the Brechtian interpretation called for a break with lyrical realism and the construction of a radically different music in the theatre with a didactic role.

Third, the ideology of the collective was beginning to emerge as a significant component of the radical aesthetic. Apart from the Eisler kind of position, the creation of 'mass songs' as part of the radical tradition was constituted by distinct ideas about the nature of the collective – both the collective that was being performed to and the collective that was performing them. The various considerations that came up in the representation of the collective through the mass song or the workers' song were the need for simplicity and accessibility for untrained amateurs, playing the role of creating the connectivities of mass gatherings while at the same time being didactic. The didactic and explanatory element of music for the revolutionary cause also came from Brecht's theatre, which developed these ideas as aesthetic devices. This meant eschewing 'lyricism' in progressive theatre music that represented expression for its own sake, in favour of 'gestic' music or music that could explain the social context of the issues taken up by such theatre. A certain version of representing the collective musically also came from the socialist realist tradition that was Soviet-inspired. It involved, from the 1930s, a greater stress on the texted genre as against purely symphonic music, on creating anthem-like music with lyrics that were uplifting, heroic and optimistic in often grandiose representations of the 'new socialist man'. Often it also meant foregoing formalism, defined officially as 'the separation of form from content' in music, which took many forms, such as a critique of atonal music as 'not comprehensible to the masses' (e.g., in East Germany in the 1950s), and an assessment of whether performers communicated with their audiences effectively or not, or got too absorbed in their own performances. Underlying these positions was, again, a didactic message for the masses which was often accompanied by arguments for simplicity and accessibility.

Fourth, the impulse towards plurality that seems to characterize revolutionary moments, pushing artistic expression in many directions, was being challenged by organizational imperatives and moves towards stricter codification and interpretation. If a new realism had to be conceptualized and theorized in the form of 'socialist realism', its practice had to negotiate the complex territory between being internationalist, recognizing the 'national' and at the same time being locally rooted. It had to contend with the variety and challenges posed by the explosion of musical expression accompanying the various revolutionary moments. With a hardline stance on socialist realism leading to a strictly limited interpretation of people's music, as in the Soviet Union and China, major challenges to artistic and personal freedom arose and became the basis for debates on the aesthetic–politics relationship, i.e. on the approaches to tradition, the constitution of modernism and the role of individuals in collectives.

Notes

1 When it was founded, the IWW was the only American union to welcome all workers, including women, immigrants, African Americans and Asians, into the same organization.

2 Bowen Struyk (2006).

3 Treece (1997).

4 Nelson (2000): 26.

5 Ibid.: 20.

6 Koenker, Rosenberg and Suny (1989): 304.

7 Nelson (2000): 70.

8 Gutkin (1999).

9 For example, Fay (2004).

10 For example, Swiderski (1979): 4.

11 Scott (1935).

12 Ibid.

13 Titus (2006).

14 Ibid.; Pearson (2009).

15 Titus (2006). Also see Fay (2004); Wilson (2006); Frolova-Walker and Walker (2012).

16 Shostakovich himself told a *New York Times* reporter in 1931, 'There can be no music without ideology. . . . We, as revolutionaries, have a different conception of music. Lenin himself said that music is a means of unifying broad masses of people. . . . For music has the power of stirring specific emotions. . . . Music is no longer an end in itself, but a vital weapon in the struggle. Because of this, Soviet music will probably develop along different lines from any the world has ever known.' (Cited in Pearson 2009)

17 Ibid.

18 Ibid.: 6.

19 Jones (2001) is an important contribution to the understanding of multiple musical genres in China from the early twentieth century until after the Cultural Revolution.

20 The term 'phonographic realism' is used by Jones (2001) to describe the relationship between commercialization in the music industry and political music in China.

21 Ibid.: 6.

22 Ibid.

23 Gong (2008). This will be dwelt upon in more detail in the next chapter.

24 Tham (2009) analyses the post-revolution musical scene in China from the point of view of socialist realism as a credo and representational technique. Her focus is on the Cultural Revolution phase.

25 Jones (2001): 41.

26 The discussions on 'yellow' or vulgar music were widespread, with questions on tradition, i.e. whether it was progressive or reactionary, asked in the context of what constituted the *true* music of the people.

27 Quoted in Jones (2001): 109.
28 Ibid.: 110.
29 Gong (2008): 29.
30 Mittler (2010).
31 Ibid.
32 Pietaro (2010).
33 Reuss and Reuss (2000): 48.
34 In the Haymarket affair of 1886, Chicago workers met to campaign for a shorter workday and against police brutality, and popularized songs promoting the eight-hour workday. The Homestead steel strike of 1892 and the Pullman strike of 1894, two watershed events in the development of American unionism, each produced a wealth of political music, some written to popular tunes such as 'After the Ball'. See Dunaway (1987).
35 Oja (1988).
36 Ibid.: 161.
37 Ibid.
38 Ibid.: 163.
39 Ibid.
40 This is a term I have borrowed from Denning (1996).
41 Donaldson (2011): 45.
42 Ibid.
43 Reuss (1979): 230.
44 Ibid.
45 Ibid.
46 Popular Frontism, as we saw earlier, was born out of Soviet influence of the 1930s. It encouraged parties in different nations to turn to their national cultures and connect with their societies, rather than operate as isolated revolutionary forces.
47 Denning (1996) and Donaldson (2011).
48 Oja (1988): 163–64.
49 Ibid.: 166–67.
50 Ibid.: 167.
51 Ibid.: 169.
52 Quoted in ibid.: 172.
53 Ibid.
54 Ibid.: 173.
55 *Gest* or *Gestus* in Brecht involves making visible or explicating clearly on stage a character's social relations and location from a historical materialist perspective, and also involves a narration technique that is 'epic' in nature, i.e. the 'showing' that is 'shown' in the 'showing'.
56 Quoted in Willett (1964): 85.
57 Quoted in ibid.: 86.
58 Quoted in ibid.: 86.
59 Eisler (1978): 59.
60 Ibid.: 60.
61 Ibid.: 66.
62 Ibid.: 66.

3

People's Music in India

By the time the Indian People's Theatre Association (IPTA) was established in 1943, a progressive literary agenda, i.e. the production of literature 'of' and 'for' the people, had already been deliberated upon, and the left cultural movement had taken shape in different parts of the country in the fields of music, dance and theatre. With the formation of the IPTA, we saw the development of a three-fold agenda for progressive art: to construct an aesthetic of nationalism or cultural expression grounded in the nation within the left movement; at the same time, to use the complex regional traditions that were not subsumed by a notion of nationhood; while being grounded in the idea of the nation even while being expressed in diverse local terms, to emphasize the radical in order to foreground exploitation, whether through colonialism or the structure of Indian society. Fundamental to all these components of a *radical impulse* in culture were conceptions of the 'people' for whom and whose art was to be discovered, preserved, represented, interpreted and (re)constructed.

Who were the 'people', and what were the appropriate musical conceptualizations and creations that could do justice to this multi-pronged project? We can clearly differentiate the 'people' in the 'national' vision from the 'people' in the 'regional' traditions. Further, whether within a national, a regional or a local vision, the 'who' of representation (i.e. who represents and who is represented) and the 'what' (whether representation means reproduction, interpretation or transformation) were important issues in the creation of 'people's music'. This, in turn, was to lead to crucial questions of authenticity of representation and the idea of the collective.

Before recounting the IPTA tradition's deliberations on people's music, it is necessary to refer to the early twentieth-century context of performance, especially musical performance, in India and the specific role of songs within it. Any intervention that aims to create a specific impact, such as the IPTA's, needs to be mindful of this context as it is critical in defining the imperatives of its visualization of musical performance. This context is summarized briefly below.

Music in Indian Performance Traditions: Songs

In performance traditions in India, a large part of music-making and singing is linked to a larger performativity linked to theatre, dance or composite performances involving dance, mime, theatre and puppetry. Deriving from the various traditions of folk theatre that exist throughout India, such music typically accompanies or describes episodes from the epics or stories of kings and conquests, dramatized in long presentations, 'often incorporating music, dance, battle-scenes, and digressive comedy'.[1] The stories themselves are often fantastic rather than realistic, relating the mighty feats of the gods, the boundless wealth of kings and the cosmic repercussions of mortal escapades. Such narrative extravagance and an 'aesthetic of excess rather than economy' has also influenced popular traditions like urban theatre and cinema, which developed to cater to new, mostly urban audiences in the early twentieth century.[2] Classical music, by this period, was an exception, i.e. it was not necessarily linked to other forms of performance and the creation of spectacle, but was performed on its own. Thus, popular commercial theatre as well as cinema contained music as an essential element even when the modern proscenium stage was adopted in place of traditional performance spaces. An actor breaking into song at any point in the performance was common, accompanied by a visible orchestra on stage or an orchestra backstage. This format could lend itself to the film format as well. While the film might be using a kind of realism, the use of music was more or less reminiscent of traditional performances. While such uses of music seem to convey that 'the psychological distance between speech and song is considerably narrower than for Western spectators', as Manuel has noted, for most Indian spectators the effect is a continuation of folk theatre traditions, where speech, song and dance are tightly integrated into a unified dramatic style, and the song constitutes a continuum between conversation and music.[3]

At the same time, the development of the recording industry from 1902 onwards and the growth in the urban audience, dominated by the middle class, wanting to establish a modern identity for itself, resulted in changes in the usual formats and grammar of musical performance. More will be said about specific musical formats further on, but here we note that from the second decade of the twentieth century or thereabouts, musical performance for large audiences was tailored more and more to a typical 'song' format with formal verse–refrain structures. Across different kinds of music, the strophic open-ended and improvisatory singing style that was characteristic of Indian music was restructured to stricter timing requirements, reducing the time available for improvisation and elaboration.[4] So, even if music was performed in 'composite' performances involving dance, theatre and other dramatic forms, it was increasingly in the 'song' format that it came to be associated with greater modernization.

In this context, songs – in shorter, 'modern' formats or in longer, open-ended ones – came to acquire special significance.[5] They could broaden an audience beyond language barriers, something that commercial cinema used very effectively to make the cinema popular. Thus, even if people did not understand the specific regional language in which films were made, their songs could often become popular outside the language group. This was seen mostly in the case of Hindi films, with the audience for Hindi film songs being far wider than those who spoke or understood Hindi. Songs could provide a convenient means by which unarticulated sentiments could be expressed, drawing from the association of modes (*ragas*) with moods. A song played on a gramophone or broadcast over the radio could reach a larger audience than via composite performances, such as music dramas, for which it might have been originally composed. It thus did not require either the staged context or the other songs from the drama to constitute an attractive package. Booth notes that the consumption of an individual recorded song required less time and less attention than did dramas, and did not depend on whether the song's consumers had seen the drama.[6] In effect, songs could live an independent existence and take on personalized emotional meanings that might supersede or simply ignore their dramatic or larger performative context, and their potential audience exceeded in size compared to even larger performances. The situation in which popular music had been located in dramatic forms and, with slightly modified structures, achieved an independent identity was thus complex and involved constant change in the early part of the twentieth century. The IPTA tradition's intervention needs to be looked at as positioned at this critical juncture, when music performance formats were being tailored to the demands of colonial modernity, rapidly changing demographies and the nationalist ideology.

In music that came out of political movements like the IPTA, often it would be a part of composite performances involving dance and theatre, such as in traditional performance. Thus, in discussions on what the nature of progressive art should be, often the focus was on theatre, with theatre necessarily meaning composite performance. Music, mostly in the song format, formed an intrinsic and very important part of performance visualized in this manner, but was rarely discussed as such. The available work on the IPTA looks quite literally at the theatre tradition, whereas a large part of it was beyond theatre in the modern proscenium sense, in the form of composite performances. It is necessary to point out that even after the songs, which were a very important component in the performance, came to acquire an identity and a shelf-life that went far beyond that of the performance, the songs or music in general were not analysed for effects, as they were conceptually subsumed under the wider umbrella of theatre. However, as happens typically with popular music, the songs became independent entities. In the endeavour to shape and respond to wider audiences beyond traditionally available means, a careful exploration of available forms, assessing their suitability to the needs of conveying political messages as well as newer or hybrid forms, became necessary.

I present below how the *national* was visualized as an essential category for defining people's music, originating in the national movement, and describe the repertoire that emerged in imagining the nation. In the following, the focus is on the emergence and playing out of the idea of a 'national radical people's music', followed by the regional strands. Through both these national and regional notions, the 'who', 'what' and 'how' of representation, along with their relationship with 'people's music', are addressed.

Imagining the 'National' in People's Music: The Bombay Central Squad

The preoccupation with the 'national' from a left-wing point of view played itself out in the creative work of the IPTA's Central Squad in Bombay more than in the regional formations. This unfolded between 1944 and 1947, the years of the Bengal famine, the Second World War and independence. The idea of the nation and its representation in music was present in the regional strands as well, but in practice, playing around with multiple ideas from different parts of the country was possible only with the Central Squad in Bombay.

The cultural movement in the city of Bombay took place within a working-class ethos and the complex social changes generated by industrialization in the city. There were three distinct, though interrelated strands: (i) poetry and music in Urdu and Hindustani, which was represented through the tradition of the Progressive Writers' Association (PWA); (ii) theatre in the Gujarati tradition; and (iii) music and theatre of the migrant Marathi working class. With the setting up of the PWA in 1936, there was an explosion of Urdu poetry (*Taraqqui pasand tehrik*) as part of the movement in north India, Hyderabad and Bombay. Jalil and Patel note that the

Urdu section of the PWA (known as the Anjuman Tarraqui Pasand Musannifin) was the most active, although what is probably also true is that it was the most obviously 'visible' segment in a national sense, its activities being prominent in cities that were prominent in the colonial structure, Bombay being one of them.[7]

In Bombay, the areas of Madanpura and Mominpura saw the political mobilization of weavers who had migrated from what is now eastern Uttar Pradesh and Bihar, to become workers in Bombay's big textile mills. This mobilization, under the leadership of the Communist Party of India (CPI), involved poetry and music as key components, and the two areas created large numbers of working-class poets and musicians from the 1930s. Along with the CPI, other organizations such as the Naujawan (Youth) Party, which functioned as a cultural organization, came into existence to harness and channelize the enormous creative impulses that were emerging spontaneously.

Parallel to this, cultural activity was building up in other areas that primarily housed the migrant Marathi working class which had migrated from the hinterland of Maharashtra into areas in Bombay such as the Matunga labour camp. Consisting mostly of Dalits, these areas saw, alongside the setting up of the Lal Bawta Kala Pathak (Red Flag Cultural Organization) of the CPI and a rise in workers' consciousness, the growth of the Ambedkarite anti-caste movement. Three great poets, songwriters in the Marathi *shahir* tradition – Annabhau Sathe, Amar Sheikh and Gavankar – came out of this ethos, representing the other strand of working-class music.

Of the three, the talented poet–performer Annabhau (originally Tukaram) Sathe hailed from a lower-caste Matang family which performed actively in *tamasha* troupes. Drought forced his whole family to migrate from Satara on foot to Bombay in the early 1930s. Learning to read and write only after migrating to the city as a teenager, Annabhau cut his teeth as a writer in the Matunga labour camp in the late 1930s and subsequently became a textile-mill worker. He was drawn to the activities of the CPI in the working-class areas of the city during the general strike of 1943 and was a founding member of the Lal Bawta Kala Pathak of the Party. Having emerged as an early radical Dalit writer, and a leading figure on the cultural and political scene in Bombay from the early 1940s to the mid-1960s, he produced four *loknatyas* or *tamashas*, ten *powadas*, plays, travelogues, twenty-two short story collections and thirty novels including the best-selling *Fakira*, and twelve screenplays.[8] Annabhau went on to become an important mobilizer in the Samyukta Maharashtra campaign.

Amar Sheikh, whose cultural roots were strong too, came from the town Sholapur, which had a strong working-class tradition and where, as early as 1934,

Clockwise, from top left: *Duniya Don Hathachi*, songbook featuring Annabhau Sathe, Amar Sheikh and Gavankar; sketch of Amar Sheikh from the cover of a songbook; Amar Sheikh with Pablo Neruda and Baba Niaz Haider at the CPI headquarters workers had held the town under siege for four days. His mother Munir Bee had been a poet, and Amar Sheikh was also conversant with the religious tradition of Eknath. Gavankar, the brahmin in the group, was a choreographer and a composer, and also functioned as the manager of the trio's performances.

By the early 1940s, therefore, Bombay had a strong multicultural, working-class tradition with substantial interaction based on larger migrant, urban solidarities that were being harnessed by the left movement. In fact, both these major areas had already become attractive for progressive artists of the middle class as well, especially with the national and the anti-fascist movements gathering momentum.

The IPTA's Central Squad came into existence in July 1944 with the staging of dancer–choreographer Shanti Bardhan's dance drama, *Hoarder*. In the first phase, Benoy Roy (songwriter–composer–singer), Usha Dutt (dancer), Reba Roy (dancer and singer), Dasharath Lal (poet–composer–singer), Appunni Kartha (dancer), Priti Sarkar (singer), Sushil Dasgupta (musician), Prem Dhawan (songwriter–composer–singer), K.M. Reddy (singer), Sachin Shankar, Nagesh, Dina Sanghwi, Shanta Gandhi, Rekha Jain and Leela Sayyed (dancers) were the prominent members of the Squad – all brought to Bombay by P.C. Joshi. At a later stage, Narendra Sharma (choreographer), Gul Jhaveri and Gangadharan (dancers), Salil Chowdhury, Jyotirindra Moitra, Ravi Shankar, Ali Akbar Khan and Annapurna Devi (musicians) joined the Squad, as did the Bombay-based worker trio, Annabhau Sathe, Amar Sheikh and Gavankar.

Shanti Bardhan

Reba Roychowdhury and Benoy Roy

IPTA Central Squad

The Central Squad was set up to bring the artistic range and spontaneous mobilization that had been seen in different parts of the country to the national stage, in the process visualizing the idea of national performances. The Bengal famine and its devastation provided the political backdrop to this need to cut across diversity, and respond across and beyond languages and cultures. At the same time, a strident critique of the commercialization of the performing arts as a late colonial 'distortion' (symbolized by Hiren Mukherjee's famous speech at the 1943 IPTA conference) and the recognition that colonialism had marginalized large numbers of indigenous and traditional forms meant that this varied group of artists had to consciously work towards creating new 'people's art', something would stand out as an alternative, that was artistically powerful, rigorous, collective, varied and, in this sense, a genuine alternative to what existed. A powerful new imagination was beginning to take shape around popular culture.

The inspiration for the creation of this kind of a squad possibly came from the mobilizational and creative experience of a group called the Voice of Bengal, which had been successful in creating awareness about the Bengal famine in different parts of the country. An IPTA document prepared in 1946 reported it thus:

> During the year 1943–44, the Bengal branch of the IPTA had organized the famous Bengal Squad which toured the provinces of Punjab, Bombay, Maharashtra and Gujerat and collected over two lakhs of rupees in aid of the victims of Bengal. At the beginning of 1944, Uday Shankar had visited Bombay with his troupe of dancers and musicians and the IPTA organized an open-air performance of his Shadow Play 'Ramleela' especially for the workers. Through this, we came in touch with many members of his troupe who became interested in our work. Two of them, Shantikumar Bardhan and Abani Dasgupta, one of the leading singers, became interested in our work and they joined up with the Bengal Squad during their performances in Bombay. The unprecedented success of the work done by the Bengal Squad and the enthusiasm shown by these two artists brought about the formation of the Central Cultural Troupe of dancers and musicians. They would work for the regeneration of folk culture and other types of dancing and music that were part of the common people of this country.[9]

For P.C. Joshi, the idea of bringing artists from different parts of the country together to spread the message wider, and to use the variety of experiences to explore new creative ideas, was a matter of urgency; and interviews with artists as well as published memoirs reveal this urgency and the conviction that it would happen. The sheer diversity in talent and regional experiences brought forth an energy that was unique, as the memoirs and interviews reveal.

The arguments for exploring, excavating and representing indigenous musical forms were important objectives with the setting up of the Central Squad, underpinned by a conceptual understanding of the need to do so. This was reflected concretely later on, in 1954, when P.C. Joshi, who was the key person in the formation of the IPTA's Central Squad in Bombay, wrote that the revival and popularization of folk culture was essential to strengthen democratic elements in the ideological struggle. The objectives of this revival, as spelt out in his document, reflect the debates that had already taken place in different parts of the country from the early 1940s onwards, on what people's music should be like and the extent to which folk music was people's music. A key objective of the revival of the folk tradition, according to Joshi, was to 'help the people of one language group in India to know the folk tradition of other language groups . . . this would weaken chauvinistic traits in all the languages. . . . Further, folk songs make the most sense to foreign readers, both the progressive in the western world and the citizens in the socialist world.'[10]

Considered relevant to the stated objectives were a wide range of songs, both traditional and completely indigenous, and modern or expressing modern ideas in the folk idiom. It is apparent that the folk tradition had been interpreted in its widest sense, while taking care not to reduce the attempt to 'mere versification of political slogans'. Apart from expressing the sentiments of the people, it was considered necessary to use the folk tradition for the creation of a larger national identity and help forge international solidarity.

Joshi's writing reflected some of the concerns that informed the collection and creation of songs in the folk tradition, and came after the cultural movement had already seen a reasonable variety within the folk idiom between the 1930s and 1950s. It had gone beyond being an expression of people's lives and their sentiments or being 'performed expression' for conveying a contingent political message, to actually being considered essential for exploring issues of national identity and, even further, internationalism. The creation of regional/linguistic identities, the search for national identity by going back to the roots, often reinventing tradition and, at the same time, dealing with complex multicultural influences, especially in music, was happening in many parts of the world from the early part of the twentieth century, and the points raised by Joshi reflected some of these debates. Joshi's vision, in several documents of the IPTA, aimed to aggregate these attempts through the pan-Indian organizational structure of the IPTA, and constituted a new imagining of the nation, i.e. from below, something that was in contrast to the mainstream national movement's notion of 'heritage'.

While Joshi provided the leadership and the vision for the establishment of the Central Squad, the idea also worked because serious artists were beginning to feel the need to take their art out into society, to express political ideas through their art. Their personal experience of and reaction to the suffering of the Bengal famine, for example, created the urge to use their art for politics in an explicit way. Jyotirindra Moitra wrote:

> The grim shadow of the great famine loomed over the whole of Bengal, particularly the city of Calcutta. It became impossible to shut oneself up indoors. Leaving behind stimulating conversations and rehearsals of plays, we came out into the streets. . . . Everywhere, it was the same – hundreds of thousands of skeletons wailing '*Phyan Dao, Phyan Dao*' (give us rice starch). Uprooting themselves from the village, compelled by pangs of hunger, the provendering *kisaan* (peasant) and the *Jagadhatri* (mother goddess like *kisaan* women) had come to the city, but dared not ask for even a couple of morsels of cooked rice. They begged for rice water. What an insult to humanity! . . . One day, I saw a woman lying dead on the street. Her innocent hungry child pulled in vain at her nipples and wept spasmodically. The massive

Voice of Bengal in Godhra: in Reba Roychowdhury's words

From an interview given to the author in January 2007. As Reba Roychowdhuri related this incident, she expressed deep anguish about the 2002 genocide in Gujarat that took place after a violent incident in Godhra.

The dance drama *Bhookha Bangal* (Hungry Bengal), the play *Antim Abhilasha* (Final Desire) and several songs like '*Purab desh mein duggi baaje*' (I hear drumbeats on the eastern side), '*Jaaga desh hamaara*' (Our country has woken up), '*Maran shiyare daladali kare*' (Death dances over my head), '*Suno Hind ke rehne waalon*' (Listen, o people of Hind) and '*Hoi hoi hoi Japan*' gave concrete shape to the Voice of Bengal Squad. We toured Gujarat and Maharashtra extensively by train. We did shows in Ahmedabad, Surat, Baroda, Anand, Nadiad and Godhra in Gujarat, and Poona, Aurangabad, Jalgaon, Sholapur and Kolhapur in Maharashtra. Bengal's famine had shaken up all of India. We would alight at stations every 80–90 miles and start performing. We were

fired by strong principles, rigour and discipline and the combination of our ordinary appearance and excellent performance would mesmerize the audiences. It is difficult to describe in how many ways audiences would appreciate and help us. Each of us would travel with a small suitcase and hold-all. Often we would spend the whole night on railway platforms and travel from one place to another during the day. We would carry bed-sheets and brooms with us, sweep the platform, spread the sheets out and sleep on the platform. Once we were returning from a show in Gujarat's Godhra. The train arrived at Godhra station where we were waiting. We knew that it wouldn't halt for more than a minute. We hurried and jumped on to the train with all our belongings. Many minutes passed and we realized that the train had still not moved. After more than twenty minutes, when the train started moving, we leaned out of the windows and saw a smiling gangman waving a yellow sign and shouting out '*Bhookha Bangal*'. Surely the gangman and his colleagues had watched our performance! We realized he was postponing our departure. By delaying our train, a whole group of railway workers were acknowledging and expressing their appreciation of our previous evening's show in an agricultural area close to Godhra.

Facing page and this page:
Members of the IPTA Central Squad
on performance journeys by train

> blow this scene struck shook my very being. I screamed 'No, no, no'. . . . As I ran with unsteady steps I muttered to myself, 'We won't allow people to die . . . we will resist it.' That was the beginning. I do not remember whose house it was that I went to and sat with the harmonium, from whom I borrowed paper and pen to write. . . . Thus began the composition of '*Nabajeebaner Gaan*' (Songs of a New Life).[11]

Shanti Bardhan, a dancer and choreographer who had been trained by Guru Amubi Singh in Manipuri classical dance, had begun to feel the need to rediscover and interpret traditional dance and musical forms, and to communicate them across the country, for which he got an opportunity as the main choreographer in the Central Squad. When his Manipuri dance troupe travelled from the northeast of India to Bombay, he found that people knew very little about traditional art forms from other parts of the country, and he felt that familiarity with these expressive forms might allow artists to enhance their expression and convey messages that were not limited to local contexts. With the growth of the national and the left movements, solidarities between people from different parts of the country needed a unique imagining of the national through creative forms. Gul Bardhan (Gul Jhaveri, when she was in the Central Squad) wrote in a memorial volume to her husband, Shanti Bardhan:

> Shantida created '*Bhookha Hai Bangal*', a programme of dance drama, so that human hearts might be moved and people might realize that the shame and suffering of Bengal were the shame and suffering of entire India; and that if help was to be extended for the sake of human dignity and basic self-respect, it was now . . . the tour extended all over India from Bombay to Punjab . . . the form in which the predicament of Bengal was conveyed showed Shantida as a true innovator . . . folk melodies and simple movements had been combined to provide poignancy . . . the theme did not demand stylized or classical treatment, yet intimate knowledge of classical lores or proficiency in classical dancing was needed . . . the melody and strains of the song '*Bhookha hai Bangal*', the words heart-wrenching in their melancholy, were augmented in their effect by the eerie movements of Death, danced by a solo figure with utter simplicity.[12]

The Indian ballet form of the dance drama, involving music, dance and acting, was considered useful as a form of propaganda to raise mass consciousness, in keeping with the composite performativity of Indian traditions. This form, which had emerged with Rabindranath Tagore and was later developed by Uday Shankar, was an innovative, composite storytelling form with dance, music and drama going together, which allowed for several traditions to be put together and still be communicable across linguistic and cultural divides, primarily because of the dramatic element involved and its direct emotional appeal. Rekha Jain, one of the main performers in the Central Squad, wrote about the creative process involved in producing the ballets:

> 1943. The country was still under foreign rule. After the mass uprisings of 1946, the terrible repressive measures of the British, the Japanese bombardment of Bengal and above all the unprecedented famine of Bengal had rocked our very foundations. . . . It was then that, for the purpose of collecting funds for the famine, the Party decided to send a troupe to Bombay. . . . Eventually our troupe raised a lot of funds by performing in Gujarat, Bombay and Maharashtra. . . . By a strange coincidence, those days the famous Uday Shankar group was being dismantled and many of its talented members were in search of fruitful work. . . . In the beginning, Abani Dasgupta gave us music lessons. Later on Pandit Ravi Shankar came as music director. Abanida was very particular about his tabla and started his practice sessions at 4 in the morning. Rabuda – that is, Pt. Ravi Shankar – could be heard practising his sitar till late in the night. Even today I can visualize him doing that on a moonlit night in the verandah. . . . Thus, some of us practised singing and others dancing. . . . Sachin Shankar gave us intensive lessons in the Manipuri style to perfect our waist movements. Narendra Sharma taught us folk dances and a variety of footwork. . . . Shantida, of course, concentrated on building up the main ballet . . . [he] was fond of listening to all kinds of folk songs. . . . If a particular tune impressed him, he immediately set about finding an appropriate dance composition for it. Once I sang a Brajbhasha song and he composed a Lambadi dance on it. This song proceeded in a slow tempo but required, by the climactic conclusion, a fast tempo tune. For this, he tried many songs and ultimately selected a Rajasthani tune. This improvisation lent great variety to that dance piece and the concluding portion became very effective due to it.[13]

The Squad was at first stationed in Bombay in Andheri, on Perera Hill Road. Their first performance was in December 1944 at a conference of the Bombay Students' Union, where more than 800 students witnessed it. Their first public performance, open to the people of Bombay, was soon after at the Cowasji Jehangir Hall, where 'was put to test the labour of five long months – and the verdict was that it was one of the best dance programmes witnessed in Bombay'.[14] The new experiment was covered in the major newspapers of the time.

Several plays, ballets and other programmes were staged all over the country, for example: *Naval Revolt*, *Amar Bharat*, *Bharat ki Atma*, etc. Dance dramas such as *Lambadi*, *Divine Musician*, *Ramlila*, *Holi*, *Collective Farm*, Jyotirindra Moitra's

Nabajeebaner Gaan, Dr Raja Rao's *Burrakatha* from Andhra, the Malabar dances, and Magai Ojha and Amar Sheikh's presentations became exceedingly popular.

The members of the Squad lived in a commune in the textile mill area, one among several in which CPI activists were organized. Nearby, there was a writers' commune and another one for other activists. Numerous memoirs describe that the artists were paid a monthly stipend of forty rupees, from which thirty rupees went towards paying for meals cooked within the commune. The training and rehearsal schedules were rigorous, and for many this was the first experience of men and women who were unrelated to one another living under the same roof, sharing responsibilities and actively cultivating solidarities through their art. Rekha Jain wrote:

> I had come from a family background where even stirring out of the house unveiled was prohibited. The face was, of course, veiled, but even the tonga was so covered on every side as to make our limbs invisible. I knew what a shameful thing it was for such a girl to seek to learn dance. This is why I felt extremely shy and diffident. My mind was guilt-ridden.[15]

Beginning with such extreme diffidence, she went on to become one of the main dancers in the Central Squad.

In retrospect, it appears that the Central Squad was an incubator for artistic expression of a kind never tried before in India, with elements drawn from extremely

IPTA Bombay singing squad, 1948: Prem Dhawan, Harshi Kashyap, Noor and others

varied backgrounds and traditions. From the assemblage of artists it can be seen that the traditions ranged from the trained and sophisticated classical forms, represented by Ravi Shankar, Ali Akbar Khan and Annapurna Devi, to the rustic and often bawdy *lavnis* and *tamashas* of Annabhau Sathe, and the *powadas* of Amar Sheikh. Most of them were from the middle class, with only a few working-class artists. There were Bengalis from Bengal and Assam, Gujaratis from Gujarat and Bombay, Purabia dialect speakers from Bihar, Malayalees, Telugu speakers and Punjabis in the group. How was a group as diverse as this, distinct from each other by language, region and class, but united by a need to respond artistically to political events, to come up with suitable responses?

One part of the mandate, as revealed in interviews and biographies of the artists, and described vividly in anecdotes, was for such new art to be rigorous, something that audiences would take seriously for their aesthetic value as well. Shanti Bardhan, who had worked with Uday Shankar, Shankaran Namboodiri the Kathakali actor, Guru Kandappa Pillai the Bharatanatyam exponent and Amubi Singh the Manipuri dancer, wanted to take the medium of the dance drama (or 'ballet' as it is popularly known in India) beyond what was popularly performed then, to use poetry put to music, and to make dancers act or 'perform' their roles more expressively than was conventionally known. It required new kinds of dancing and a new musicality: music that would enable and enhance performance and be performance itself. The IPTA produced six ballets between 1944 and 1946, *Spirit of India* and *India Immortal*, being two key examples. These dance dramas, as their names suggest, attempted to present a national vision through bringing together, synthesizing and presenting forms from different parts of the country, and through them, to convey political messages. In music, apart from the music that was composed for the dance dramas relating to various dance forms that were used, the already prevalent nationalist idiom in music was explored as well, as in some of the songs composed by Ravi Shankar. Two examples – the song '*Jaaga desh hamaara*' and the songs from the film *Dharti ke Lal* – are discussed below.

'*Jaaga desh hamaara*' can be categorized as a classical music-based song in the nationalist music tradition, which was reasonably well established as a genre by the first couple of decades of the twentieth century, its hallmark being its upbeat and heroic quality, both in terms of its lyrics and in the structure and orchestration of the tune.[16] It is a group song composed in the *raga* Brindavani Sarang (which consists entirely of major notes and thus is amenable to creating an uplifting mood), and is sung at a high tempo accompanied by several instruments like the sitar, violins and the bugle.

jaaga desh hamaara jaaga jaaga desh hamaara
goonj utha hai har kone se azaadi ka naara
yeh sadiyon ka behta paani
phoota jal ki dhaara, phoota jal ki dhaara

maidanon mein jhoom ke nikle laakhon hi mastaane
talwaaron ko choom ke nikle laakhon seena taane
har baagairat peshaani pe khoon se yeh likkha hai
woh jeena hi kya jaanega jo na marna jaane
jo na marna jaane

Our country has awakened at last,
The call of freedom resounds in every corner,
The waters that have been flowing quietly
Have burst into strong streams.
Our country has awakened at last.

Lakhs of strong youth throng the battlefield,
Lakhs of people kiss their swords and surge forth resolutely,
Every martyrdom is marked in blood,
Who can know about life if he doesn't know how to die?
Our country has awakened at last.

These are the lyrics of the first verse, clearly demonstrating the song text markers of typical nationalist music and the IPTA's engagement with that idiom. These markers are references to the country waking up, to still waters turning into vibrant rivers, to millions of freedom fighters emerging with swords in their hands to fight for freedom, and other similar heroic acts.

The music composed for *Dharti ke Lal*,[17] a film on the Bengal famine, was a combination of a traditional boatman's song ('*Suno manwa naiya re*' – Listen, o boat-like mind), theatrical music coming into existence at the time with the use of the classical idiom for the proscenium ('*Jai dharti maiya jai ho*' – Praise be to mother earth; '*Bhookha hai Bangal*' – Bengal is hungry) and two classical *thumris* ('*Ka se bataun ye man ki batiya*' – To whom can I tell my feelings; '*The beete sukh ke din*' – The days of happiness have gone past), with the latter two being part of the classical music-based sub-genre reproduced on the celluloid screen.[18] Three of the songs were performed by the Central Squad's ballet troupe and rendered by trained choruses along with dances, and theatrical entries and exits.

Ravi Shankar's music often used classical forms such as the *thumri* or compositions with complex phrases, and needed to be rendered by large trained choruses that could negotiate the *taans*[19] and *mudkis*[20] easily. For him, rigour and complexity in composition, orchestration and rendering, drawn from the classical tradition, were a fundamental aspect of music-making, irrespective of the purpose. His response to a radical call to artists for participation in a new cultural awakening, symbolized by the IPTA, was through exploration of his own craft with all its existing characteristics.

In the same idiom Amar Sheikh composed '*Janani janmabhoomi*' (Motherland), and Iqbal's '*Saare jahan se acchha Hindostan hamaara*' (Our Hindostan is better than other nations) was set to tune by Ravi Shankar. These songs were openly mobilizational, exhorting people to rise up against colonialism and oppression, and all of them addressed the country as a whole, not to particular regions or nationalities. The fact that '*Saare jahan se acchha*' was composed and performed by the IPTA was hardly known, especially after the communists (and the CPI) were accused of being anti-national as a result of their not openly participating in the Quit India movement of 1942.[21]

Jyotirindra Moitra, like Ravi Shankar, came from a background of classical music training. His long composition, '*Nabajeebaner Gaan*' (Songs of a new life), in Bengali was sung extensively by the Central Squad. The composition, involving several songs sung one after the other, employed techniques from the Bengali theatre of the late nineteenth century. It was marked by a highly emotive theatricality, which is strongly suggested in the extract from Moitra's writing reproduced earlier. The creative process came to him from a strong sense of identification; his music was written emotively and spontaneously as a deep personal process, involving a highly refined craft. The wails of famine-struck people saying '*Phyan dao*' (Give me rice starch) were musicalized and were an intrinsic part of the composition. This direct and, at the same time, highly stylized composition was strongly rooted in a theatre tradition that was specifically Bengali, representing the Bengal modernist tradition, but in the Central Squad it was sung by trained non-Bengali singers as well.

naa, naa, naa, maanbo naa maanbo naa
koti bik kore kine nebo praan pone
bhoyer rajye thaakbo na

obhoy peyechhi nuton diner kaachhe
dike dike taai aashaar potaaka naache
peshite peshite rokter laal aalo
dhue debe omaabaashyar joto kaalo
bhoyer rajye dhukboi mora thaambo na

No, no, never will we accept this,
We won't inhabit the land of fear.

We found fearlessness in the new dawn,
The flag of hope flutters all around us.
Hues of red blood colour our sinews,
They will wash away the darkness of the dark moon night.
We will fearlessly enter the land of darkness,
We cannot be stopped.

The 'national' was also imagined in the way in which performances were structured. It is apparent that the 'showcasing' of regional dance and music forms as part of large performances took place consciously so as not to lose sight of the regional. What was to become a natural part of public entertainment in independent India, a showcasing of dances and music from different parts of the country, took place probably for the first time with the work of the Central Squad. A description of the performances that the Squad would typically put together, publicized before performances in the form of souvenirs or notices published and distributed, will illustrate this point.

The first souvenir, with Congress leader Sarojini Naidu's message printed on the back cover and artist Chittaprosad's sketch on the front cover, listed the programme as follows:

> *Saare jahan se acchha* – the national song by poet Iqbal set to a new and rousing tune by Ravi Shankar, the famous musician, 'Call of the Drum' – Dance of Invocation for the youth of India rousing them to patriotism, Lambadi Dance – a simple folk dance of the *lambadis*, a gypsy tribe living in Hyderabad state, 'She Died of Hunger' – a solo dance in classical style performed by Sachin Shankar, portraying the sorrow of a peasant of Bengal who arrives home to find that his wife and companion has died of hunger, Dhobi Dance – a folk dance commonly seen among the Dhobis of Andhra, 'They Must Meet Again' – a ballet in folk form on the recent Gandhi–Jinnah meeting, Collective Farmers' Harvest Dance – incorporates folk dances and music of more than one province of the Punjab, of Bengal, of Andhra and of the UP, *Ramleela* – a scene from the story of Ramchandra in a folk form very commonly seen in the UP villages, 'The Spirit of India' – a ballet based on the story of India since the advent of the British and *Jana Gana Mana* – National song by Rabindranath Tagore.[22]

The second souvenir listed ten new items, of which eight were dances, one was a play and the last item was a dance drama. The dances included *Gaajan* (based on a form from Bengal around the relationship of the Hindu god Shiva with his wife Parvati), *Nauka Bihar* (around boatmen's traditions), *Divine Musicians* (based on stories about *gandharvas*, celestial musician beings in mythology), and *Khadaun* and *Chaturanga* (classical forms of dancing from Tripura); the dance drama was an iconic Central Squad creation titled *India Immortal.*[23]

In addition to those listed above, numerous songs were performed as well: for example, Benoy Roy's '*Suno Hind ke rehne waalon*' (Listen, o those who live in India), Priti Sarkar's '*Din khoon ke hamaare*' (Our days of blood) and Amar Sheikh's '*Naya zamaana laayein*' (Let us usher in a new era). '*Din khoon ke hamaare*' (Our days of blood) was written and composed by an anonymous artist after the brutal massacre of thousands of people in Jallianwala Bagh, in Punjab in northern India in 1919, and it used to be sung by Priti Sarkar.

din khoon ke hamaare pyaare na bhool jaana
khushiyon mein apne hampar aansoo bahaake jaana
din khoon ke hamaare

saiyaad ne hamaare chun chun ke phool tode
veeraan is chaman mein ab gul khilaake jaana
din khoon ke hamaare

Do not forget my dear, our days of blood,
Shed a tear in their memory even amidst happiness.

Destiny plucked and took away our dearest flowers,
Do let more flowers bloom in the barren garden.

With such a range, it was essential for artists to learn each other's forms and create new ones through imitation, adaptation or interpretation. For artists of certain backgrounds, going beyond their own idioms and forms came naturally, as there was a history of doing so where they came from. For example, Salil Chowdhury, the versatile genius trained in western classical music and at the same time widely conversant with Bengal's indigenous forms, converted tunes from one region into songs in another language effortlessly. His very well known '*Manbo na ei bondhoney*' (We will not accept bondage) is composed in a peasant tune from Andhra, from a song called '*Levaraa o karshaka*' (Wake up, o peasant), and came into existence when he was with the Central Squad in Bombay.[24] Amar Sheikh, who belonged to the Marathi tradition, edited a songbook consisting of songs in Hindi and Marathi which was later used by trade unions. This included '*Ye jang hai jang-e azaadi*'

'*Parna Jhanda*': Biography of a Song

In September 2009 I was invited to attend a commemorative conference on the centenary of the South African Communist leader Yusuf Dadoo in Johannesburg, South Africa. On a request by Omar Badsha, the anti-apartheid activist and a leading photographer, who was one of the organizers of the conference, I sang '*Din khoon ke hamaare pyaare na bhool jaana*' (Do not forget my dear, our days of blood), a song that used to be sung by Priti Sarkar of the IPTA's Bombay Central Squad, one that had been written after the Jallianwala Bagh massacre in Amritsar by an unknown poet. I had learnt the song from Sarkar in 2007 and it is an important part of my archive. The song met with a very interesting response from a group of South Africans of Indian descent, who told me that it reminded them of a song '*Parna jhanda*' that travelled from India at some point in time and played an important part in mobilizing people of Indian descent in the Transvaal region and was also popular with non-Indian-descent South Africans fighting apartheid. When I heard the tune of the song and also looked at the lyrics carefully, it was apparent to me that this would have been part of the IPTA tradition and would not have travelled as part of the mainstream national movement's influence, contrary to what the South Africans assumed. The tune, like that of '*Din khoon ke hamaare*', is one that is typical of the Urdu/Hindustani ethos and the lyrics make it clear that it comes from a working-class tradition.

My enquiries with several people in South Africa, including the African National Congress veteran Ahmad Kathrada, revealed that the song was sung during the passive resistance movement of 1941 in South Africa, which meant it had arrived there earlier.

The second verse refers to the Jallianwala Bagh massacre and I learnt that after the Sharpeville massacre in South Africa in 1960 there was an addition, a reference to

Sharpeville as well. The verse in the post-Sharpeville period runs as follows:

jab azaadi ki bhookh lagi thi
goli Jallian mein yoon chali thi
jab azaadi ki bhookh lagi thi
goliyan sharpeville mein yoon chali thi

When the hunger for freedom grew,
Bullets were fired in Jallian.
When the hunger for freedom grew,
Bullets were fired in Sharpeville.

Cover of songbook published by the Transvaal Indian Youth Congress during the anti-apartheid movement, containing songs in Hindustani and Gujarati as well

The parallel being drawn between the freedom movements in the two countries through a working-class song was clearly indicative of connections that had not been officially recorded anywhere. Once back in India, I asked several of the people I had contacted during my field research about whether they had heard the song, and was unable to find anyone who had. It was almost a year later that I found the original lyrics of the song in a songbook edited by Amar Sheikh, the worker–poet from Maharashtra, which was given to me by the trade-unionist Subodh More. The song, written by the worker-poet Bhagwan Singh Bagi, was sung regularly as part of the trade union movement in Bombay, according to More, and it is not known how it travelled to faraway South Africa.

August 1981

Song of Resistance

PARNA JANDA

Bazi e jane ispe lagana
Parna janda ye niche jockana

Ye mehnat ka soonka sahara
Jisne chamke diya he sitara,
Ispe aa e moseebut [illegible]othana
Parna jande ye niche jockana

Ye mezdoore ke he nishani
Is ki darde babri he kahani
Ye Rahe to, rabe zindegani
No jooke to mitado jewani,
Ooski Soorkhi ke khoonse barhana,
To no janda ye niche jookana

Jab azaadi ki booke lagi thi
To goli Jalyan me chali
Yad ho golio ka wokana
To na janda yo piche joockana

Oon shahidon ki kabraw pejane
Phoole sansoo ke oonpor charana
Oon ke barsal jalse manana,
Jispo khoonki kahani soonana.
Soonker kanpe ka zaalim zamana,
Perne janda ye niche jookana

TRANSLATION

Put your whole being into this struggle
But don't allow your spirit to be conquered.

This is the fruit of our labour
it is the shining star of our existence
For this we must bear all hardships
but we won't allow our spirit to be conquered

This is the symbol of the workers
whose tale is filled with sorrow
What is youth
to achieve our goal we will sacrifice our lives
We will colour our lives with our blood
but we won't allow our spirit to be conquered.

When we cried out in hunger for freedom
bullets tore our flesh.
We remember being fed with those bullets
but we won't allow our spirit to be conquered.

Go to the graves of those Martyrs
and strew them with wreaths of tears
Commemorate their sacrifice every year
and tell the tales written with their blood
So that hearing them, the oppressors will trembl
we won't allow our spirit to be conquered.

जानकी इस पे बाजी लगाना
अपना झंडा न नीचे झुकाना

[भगवानभाई बाग़ी]

जानकी इस पे बाजी लगाना
अपना झंडा न नीचे झुकाना
सुर्ख़ रंग का है झंडा हमारा
बीच हंसिया हथोडा है प्यारा
है ये मेहनतकशों का सहारा
इसने चमका दिया है सितारा
जो भी आये मुसीबत उठाना
अपना झंडा न नीचे झुकाना—
है ये मेहनतकशों की निशानी
खून से तर है इसकी कहानी
ये रहे तो रहे ज़िंदगानी
ये मिटे तो मिटा दो जवानी
इसके लालीको खूँसे बढाना
अपना झंडा न नीचे झुकाना—
झंडा लेकर के आगे बढो तुम
इसको लेकर किलों पर चढो तुम
हर जगह अपनाही राज होगा
फिर ये दुनिया का सरताज होगा

अब तो आया है इसका जमाना
अपना झंडा न नीचे झुकाना—

अपनी हडताल जिस दम चली थी
तब मची शहरमें खलबली थी
लाठियाँ गोलियाँ भी चली थी
खून से तर वह सारी गली थी
याद हो गोलियों का वह रवाना
तो ये झंडा न नीचे झुकाना—

चंद मज़दूर जो मार डाले
यूँ कहते थे वे भोले भाले
खूब दिल भर के जालिम सता ले
बेगुनाहों पे गोली चला ले
रंग लायेगा यह खूँ बहाना
अपना झंडा न नीचे झुकाना —

मस्वरा आप बागी का मानो
सुन लो मज़दूर और ऐ किसानों
एक हो जाओ सब नौजवानों
एक हो जाओ अब नौजवानों
आ गया वख्त जौहर दिखाना
अपना झंडा न नीचे झुकाना—

★

Facing page: Lyrics and translation of 'Parna Jhanda' in a South African publication, dated August 1981
This page: The original song lyrics from a songbook titled *Waqt ki Aawaaz*, edited by Amar Sheikh

(This is a war for freedom) and '*Jaane waale sipahi se poochho*' (Ask questions to the departing soldier) written by Makhdoom Mohiuddin, and '*Jhanda na neeche jhukaana*' (Do not lower the flag) by a worker–poet Bhagwan Singh Bagi – a song that was to travel to faraway South Africa around the same period and animate Indians there to fight apartheid later on.

As part of the alternative imagination of the nation, a large number of songs of the Central Squad used indigenous music from the regions of the country that members of the Squad came from, such as *powadas* and music from the *lavnis* and *tamashas* of Maharashtra, or the dance music from Andhra.

There also came into existence another category of songs based on indigenous forms. Prem Dhawan, the songwriter from Punjab, wrote and composed satirical songs about British rule in a simple, call-and-response mode. Three songs that he wrote when the Cripps Mission visited India, asking its representatives to run away, run back to London, used known styles from rural Uttar Pradesh such as the *aalha*, which were very popular street styles. One of the Cripps Mission songs went as follows:

ab bhaago london bhaago
kaahe sau sau maker banaao
bhaago london bhaago

kaise bhoolein jallianwaala bagh ko kaise bhoolein
aur kaise bhoolein itne gehre daagh ko kaise bhoolein
jaag uthe ghar ke rakhwaale
apni khair manaao
bhaago london bhaago

Run away to London, run back!

How can we forget Jallianwaala Bagh?
How can we erase our deep wounds?
The people of the country have woken up,
Run away to London, run back!

Another song went like this:

arre jab bharat mein garam siyasi
mausam ho jaata hai
aur jab gori chamdi waalon ka dum
ghutne lag jaata hai

arre london se bheji jaati hai
fauran yeh madaari
aaye teen madaari, aaye teen madaari

When political temperatures are running high in India,
Whilst white-skinned people suffocate,
Three magicians are sent from London.
Here come the three magicians!
Here come the three magicians!

In fact, when the street theatre tradition came into existence in northern India in the late 1970s, particularly with Safdar Hashmi's Jana Natya Manch, it used this satirical style extensively.

The Central Squad's cultural work took place in an atmosphere of great autonomy for the group, primacy being given to creation, rehearsals and performance, and this allowed for a variety of new kinds of performances, as seen above.

IPTA Delhi performing the song '*Churchill ki chori*'

The autonomy came as a result of the conscious design of P.C. Joshi, General Secretary of the CPI, who, as we have seen, was instrumental in setting up the IPTA and specifically the Central Squad, to begin with. Joshi's position on the role of cultural workers was subsequently critiqued within the Party, and was possibly one of the positions that was referred to in the IPTA conference resolution of 1949.

Gana Natya Sangeet: People's Music in Bengal

If there was one province where the repertoire could be compared to that of the Central Squad in terms of diversity, it was in Bengal. In fact, it was probably more varied in terms of musical innovations, as the description below seeks to demonstrate.

Bengal was poised to explore new forms and interpretations of 'people's music', with syncretic forms involving Indian and western idioms already having come into existence with Rabindranath Tagore and Dwijendralal Roy.[25] Jyotirindra Moitra, who was with the Bombay Central Squad for a few years, was a representative of this carefully developed nationalist music tradition in terms of its form; he went on to use the idiom to compose music around the Bengal famine, as has been mentioned earlier. One of his most important contributions was the twenty-three-song dance drama, *Nabajeebaner Gaan*.

There were at least four other distinct types of musical idioms that constituted alternative definitions or interpretations of people's music in Bengal. The first was represented by what can be termed the 'indigenous or folk music' group, consisting of Bijon Bhattacharya, Paresh Dhar, Hemanga Biswas and Nibaran Pandit among its prominent members, which consciously focused on rediscovering, reclaiming and presenting indigenous musical traditions, many of which were getting lost or being overshadowed by modern, urban-based forms. What was common to all of them was a belief that colonialism and modernity had caused the music of the boatmen (the *bhatiali*, for instance), peasants (sowing and harvest songs), itinerant wandering mendicants (*baul* and fakir songs) and other groups of rural people to either become insignificant in public performance, or to be limited to a museum-display kind of performance. Documenting them, reclaiming them on behalf of the people and performing them in ways that would allow for a depiction of ordinary people's lives was essential, and thus constituted the basis for works by this set of composers. In other words, they were 'being a phonograph', as the Chinese songwriter Guo Moro urged in the 1920s. There were differences between what each of them did, with Bijon Bhattacharya's music being mostly for the theatre, whereas the other three were exclusively songwriters and singers.

Two examples of Bijon Bhattacharya's music are from the play *Nobanno* and the dance-drama *Jeeyan Kanya*, both written by him. *Nobanno*, a realist play, had music that used simple tunes from praise song traditions like the *kirtan* or songs by religious mendicants (*pirs*) called *pirer gaan*, converted into the satirical format.

aapni baanchle to baaper naam eelaashe boyaan
hindu muslim jopero chaashi
eesha naai upaai naai
aaji jodi shikkha naai shikkha hobe kobe
aapni baanchle to baaper naam eelaashe boyaan

kaalaanto aakaale ekhon koto chaashi bhai
aukaale praan haaraailo lekha jokha naai
oi goroo koto baanchlo koto morlo
hishaab ke aar raakhe, praan haaraailo laakhe laakhe
aapni baanchle to baaper naam eelaashe boyaan

You can proclaim your father's name only if you survive.
O peasants, Hindu and Muslim, those left with no hope, no way out,
When will we ever learn, will we learn our lesson today?
You can proclaim your father's name only if you survive.

How many peasant brothers have we lost in the famine!
How many cows have died, how many survived!
Who will keep count? Lakhs of lives have been lost.
You can proclaim your father's name only if you survive.

Jeeyan Kanya's narrative was built around a congregation of different kinds of snakes and snake charmers, with relatively unknown folk melodies from different parts of Bengal representing each kind. These songs were reproduced as they were and constituted an exercise in 'presenting' lost indigenous song traditions to wider audiences; however, they were put together in a way that constituted a script and a storyline for a play. The play told the story of two tribal clans at war with each other and extensively used imagery from the snake-myth traditions of Bengal and surrounding areas. Unfamiliar to those living in Calcutta, the collection of songs displayed a wide diversity in dialects, instrumentation and also modes of singing. In 1954, Hemanta Mukherjee (known as Hemant Kumar outside Bengal), a singer–composer and IPTA activist from Bengal, composed music for a Hindi film produced in Bombay titled *Nagin* (Snakewoman), which adapted tunes from *Jeeyan Kanya*. It was not only Hemant Kumar who shot to fame with his compositions and his own singing for the film, but the film itself was a pioneer in creating some of the iconic snake-myth idioms of popular Indian cinema.[26] The soundtrack of the dance drama *Jeeyan Kanya*, which was possibly staged only twice, once in the 1940s and later some time in the 1960s, consists of a large number of songs sung one after the other, each with a complex tune in a local dialect. This stood in contrast to a lot of the music that was being composed and performed in Calcutta, including on left-wing platforms, bringing the high-pitched, earthy mode of singing into prominence in urban stage performance. Ritwik Ghatak used music of similar style later in his film *Titash Ekti Nadir Naam* (Titash is the name of a river).

Paresh Dhar was a composer who made the transition from singing heavily classical songs to disavowing them subsequently because he considered them too sophisticated and alien for rural audiences, employing instead indigenous forms that used call-and-response mechanisms to interact with audiences.[27] Prominent among his compositions are a whole set of songs referred to as the *Sukh–Sharee* songs, which traditionally involve a conversation between two birds called Sukh and Sharee who tell the story of the *Ramayana*. Musical dialogues between the two dancer–actor–singers would throw questions at the audience, and the immorality of exploitative landlords and moneylenders, or of British rule would be counterposed with the possibilities of attaining a just and free world, a '*Ramrajya*', through use of short musical phrases that were also conversational.

Hemanga Biswas similarly used relatively simple, satirical indigenous forms that involved audience participation, like the *kirtan* or praise song. One of his best-known compositions of this type is '*Mountbatten mangal kavya*' (In praise of Mountbatten), imitating the well-known '*Raghupati Raghava Raja Ram, Patita Paavana Sita Ram*' sung in praise of the Hindu king Rama. It went thus:

mountbatten mongol kaabyo
hethaai shaango holo
premaanonde baahutule raamo raamo bolo

deshobaashi gaan gao shoraajo bhojon
raghupati raaghava mountobaton
tata birla tero naam
jai vallabh gopal rajaram
jai jai raghupati raghava mountobaton
raghupati raghava mountobaton

Here begins the Mountbatten praise song,
Raise your arms in salutation and chant Rama Rama!

Countrymen, sing the *swaraj bhajan*
Raghupati Raghava Mountbatten!
Your name is Tata, your name is Birla,
Praise be to Krishna and Lord Rama!

The significance of this sort of satirical form taken from indigenous singing traditions lay in its ability to accommodate verbal content flexibly and being able to connect to audiences quickly. In this so-called praise song, for example, Hemanga Biswas caricatures the newfound friendship between Lord Mountbatten, the nationalist leaders, and the capitalists Tata and Birla. His use of the Bengali-accented 'Mountobaton' in place of Mountbatten accentuates the caricature.

Hemanga Biswas also sang many *bhatiali* boatsongs as part of his repertoire, attempting, like Bijon Bhattacharya, to introduce these as legitimate performance and explicitly as 'people's music' to urban audiences which had already experienced 'new' forms of music.

The revival and interpretation of indigenous music outlined above also reflected a serious archiving and documentation effort that was undertaken furiously all over Bengal after the IPTA's formation. District committees collected hundreds of songs, dances and theatre forms that existed in the provinces, reviving them through festivals held in villages, featuring artists who traditionally performed these forms. These performances under the aegis of a left-wing organization, even if the artist, form or message was not explicitly political, were an innovation in themselves since the 'common people' and their art were not usually part of political platforms until then in India.

The IPTA in Bengal also introduced another idiom into performance involving a democratization of musical forms that were part of a 'citadel', like Rabindra Sangeet, the music of Tagore. Tagore's music used written notation, a major innovation in comparison to the traditional codification of Indian music, and this reflected Tagore's comfort with western structures of music-writing and notation, in addition to his command over *raga*-based Indian classical music systems and folk forms.[28] Rabindra Sangeet, similar to elements from the classical tradition, had become canonized, strictly codified and interpreted rigidly, and often mechanically, and its singers had to adhere to strict standards that were set by his followers. It was with Jyotirindra Moitra, Hemanta Mukherjee and Debabrata Biswas, all virtuosos in Rabindra Sangeet and strongly committed to the IPTA's ideology, that Rabindra Sangeet came to be performed with other kinds of music, and often sung with greater spontaneity and not necessarily following all the rules that were held dear in the canonized form. In fact, apart from these people who were active in IPTA, the IPTA's platforms also featured popular and iconic Rabindra Sangeet singers like Suchitra Mitra and Dwijen Mukherjee.

An example from a large performance at a peace conference held in Calcutta in 1952 will illustrate this point. Suchitra Mitra and Salil Chowdhury, both on stage with two harmoniums, sang two songs, one after the other. The first was Tagore's '*Krishnakali aami tarey boli*' (Krishnakali, let me talk with you), an evocative depiction of a dark, beautiful girl, by then an iconic image of a rural woman in the Bengali imagination. The second, '*Shei meye hoyto taare dakheni keu*' (That girl, no one has possibly seen her before), written and composed by Salil Chowdhury, continued the story of the dark girl in Tagore's poem, starving as she struggles through the Bengal famine, an image that connected to the present immediately. The juxtaposition of an image from Tagore with a contemporary image reportedly electrified the tens of thousands of people in the audience, who were witnessing something like this for the first time.[29]

The music of Salil Chowdhury, in fact, constituted the third distinctive idiom that came from Bengal. The harmonic tradition of his music can be considered a major innovation within the IPTA tradition, marking a complete departure from the existing music, even that which existed in India's 'westernized' tradition. The use of western tunes as well as western orchestration in predominantly Indian melodies was common in urban Bengal from the early twentieth century. However, these innovations continued to retain the 'modal' nature of the Indian musical tradition, where a basic melody uses a certain combination of notes, whether *raga*-based or based on western tunes. When western orchestration was used with the main melody, what made it as pleasing as the original melody was the exploration of harmonic notes in the orchestration, even though the instruments might explore notes not contained in the dominant melody. Salil Chowdhury's compositions for the IPTA, exemplified by '*Dheu utchhe*', on the Naval Mutiny of 1946, moved away from the modal structure by using a series of modal melodies, each with its own given combination of notes and accompanied by harmonic orchestration, but such that each piece of the song sounded very different from the other. He also introduced significant silences, varying speeds in the different sub-melodies, harmonies in singing, superimposition of one scale upon another and such other features that went on to become the hallmark of the Indian choir tradition, first in Calcutta, and later on in Bombay and Madras.

Writing about one of the popular songs, '*Gnayer bodhu*' (The bride from the village) that he wrote during the Bengal famine, Salil Chowdhury noted: 'The success of *Gnayer bodhu* did a very wonderful thing. It heralded a new era in Bengali contemporary music. It was a completely unconventional song having no traditional *asthayee* (refrain) and *antara* (verse), and its movement from phrase to phrase was symphonic in form, with two distinct movements.'[30] In his study of the urban folk genre that became very popular in Bengal from the 1970s, Avishek Ganguly argues that Salil Chowdhury was one of the greatest influences on the later urban folk tradition through his extensive use of the back-up orchestra, which set the stage for the emergence of band music. In his work, the 'orchestra achieved its much needed liberation' and, along with innovative use of percussion, he accorded the accompanying instruments the status of voices capable of making statements to qualify or modify those made by the human voice.[31] The foregrounding of the orchestra was to become the 'ubiquitous feature of the musical arrangements of band music later'.[32]

Apart from this, Salil Chowdhury's work was characterized also by his brilliant reworking and interpretation of traditional folk tunes to convey explosive political messages. In one of his most remembered early protest songs, '*Bicharpoti tomar bichar korbe jara*' (O lawkeepers, you will be judged), a song against the brutality of the colonial law courts, Chowdhury used a popular Bengali *kirtan* tune, traditionally devotional in character, and laced it with an explicit political text, thus transforming an soft melody of devotion into a statement of explosive protest and anger. The intimate and personal–traditional aspect of the same *kirtan* had been adapted in a Tagore song before, with which audiences were familiar, and the transformation in its interpretation again was unique and electrifying. For Salil Chowdhury, the creation of a new aesthetic involved innovation not only in the poetic content of the composition but also in its form.[33]

The IPTA tradition's Bengali instances also introduced a new kind of music that came to be seen as the 'voice of the collective', a completely newly crafted group voice, a new use of the chorus. Exemplified by Ritwik Ghatak's music for his film *Komal Gandhar*, which narrates the story of a theatre group modelled on the IPTA, it consisted of choral pieces using short, staccato musical phrases, with each phrase made up of two or three notes. The pieces were sung by numerous male and female voices in unison in a hollow sort of way, often accompanied by atonal uses of tightly-strung instruments like the sitar or veena, dramatizing particular, often personal situations. It can be argued that the use of voice and instruments in this way musically evoked the social world, and helped locate the individual's dilemmas, conflicts and constraints within a turbulent, transforming social context.

It is obvious that the IPTA in Bengal brought in tremendous variety and innovation through its music, whether for the stage or as music itself. The debates were intense and often transformed into bitter rivalry between the artists. Reading into the arguments, what one sees is varying notions of people's music and each artist's justification for his own work as 'people's music'. In 1948, Charu Prakash Ghosh, the then Secretary of the Bengal IPTA, wrote in a report:

> Two trends of thought have been expressed within IPTA. One group, which we will call the first group, is represented by comrades like Sambhu, Bijon and the other one is represented by Comrade Sudhi Pradhan. The first group feels, art and literature are reduced to artificiality by reactionaries. So they want to create progressive people's art. To do this they think: (a) they should be given absolute freedom in developing their talents; (b) they give important stress on 'form'. They suggest that it would be better not to stage plays than to leave 'form' incomplete and (c) they do not have any faith in the guidelines of the party, as regards art. The second group, it seems, feels that the need for the IPTA lies in the spread of the mass cultural movement, in serving the masses through art and literature, and that through living contact with the people satisfactory art can develop. So they consider the role of 'form' a secondary one. Probably they feel that undue stress on 'form' is the result of bourgeois ideas.[34]

This fundamental difference of positions, one emphasizing 'form' and rigour *as* politics, and the other questioning the autonomy of cultural production that the former demanded, instead focusing on the need to build a large mass cultural movement and rendering form secondary, was what Ritwik Ghatak was referring to in his 'On the Cultural Front' document referred to earlier. Ghatak's position, while stressing artistic autonomy and form, was in fact also laying out what might be an appropriate organizational structure that would allow for autonomy, but not compromise the need to convert it into a mass movement. It may be recalled, Ghatak was not expressing a lack of faith in the CPI as such, but rather, in the idea of the non-artist organizer of the cultural front who might not possess artistic sensibilities. However, as with the PWA, the disagreements translated into conclusions about 'correct' and 'wrong' art, particularly in the Bengal IPTA.

What was unfortunate about the spate of disagreements that arose was that some of the most creative people broke away from the organization and the CPI. Later, the differences in positions translated into bitter inter-personal attacks that turned attention away from the fundamental aesthetico–political issues involved.

Naataka Gaanangal, Viplava Gaanangal (Theatre Songs, Revolutionary Songs): People's Music in Kerala

Kerala's left-wing musical repertoire was not as varied as that of Bombay or Bengal, and until the early 1950s, when the KPAC (Kerala People's Arts Club) was formed, it was quite autonomous of the organizational structure and deliberations of the IPTA, although there were links between cultural activists and the IPTA through the CPI and the Party's mass organizations such as the All India Kisan Sabha. However, the links of the existent cultural movement, which took shape from the 1930s, with the CPI, and the rapid growth of the communist movement in all three regions that were to constitute the state of Kerala from 1956, resulted in a vibrant music and theatre movement by the 1940s that led to the formation of the KPAC in 1951. So, although work on Kerala's left-wing cultural history often tends to get over-identified with that of the KPAC, the period we cover here is from the 1930s until the late 1950s.

Further, unlike in the other regions and provinces that this chapter details, there is a greater need to engage with music emanating out of the theatre tradition in Kerala, even if, as argued earlier, the shelf-life of theatre songs is far greater than that of the plays themselves. To the extent that in common usage in Kerala to this day, *viplava gaanangal* (revolutionary songs) and *naataka gaanangal* (theatre songs) are often used as emblems for the decades that this book deals with, these songs will be discussed in the context of the theatre in Kerala in greater detail.

Kerala's progressive cultural history over the same period stood in contrast to that of Bombay, with its rural characteristics in the regions of Malabar and Cochin, and even where an incipient working class had emerged in Travancore, in the coir factories of Alleppey. The case of all these three Malayalam-speaking regions, which later officially became the state of Kerala, was also distinctive in the sense that the cultural movement emerged as part of a widespread '*literization*' or education movement that was an integral part of political mobilization.

A year after the PWA was set up, the Jeevat Sahitya Samity or Committe for Life-oriented Literature in Kerala converted itself into the Purogamana Sahitya Sanghatana (the Malayalam version of the PWA).[35] From the 1930s, the Congress Socialist Party (CSP) and later the Communist Party of India (CPI), used a variety of media for political mobilization aimed at mass education, publicity and dissemination of information/knowledge. The cultural movement emerged as part of the need to educate and disseminate knowledge on the one hand, and the need for actual political action on the other. The founding of newspapers which would raise issues of the working class and other disadvantaged sections was an active intervention towards the 'creation of an oppositional language', a part of creating 'mass media that was not just an institution of dissemination in an already historically evolved, naturalized system, but one that disseminated information and oppositional culture of particular kinds'.[36] Another step in this literization was the setting up of rural reading rooms/libraries or *vayanashalas*, which provided the public access to reading material and promoted sociality in the dissemination of news and ideas.

Malabar, the most economically backward among the three regions, was directly under British rule as part of the Madras presidency, and Cochin and Travancore, which were more developed, were princely states obedient to the British Crown. Malabar was industrially backward, but it had various traditional industries and a sprinkling of small modern industrial units. It saw, between the early 1930s and the late 1940s, the rise of major peasant movements against highly exploitative landlordism and also the development of a working-class movement, along with the national liberation struggle.

One of the main currents that crystallized the growth of peasant and working-class movements in Malabar was the 'leaning to the left' of the Indian National Congress, discussed earlier, and the subsequent formation of the breakaway CSP. In Malabar, the formation of the CSP was set against the background of an unprecedented agrarian crisis during the Great Depression, after a whole generation of young men from Kerala, who had entered the political arena during the Civil Disobedience Movement of 1930–32, came out of jail in 1933–34 dissatisfied with the Gandhian leadership for withdrawing the struggle. Many of these men had been in touch with terrorist-detenus imprisoned in the Cannanore Central Jail, who gave them their first exposure to a political philosophy radically opposed to Gandhian ideas. The CSP radicals organized tile, *beedi* and weaving workers, and led strikes in the cotton and weaving mills. This was also the period of the organization of the peasant movement both independently and through the Kisan Congress, with the agrarian crisis providing the background, for campaigns for the reduction of land rent. These campaigns in 1935–36, comprising walking squads of activists touring across several areas at the same time, village meetings and local conferences, led them to an understanding of the degree and nature of landlord–tenant relations,[37] which in turn provided the information for designing a radical agenda subsequently that would make the province of Kerala stand out.

These years also saw the growth of youth leagues which carried out the campaigns. These youth leagues were closely linked to the *vayanashalas* (reading rooms) that had begun springing up in village centres and the involvement of hundreds of teacher-volunteers in the literization process. The *vayanashalas* became meeting points for the youth to discuss and read political literature. In the years 1934–36, a spate of *vayanashalas* were opened by young Congressmen at village and taluk centres. The network of reading rooms soon took on the shape of a movement and, as Jussy notes, by 1937, their spread was significant enough to merit a Malabar Vayanashala Conference in Calicut. Further, the CPI's newspaper, *Deshabhimani*, was read aloud at factory sites – for example, in *beedi*-rolling centres – that saw the rise of the trade union movement, and workers who were assigned the job, by rotation, of reading out the newspaper were paid wages as if they had been rolling *beedis*. As part of this process, Kerala also saw a striking innovation in the form of a writers' cooperative set up in 1945.

In 1936, a further front in the rural campaign of the CSP was opened with the movement against unemployment and hunger. On the same lines as the 'hunger marches' that were taking place even in advanced capitalist countries such as Britain in the aftermath of the Great Depression, '*pattini jathas*' (hunger marches) and '*thozhilillaima jathas*' (marches of the unemployed) were organized in Malabar by A.K. Gopalan and Chandroth Kunhiraman Nair. These marches were characterized by meetings, the publication of booklets and the singing of *pattini* (hunger) songs.

Thus, in Malabar, performances were a part of demonstrations against landlords at the village level, i.e. were political action, or part of the education process at the workplace, or at nightlong 'reading, discussion and performance festivals'. Several plays of the early 1940s, such as *Paattabaakki* (Rent Arrears) and *Nammalonnu* (We Are One), depicted the conditions of the peasantry and called for overthrowing landlordism. A major characteristic of these plays was that they were improvisatory, often being tailored to suggestions from audiences and creating a strong sentiment of joint authorship. Those who acted in the plays were often Party leaders themselves, and there was very little distinction between cultural workers and other mass workers of the Party.

Theatre, music and other kinds of performances formed an integral part of this disseminative–mobilizational strategy that had a wide mass base in Kerala, and the performance modes that came into existence were influenced by these larger imperatives. The music that came out of the political mobilization in Malabar in this period was mostly spontaneous, being part of marches or *jathas*, involving collective participation, and based most often on local customary tunes and ritual music.

Travancore, constituting the southern part of what later became the state of Kerala, was relatively more advanced than Malabar, particularly due to high levels of literacy, and the left cultural movement developed there primarily around trade union struggles from the 1930s onwards. In both Travancore and Cochin, which were princely states, the Congress agitated for 'responsible government', which was supported by the CSP and the communists who worked closely with it, as in Malabar, but major mobilizations also took place around the coir factories in Alleppey district. Political consciousness was high as a result of social reform movements spearheaded by the backward-caste Ezhava community in the first two decades of the century. Prominent among these was the Vaikom Satyagraha in 1924–25 against untouchability and for the entry of Ezhavas into temples. With Ezhavas constituting 80 per cent of the coir workers, and with other communities such as upper-caste Nairs also seeing major changes in their social systems, the formation of the Travancore Labour Association allowed for the creation of solidarities across communities. Anti-colonial nationalist sentiment and trade union consciousness grew simultaneously, and by the mid-1930s, the trade union movement had changed from being welfarist to becoming militant, especially under one of its General Secretaries, Kesava Dev, a quixotic, firebrand communist organizer who was also one of the founders of the PWA in the region. The militant political mobilization centred around the coir workers of Alleppey also got involved in the opposition to atrocities committed by Sir C.P. Ramaswamy Aiyar, Diwan (Minister) to the Maharaja, and the call for overthrowing landlordism in the region. By 1938, when a massive general strike of coir workers took place, the radical political movement was firmly established under the leadership of the communists.

Progressive literature and music arose as responses to these specificities. Literature published in the 1940s, such as Kesava Dev's *Odayil Ninnu* (From the Gutter, 1942) and Thakazhi Sivasankara Pillai's *Thottiyude Makan* (The Scavenger's Son, 1947), focused on the lives of people belonging to the lower castes. Songs written in the Travancore–Cochin region – by P. Bhaskaran, Ponkunnam Damodaran and others – were often militant, satirical or in the agitprop mode, ridiculing the Diwan, strongly attacking particular landlords or capitalists, and often openly confrontational.

The cultural movement in Malabar thus took shape around literization initiatives, the library and reading room movement, hunger marches and processions, and the peasant movement, from the early 1930s. In Cochin and Travancore, struggles against the intransigent monarchies that ruled the two regions as well as the growth of class consciousness through peasant and working-class organization resulted in a vibrant theatre movement. In Cochin and Malabar, the social reform movements of the Namboodiri and Ezhava communities, even if directed within the communities themselves, included radical activists who later became active communists. The plays that came out of such movements were some of the earliest to put across an alternative role for theatre in society.

In 1929, V.T. Bhattathiripad's play *Adukkalayil Ninnu Arangathekku* (From the Kitchen to the Stage) protested against the repressive marriage practices and the purdah system in the Namboodiri community that subjugated its women, and campaigned for school education. It was considered a milestone in the history of Malayalam theatre, and in fact was followed by other plays that carried similar social messages, such as *Marakkudakkullile Mahanarakam* (The Hell Behind the Wooden Umbrella, 1931) and *Ritumathi* (The Pubescent, 1938) by M.P. Bhattathiripad, both dealing with the degradation of Namboodiri women.

The first among the plays to define the contours of the radical aesthetic in Kerala was *Paattabaakki* (Rent Arrears), written in 1936 by K. Damodaran, a leader of the CSP and later the CPI, which was staged in hundreds of villages over the next ten years. Written and performed to organize landless agricultural labourers, the play addressed agrarian class issues and brought socialist dreams to the theatre. Interestingly, copies of the playscript were confiscated by the police of the Cochin government in 1950, three years after independence. Two other plays by K. Damodaran, *Panimudakku* (Strike) and *Rakta Panam* (Blood Money), were also staged all over Malabar, but were banned by the government in 1939.

Theatre and music (as part of plays) were an important part of political mobilization in Travancore too, developing around the vibrant trade union movement. The first labour organization formed in Kerala was in Travancore in 1922. It was called the Travancore Labour Association. Started by two workers of the Empire Coir Factory in Alleppey, it gradually came to represent workers of all coir factories in Alleppey, and was registered as Kerala's first trade union after the Travancore Trade Union Act came into existence in 1938. Later, it came to be known as the Travancore Coir Factory Workers' Union. In the meantime, the coir workers' movement had turned militant with the writer Kesava Dev being one of its main leaders who organized a strike in 1925–26. By the early 1940s, with the coming into existence of the CSP and later the CPI, the trade union movement was established among almost all coir, *beedi*, tile, port, cashew, paper mill and headload workers, as well as coconut tree climbers, toddy tappers and boatmen, spreading to the neighbouring Quilon district as well.[38]

Music of the 1930s and 40s in Kerala was largely of three types. The first type came from local musical traditions like harvest songs, festival songs and songs of celebration of different religious groups, with the lyrics containing political messages. In most cases, these tunes and melodies were musically simple and limited in terms of the range of notes, this being a characteristic of music in the whole region. Folk melodies from the region typically employ pentatonic scales (using five notes), are rhythmic and often with short cyclical movements. Probably because of the simplicity in structure, they were amenable to being sung by large numbers of people with little or no training, familiarity allowing for easy reproducibility. These songs were typically used and performed in processions, worker and peasant gatherings and marches.

The second kind of music consisted of marching songs of the nationalist or western genres that often imitated songs in Hindi or Bengali, songs that activists picked up from Party or Kisan Sabha conferences. P. Bhaskaran, for example, wrote a song, '*Padam padam*', in the tune of the rousing nationalist Hindi song, '*Kadam kadam badhaaye jaa*', which was a regimental marching song of Subhas Chandra Bose's Indian National Army (INA), written by Pandit Vanshidhar Shukla and composed by Ram Singh Thakur.

padam padam urachhu naam
paati paati povuka
paarilaikya keralattin
kaahalam muzhakkuvaan
navam navaranangalil
nammalthan thyaagangalil
naam rachikkum aa puthiya
keralam manoharam

With firm steps we surge forward, singing,
The songs of united Keralam resound.
With our sacrifices we craft the new,
We craft a new beautiful Keralam.

Whether based on traditional tunes or marching songs, these two types of music from the repertoire in Malayalam until the late 1940s might be categorized under the category of '*patappattu*' or 'procession song'. There was no conscious search for 'roots' or indigenous music as in Bengal, with conscious archiving, documentation and preservation objectives, but instead a spontaneous 'use' of easily reproducible local melodies imbibed with political lyrics. This happened, as described above, alongside a theatre movement that saw the writing and staging of plays on topical social issues, and highlighted backward social practices, landlordism and, in the case of Travancore, the cruelty of the Diwan. Like music, the theatre was spontaneous; the productions were often tailored to responses and suggestions from audiences, which transformed them substantially in the process. It must be remembered that the cultural movement also grew alongside the literary and library movements, with mass participation being the hallmark rather than specific autonomy for the cultural fronts.

An example of the marching *patappattu* is a song titled '*Janmitwam nashippikkuka*' (Destroy landlordism) by V.T. Achuthan Nair, whose lyrics are as below:

varika varika sahajare, samayamaayi karshaka
varinirannu varinirannu munnilaanjadukkanaam
duritapoornamaakumee mainajeevitattine
adi tutacchhu pizhuthetuttu neekkuvanorunganam

aniniranniranganaam
aniyuvaanatarkkalam
duritapaathakatthotettu
porutuvaaniranganam

Come forth, move on!
It is time to move, o peasant!
Let us uproot and clean up!
Let us shake up and change this misery-filled life!

A variation of the *patappattu* based on a folk tune and employing typical chanting patterns, titled '*Njangal varunnu*' (We are coming), written by Vaikom Chandrasekharan Nair, runs as follows:

timitimtimi teyyannam taara
timitimtimi teyyannam taara
timitimtimi timtimi timtimi teyyannam taara

kalachoodiya kaittiri neetti
maniveenayil gaanangal meetti
alayaayi putulokam rachikkan
o njangal varunnu
chiri tookunna chenkotiyenti
arivaalukal maanattuyarti
aniyaayi patapattukal paati
o njangal varunnu

timitimtimi teyyannam taara
timitimtimi teyyannam taara
timitimtimi timtimi timtimi teyyannam taara

With our arms outstretched,
Playing songs on our veena,
Like waves we surge forward,
We are coming to craft a new world.

We raise the red flag,
We raise our sickles to the sky.
Together we sing our songs,
Here, we are coming.

(The '*Timitimtimi teyyannam taara*' refrain is a typical rhythmic call-and-response chant that has no specific meaning, but can be employed in a rousingly celebratory manner.)

The third type of music consisted of songs that may be considered precursors to the hallmark '*naataka gaanangal*' (theatre songs) of the KPAC, and what I characterize as a 'crafted' resistance song idiom. They were beginning to be written by songwriters like Ponkunnam Damodaran and P. Bhaskaran, expressing sentiments of rural life and the aspirations of ordinary people – quite different from the *patappattu*, whether traditional or adapted. One of the major singers who came out of the trade union movement, P.K. Medini, spoke to me at length about the performance of such songs. Medini, a coir worker, who became famous for a song called '*Pachhapanamtatte*' (O, green parakeet) in Alleppey in the 1940s, recounted how popular her songs had become during those years and how people would come from as far as fifty miles to hear her sing. In fact, she came to be known as the green parakeet herself.

Performance contexts in the pre-KPAC period were provided by trade union and CPI meetings, strikes and agitations, particularly the Punnapra Vayalar revolt in Alleppey. The revolt, which lasted for ten days in October 1946, and consisted of a general strike called by the ATTUC (All Travancore Trade Union Congress) and an armed uprising by the agricultural labourers and industrial workers of the area, shaped the political ethos within which the cultural movement developed.

By the late 1940s, strong links had been created between the cultural movement in various parts of Kerala and the IPTA. In 1949, Achyuta Kurup, K.P. Namboodiri and K.P.G. Namboodiri represented the Malabar province at the first all India IPTA conference in Bombay and presented their provincial report. The report stated:

> [T]he arts forms like Kathakali, Ottamthullal, Kolkali, Poorakali, etc. have been taken out of their outworn temple surroundings and have been staged before large masses of people, with a new theme portraying the people's struggle . . . about two hundred songs have appeared since August expressing the people's demands. 'You who write in your own blood the history of modern India', 'Keraleeyan's Release, Release our great heroes Nehru and Gandhi,' are two of the most well known songs which are sung all over Malabar. . . . Those songs which are printed like K.P.R. Gopalan's 'Call for battle', 'Unite to defend the motherland' and Bhattathiripad's 'Strange times' have been sold in thousands.

With the KPAC's establishment in 1951 cultural activism acquired a distinct identity at the state level in Kerala, and conscious deliberations on people's music

Members of the Kerala People's Arts Club (KPAC)

'*Pachhapanamtatte*': Finding the Green Parakeet

P.K. Medini

In 2006, a Malayalam film *Nottam*, directed by Sasi Paravoor and depicting the life of a Koodiyattam artist, used a song titled '*Pachhapanamtatte*' in the picturization of a romantic song-and-dance sequence. When the film was released it created a stir in Kerala, with senior activists from the left cultural movement identifying it as their song from the 1940s and objecting to the way it had been changed and used in the film. Their claim was that the use of the song in a different tune, created by the music director M. Jayachandran for the song-and-dance sequence, was objectionable and rendered it trivial. Jayachandran responded by stating that he had at least brought back a forgotten song and made it popular again. I came upon this controversy when I visited Kerala in June 2006. While several people, including my parents, remembered having heard the original song, no one could recall the tune beyond the first four lines or so. I was fascinated by whatever little I heard of the song's original tune and asked a large number of activists from the period of the 1940s and 50s, but in vain, if they could reproduce the song. A few weeks later I travelled to Alappuzha (Alleppey) to meet Anasuya and Medini, singers who had emerged from the working-class movement around the coir factories of Alleppey in the 1940s. As part of a long conversation with them, I hesitantly asked whether they knew the song. Medini *chechi* laughed and said, 'Of course. I sang the song and used to be known as *pachhapanamtatta* in those days.' She recollected the song being very popular in trade union and Communist Party meetings.

I found out from her that the song '*Pachhapanamtatte*' was written by Ponkunnam Damodaran and set to music by the composer Baburaj; it was first used in the play *Nammalonnu*, by the writer and playwright Cherukad. The song's lyrics refer to a young peasant girl addressing a green parakeet, thus:

pachhapanamtatte punnaara poomutte
poonellin poonkarale
uchhakku neeyente kochhuvaazha toppil
onnuvaa ponnazhake
pachhapanamtatte

teyyannam teyyannam paatana paatattu
neeyonnu paatazhake
koyyunna koittarivalinnu kikkili
kollunna paattupaadu, kollunna paattupaadu
pachhapanamtatte

My dear green parakeet, my beloved parakeet,
Will you come in the afternoon to my banana grove, my love?

Will you come and sing in the dancing fields?
Will you come and sing a song
That tickles the sickle I hold in my hand?

Medini *chechi* also recalled how she was expected to sing this song by audiences who came to attend public meetings of trade unions in the coir factories, where music performances were also organized as part of the mobilization. One of the stories she recounted of how popular she was in the 1940s is fascinating in helping to understand how audiences get shaped by the exercise of reaching out through cultural means. For one of the trade union meetings, Medini's singing was advertised through handbills that announced that she would be singing with a microphone, a new acquisition by the union. The word that was used for microphone by the union was '*ucchabhashini*' (which literally means 'she who can speak loudly'), with the handbill announcing the highlight of the evening as '*Mediniyum Ucchabhashiniyum*' (performance by Medini and *Ucchabhashini*). When Medini finished her performance and once the meeting was over, an old man who had travelled from afar came over and asked her why her sister had not performed with her. He had assumed that 'Ucchabhashini' was her sister's name!

I learnt the song '*Pachhapanamtatte*' from Medini *chechi*, and was thrilled to realize later on, when I started performing it, that it uses a light-footed waltz form to depict a peasant girl singing to a green parakeet. To find such a lyrical song, that explodes all stereotypes of the protest song, that was an important part of the protest music repertoire of the trade union and peasant movement, and to reconstruct the context of its performance, has been a fulfilling experience as well as illustrative of the methodology used herein.

and theatre took place. Soon after the KPAC was formed, it formally became the Kerala branch of the IPTA. Its formation was marked with the performance of a *nizhal naatakam* (shadow play) by four students of the Ernakulam Government Law College – G. Janardhana Kurup, P. Narayanan, K.K.K. Kurup and Sukumaran. Subsequently, the group performed another shadow play titled *Poruthunna Korea* (Fighting Korea) and the first of KPAC's proscenium plays, *Ente Makanaanu Sari* (My Son is Right).

The play that catapulted KPAC into immense popularity spanning the entire province was *Ningalenne Communistaakki* (You Made Me a Communist), written by Thoppil Bhasi and first staged in December 1952. This iconic play, considered the most successful political play in the history of Kerala, was banned by the Congress government in Travancore state in March 1953, after it had played for 85 days. The ban was met with massive people's protests all over the state, and activists of the KPAC continued to stage the play despite the ban. It also caused tumultuous scenes in the Travancore–Cochin Legislative Assembly. KPAC activists then decided to file a petition against the ban in the Kerala High Court, with G. Janardhana Kurup, the President of KPAC, taking up the case as an advocate. Within two months, the High Court revoked the ban. *Ningalenne Communistaakki* is a stellar example of

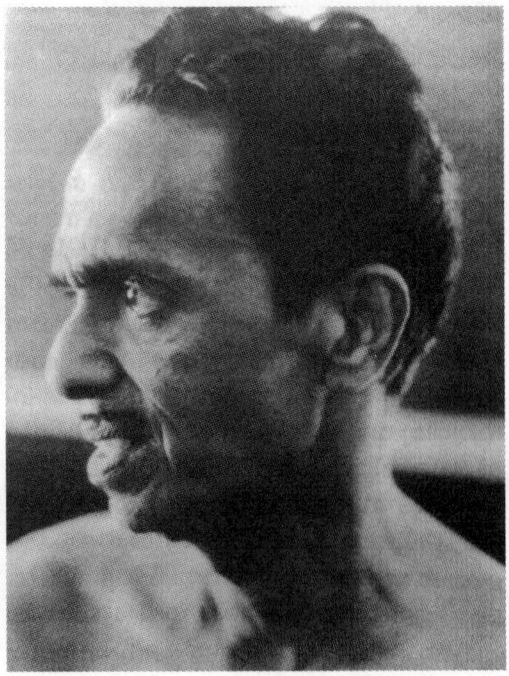

the style and structure of the KPAC's plays, which crystallized a trend of political theatre and music in Kerala that drew strongly from the cultural trends of the two decades before the 1950s, but also brought a new idiom of language, voice and gesture to the state's theatre tradition. Music was a significant part of the play, which contained twenty songs, as did the subsequently performed plays of the KPAC; the songs in the play reflected the conscious crafting of an alternative radical aesthetic in Kerala.

The music of KPAC came out of intense discussions among its activists about 'people's music'. It came out of a need to break, at least partially, with the established kinds of political music described above, a perceived aesthetic inadequacy and a related fear of political ineffectiveness. The discussions centred around how best to depict the conditions, hopes and aspirations of the Malayali people, i.e. around the linguistic identity. The publication of E.M.S. Namboodiripad's *Keralam, Malayalikalute Mathrubhoomi* (Kerala, the Motherland of Malayalis) was in response to the CPI's call for liberation of all those who lived within the geographical boundaries of Kerala, an appeal to overthrow landlordism and vote a Communist government to power. Not only was expressing '*Malayalattanima*' or 'Malayaliness' essential to the establishment of the Malayali linguistic identity, but the left's role in this was also considered critical.

In theatre and music this was seen in the need to express '*Malayalattanima*' aesthetically and also propagate an ideology to oppose exploitative land relations. Two of the main songwriters of the KPAC, O.N.V. Kurup and Vayalar Rama Varma, and the composer G. Devarajan, were middle-class artists who came from the student movement of the late 1940s. What began for them as theatre to mobilize students

Facing page: (left) Sulochana; (right) K.S. George
This page: O.N.V. Kurup

against the post-independence government, resulted in the experiment described below, which slowly established links with the cultural movement that had come into existence around the coir factories and cashew plantations of Travancore. That, as the earlier chapter has described, was spontaneous, participative and used for mobilization in meetings and demonstrations.

It was considered essential to counteract the effects of the dominant popular commercial theatre, which drew huge audiences, especially in Travancore, and consisted of music and theatre in the '*sangeetanatakam*' (music theatre) tradition that drew heavily from Tamil culture. Theatre and music in these productions tended to be ornate and bombastic, which, it was felt, could not represent the people. The new folk idiom that was crafted in the definition of the identity of Malayaliness needed to be both simple enough to express the feelings of the common people, and, at the same time, expressive enough to convey a range of emotions.

In terms of form, that which was easily available – the folk music of Kerala on the one hand, and music from the Carnatic tradition on the other – was seen as constrictive. In the case of a large number of indigenous forms, the dominant perception was that they would not attract the people to 'think new', since folk music from Kerala, unlike in many other parts of the country, is fairly limited in terms of pitch, the range of notes explored and variety in melodic forms. At the same time, use of Carnatic music was not only considered much too ornamental and elaborate to express simple feelings, but also constrained by its structure and rules of rendering. It was felt, instead, that Hindustani music, or the north Indian tradition, offered greater freedom and variety of expression because it allows for rendering the same *raga* or combination of notes to suit variations in moods, which is not allowed in the Carnatic tradition.[39] In addition, there was sufficient familiarity with the north Indian tradition in Kerala because of a thriving *ghazal* culture in Malabar, and also because of the growing popularity of Hindi film music. The songs of the KPAC reveal both a 'beautification' of hitherto fairly monotonous folk melodies making use of principles from north Indian singing, and the creation of new melodies that were more expressive without being ornamental. In fact, in the initial stages, composers brought in what they had heard elsewhere quite blindly, as O.N.V. Kurup noted in his interview to me, because they happened to like the tunes – and the songs were mere imitations, direct reproductions of tunes with hardly any interpretation. The innovations happened subsequently, with interpretations of accents, different crooning styles from what was being imitated and adoption of the ostensible flexibility of other forms.

This innovation in form was also accompanied by fresh lyrics that reflected the same objectives. Again, in contrast to Sanskritized and Tamil-based lyrics, there was greater emphasis on colloquial usages while consciously eschewing anything that might sound like sloganeering. These songs typically talked about the lives of peasants and their families, and often did not directly refer to class relations or exploitation except through symbolism, such as references to the 'sickle-shaped moon' that attracts a poor peasant girl. An example of this that provoked serious debate was the song '*Ponnarival ambili*':

> *ponnarivalambiliyil kanneriyunnole*
> *aamarattin poontanalil vaatinilkkunnole*
>
> *pulkudilin polkkatiraam kochhuraaniyaale*
> *kankulire ninakkuvendi nammalonnu paadaam*
>
> O woman who gazes at the golden sickle-shaped moon!
> O woman who stands under the shade of that tree like a faded flower!
>
> You are the queen of your grass hut,
> Apple of my eye, let me sing for you.

The love motif, invoking 'pure love between ordinary people', became a hallmark of KPAC songs. This new 'language of the people' drew a tremendous response, and plays and songs of the KPAC were performed to large audiences all over the state. However, they were ridiculed as not sophisticated enough in the 'high art' circles of the 1950s in Kerala, and much later as not representative of 'the collective' because they were crafted and artificial.[40] I have referred to this earlier in connection with the authenticity debates, and I am pointing out here the connection between arguments for autonomy in cultural movements and for a vigorous reinterpretation of existing idioms in defining music 'for the collective'. What is interesting to note is that the popularity of this new idiom was such that despite a directly unfamiliar format, the KPAC's repertoire was converted from a 'new' kind of music to one that a large number of people sang along to for decades afterwards.

People's Music in Assam

Assam was a province where the cultural movement took shape spontaneously from the 1930s onwards, but it grew exponentially and in fact expanded very consciously through music. Jyotiprasad Agarwala, Bishnuprasad Rava, Bhupen Hazarika, Dilip Sharma, Sudakshina Sharma and Keshav Mahanta, to name a few, came to be known as the faces of the IPTA in Assam from 1945, when it was formally established there. They were all singers and musicians, as was the inimitable

Hemanga Biswas, who had lived in his childhood and youth in Assam and was instrumental in setting up IPTA's Assam unit.

The IPTA in Assam was formally established in 1945, when Hemanga Biswas and others went on a forty-day cultural tour all over the state with the 'Surma Valley Cultural Troupe'.[41] In his secretarial report to the Third State Conference of the IPTA, Assam (1955), Biswas recollected:

> Year 1943–44. World War was inflicted upon Assam border. . . . The British imperialist rulers clamped public opinion of enraged India. A strange thing came into the economic life: black market, blackout got set in the life of the citizens. The curtain of blackout was dropped on the platform of cultural life. Subsequently, a small cultural troupe of students from Kolkata came down seeking help for the victims of Bengal famine and performed various programmes at different places ranging from Dibrugarh to Silchar with the message of freedom and peace against war. Their leading slogan was 'Bengal is hungry o friend, Bengal is hungry'.[42]

Hujuri notes:

> The mobile squad performed 27 cultural items in different places which included demonstrations on the Naval Revolt, a shadow play on the theme of the hanging of Kushal Konwar, cartoon dance of the Cabinet Mission, a ballet on the Bengal famine entitled *Bhukha Nritya* (by Purnendu Pal and Usha Dutta) and such other items on socio-political issues. A few Assamese songs composed by various lyricists including Jyotiprasad Agarwala were also included in their programme schedule.

In the course of this tour, the troupe also went to Tezpur, where Biswas met Jyotiprasad Agarwala and Bishnuprasad Rava, who were already major cultural figures of left politics in Assam. The IPTA's Assam State Committee was established in 1948 with Agarwala as President and Rava as Vice-President.

As with other provinces, and as seen from Hemanga Biswas's memoirs, and work by Dewri and Hujuri, a vibrant culture of people's music from the left movement existed in Assam from the 1930s.[43] Assam's radical cultural movement, exemplified by interventions of the IPTA, but also through specific cultural explorations of the people involved, had several dimensions, with music being a significant part of all. Artists from Assam were excavating numerous indigenous forms and in that sense were strongly locally rooted, but were also engaging with questions of the national in translocal ways that were quite distinct. I would argue that as in the case of the Central Squad whose activities were detailed earlier, Assam's artists were imagining the nation in a very distinct way.

Left: Bishnuprasad Rava
Below: All India IPTA Conference, Assam, 1955: (in the foreground, left to right) Hemanga Biswas, Bhupen Hazarika and Balraj Sahni

We can see two kinds of impulses. The first came from a variety of indigenous traditions that influenced individual artists substantially, as is described vividly in Biswas's memoirs and Dewri's research into Bishnuprasad Rava's life and work. The second came out of conscious experiments with interpretation, and the transformation of such forms into 'modern' formats and media, such as film. And interestingly, it came also with theorization – by people such as Biswas, Agarwala and Rava, of the role of the artist in society and of themselves as creative people.

It is possible to identify three kinds of people's music in Assam. First, as in Bengal, Assam's IPTA tradition engaged very intensively with indigenous forms like *bargit, naam, kirtan, bihu, goalpariya lokageet, boragi geet, bangeet, aainaam* and so on.[44] As with the Central Squad, the examples of gatherings and festivals that showcased these forms through performances by indigenous artists are numerous.

Second, dance traditions, and the music involved, were also harnessed substantially. Three types of dance traditions were worked with: classical forms like Manipuri and hybrid forms such as those from the Uday Shankar tradition; traditional religious forms like *satriya nritya* that were part of religious practices and based in monasteries; and folk forms like *bihu*. Shanti Bardhan of Bombay's Central Squad, who belonged to Bengal but whose training in Manipuri classical dance was from Assam to some extent, and numerous other dance maestros and veterans from the Manipuri classical tradition, such as Amubi Singh, Gour Nitai Singh and others, were a part of the left movement's cultural activities.

Third, music born out of the complex interface between tradition and modernity, mediated in interesting ways by emerging technologies like film, was one kind of people's music in Assam, with Bhupen Hazarika and the Agarwala–Rava partnership in theatre and film representing this strand.

The partnership between Jyotiprasad Agarwala and Bishnuprasad Rava, established in the 1930s, played a significant role in creating people's music. Rava, who was a dancer, singer, actor, playwright, filmmaker and litterateur, was involved in the Civil Disobedience Movement during the freedom struggle, and he later became a communist leader who played an active role in mobilizing the peasants of Assam to rise up in armed struggle against the *mouzadars* (landlords). His studies took him to Calcutta in the 1920s, where he was influenced by the works of Rabindranath Tagore; he also met the Russian ballerina Anna Pavlova there, who urged him to return to Assam and study the traditional music and dance forms that originated in temples and other religious centres. This, as he has acknowledged, was an important event in his life, and was crucial in leading him to extensive documentation and work with forms such as *satriya nritya*. He was an active member of the Revolutionary Communist Party from 1945 onwards, and later joined the CPI. Dewri notes:

> [W]hen he finally had to return to Assam in 1930, he began to tour composite Assam, which at that time consisted of present-day Assam, Greater Sylhet district of East Bengal (now Bangladesh), Meghalaya (Garo Hills district and Khasi and Jaintia Hills district), Nagaland (Naga Hills district and Tuensang area), and Arunachal Pradesh (Sadiya Frontier Agency and Balipur Frontier Agency). He visited all the Vaishnav religious centres, or Satras, and started studying the Satriya culture. This is when Rava began to secularize and popularize the Satriya culture. He was responsible for bringing Satriya dance and music out of the confines of the Satra. He was himself a dancer, and performed Satriya Nritya in various places in Assam as well as outside it; for instance, he performed the Tandav Nritya in Benaras Hindu University in 1939 during an all India dance exhibition. He also discovered and trained talented dancers (such as Jatindranath Goswami), who later went on to become consummate practitioners. Rava also explored the cultures of the various ethnic groups of the region, wrote extensive ethnographic notes on them, and incorporated them in his creations.[45]

Jyotiprasad Agarwala came from an affluent family of Tezpur which was also involved in literary and cultural activities for at least two generations. Agarwala, who had travelled to the University of Edinburgh in the 1920s, came into contact with the filmmaker Himanshu Rai and other prominent artists, and also came to be conversant with western classical music and filmmaking. In 1934, Rava and Agarwala collaborated in the staging of Agarwala's play, *Karengar Ligiri* (The Maid at the Palace), where the audience heard 'typical' Assamese tunes played with a combination of indigenous and western musical instruments for the first time. This performance was also significant because the orchestra was an all-woman one. Dewri notes that from 1935 onwards they began recording their songs, which became very popular in the region.[46]

By the late 1930s, Soumendranath Tagore of the Communist League (later named the Revolutionary Communist Party) established the Radical Institute in Guwahati, which became a major centre for radical politics. With the Assam branch of the CPI being established in 1943 in Guwahati, both Rava and Agarwala, influenced by Marxist politics, were to begin to locate their art within a theoretical framework, and begin speaking and writing about the role of the *shilpi* (artist) and of culture in society.[47] Given the multiple media and forms they were working with, it meant a critical engagement with indigenous forms in the context of colonial modernity and the development of new technologies, such as film. For example, Rava, who spent many years working with *satriya nritya*, the dance form that came out of the monasteries of the Vaishnavite tradition of Shankardeva, argued that *satriya* belongs to the common people of Assam,and hence his attempt to secularize the dance and music of the *satra*.

When the Communist Parties of India were banned in 1948, Rava went underground, travelling from village to village while in hiding. Most of his songs that drew from different folk traditions, primarily from the peasantry, were composed during this period. Consciously writing and speaking about the need to work with and revive indigenous forms, Rava was involved with legitimizing and working with *bihu* music and dances, and also another form known as *bangeet* which came out of *bihu*. Shunned or considered inferior by the urban middle classes due to association with groups belonging to the lower strata and their eroticism, *bihu* was brought into the limelight as an example of engaging with the folk tradition.

Both Rava and Agarwala worked with transforming indigenous melodies into rousing and mobilizational songs for the peasantry and other ordinary people. Dewri mentions two songs, Rava's '*Bol bol bol*' (based roughly on Shelley's 'Song to the Men of England') and Agarwala's '*Tor mor alokore jatra*', as examples of this.[48] '*Bol bol bol*' goes as follows:

bol bol bol krisak sakti dal!
o'bonua samaniya agbarhi jao bol
jag jag jag mazdur na-joan.
nirjatita nipidhita krisak saktiman!
tor bahute ase lukai oshim sokti bol
ranar singa baje sun oi agbarhi jao bol

Onward, valiant peasants, onward!
Oh toiling comrades, let's march forward!
Rise up! Rise up! O young toilers!
And the brave tillers of the soil
Who suffer oppression,
In your arms is great strength.
Listen to the trumpets of war blow! Let's march on!

Others who were involved with the revival of indigenous music in Assam were Bhupen Hazarika, Anandiram Das, Rudra Baruah, Pratima Baruah Pandey, Nizamuddin Ahmed and Nileswar Brahma.

Bhupen Hazarika, who was greatly influenced by the work of Rava and

Agarwala,[49] was a child-artist who wrote and performed music when he was as young as fourteen years old. '*Agni jugarphiringati mai*', which he wrote in 1939, when he was about fourteen, was a song dedicated to the *sarbahara* (proletariat). His iconic song, '*Bistirno parore*', was written in the 1960s, influenced by his meeting with Paul Robeson when he went to Columbia University to do a PhD in Mass Communications in the early 1950s. Robeson's 'Ol' Man River' about the Mississippi river provided the idea as well as the basic melody for this song in Assamese about the Luit (Brahmaputra) river, which Hazarika later sang in Bengali about the Ganga, and is an interesting example of a western tune being adapted to an 'Indian' format.

bistirno parore oxongxhyo jonore
hahakaar xuniu nixobdde nirobe
burha luit tumi burha luit boa kio

With innumerable people on your droves,
How do you flow silently hearing their cries?
O, Old Man Luit?

After Hazarika returned to Assam in 1953, he became an active member of the IPTA.

People's Music in Andhra, Telangana and Rayalaseema

Andhra's case was similar to Kerala's in the sense that its territory, consisting of three regions – coastal Andhra, Telangana and Rayalaseema – were administratively differently located in the colonial administration, with Telangana being under the Nizam of Hyderabad and the other two being part of the Madras presidency. Before the left-wing cultural and literary movement emerged in these regions, in the 1930s primarily, the national movement and social reform movements had set the scene somewhat for cultural interventions for social change. From 1870 onwards, social reform themes that questioned retrograde social practices appeared extensively in literature. Political literature with nationalist themes came into existence from 1920. In the early 1920s, a novel that was banned by the British (*Malapalli*, written by Unnava Laxminarayana) talked about socialist principles, and of economic and social equality; and a play (*Ryotu Bidda* by Sabnavis Rama Rao) talked of the problems faced by the peasantry. From around 1934, literature started acquiring a distinct left-wing tilt, with novels and plays being written on socialist themes. Magazines such as *Jwala*, *Prabha* and *Vauhini*, published between 1930 and 1935, discussed Marxist ideas and published translations of key Marxist texts. An anthology of poems titled *Ryotu Bhajanavali* (Praising the Peasant), published in 1934 and edited by N.G. Ranga; short stories regularly published as pamphlets by Kaarmika Sangha (Workers' Association) from 1933; and the magazine *Prabha* which was considered the first communist magazine, are important examples. Highly influenced by Bolshevik literature, which made an appearance in Andhra by the late 1920s, these works attempted to evolve a 'new, simple language' of the peasantry and used traditions of indigenous oral poetry. Between 1934 and 1943, there was an explosion of such literature, printing presses and publishing houses, and the setting up of the PWA and the Praja Natya Mandali (PNM, which aligned itself with the IPTA) in Andhra in 1943 signified a consolidation, expansion and wider interpretation of the already prevalent idea of cultural intervention in politics.

Examples of songs written in the mid-to-late 1930s are '*Kaarmika sodara*' (Worker brother), '*Kadupu manta*' (Hunger in the belly) and '*Coolie*'. The lyrics of '*Coolie*', written by Vasireddi Nageshwara Rao and published in *Prabha* in 1935, are as follows:

maamsaheenamu nee sareeramu
makili nindenu nee tanuvuna
raktaheenamu needu mukhame
vyaktta parachunu ninnu, coolie

Devoid of flesh on your body,
Hardly any blood in your face,
I talk about you, o coolie.

Apart from the literature in Telugu mentioned above, Hyderabad city emerged as an important centre for Urdu literature, Makhdoom Mohiuddin being the most prominent of the poets writing in Urdu. As part of a radical group constituting stalwarts like Ravi Narayan Reddy, Rajbahadur Gour, Baddam Yella Reddy and others, a vibrant trade union movement built up in Hyderabad from the late 1930s onwards, along with an explosion of literature.

The creation of people's music in the Telugu-speaking regions took place far more as part of composite performances by the Praja Natya Mandali and its numerous units all over the region, involving dance, theatre and music, and in turn performed by large groups called *sanghams* or *dalams*. These units were constituted by drawing people from several mass organizations of the CPI, such as the Youth Association, the Students' Association, Mahila Sangham (Women's Association) and Bala Sangham (Children's Association).[50]

As early as 1935, a youth meet was organized in the coastal city of

Visakhapatnam under the aegis of the Congress Socialist Party (CSP). By 1937, political schools were being organized targeting the youth, which imparted lessons in Marxism, history and geography, the major world revolutions, class struggle, and social reform themes such as widow remarriage, inter-caste marriage, critiques of untouchability and superstition. Cultural intervention took place along with literacy campaigns, and involved large numbers of people in camps where music, dance and theatre teaching went side by side with actual performances. As in Bengal, there was an extensive documentation exercise and an elaborate exploration of indigenous forms.

What perhaps marks out the Andhra case is the extent to which large and numerous cultural collectives were organized, and how the cultural movement acquired the nature of a mass movement on its own. At the cultural programmes organized in camps, performances of indigenous forms like *jamakula katha*, *buda-bukkala*, *chencheeta*, *lambada* dance, fakir dance and *anna chellala samvadam* were staged. Plays like *Kanya Sulkam* (dealing with a range of gender issues including child marriage, widow remarriage and sale of brides), *Prahasana* (against corruption in government), *Veluguloki* (against child marriage) and *Innemma* (promoting inter-caste marriages) were performed advocating social reform.[51] Noted *burrakatha* artists such as Nazar, Kosuri Punniah and Koganti Gopalakrishnayya came from such youth mobilization.

These cultural collectives were also established through the creation of camps for specific purposes and around pertinent events. For example, Sailaja notes that with the threat of a Japanese attack on India, the CPI in Andhra established sixteen 'people's protection and training camps' through student and youth associations all over the region in the year 1943.[52] Anti-fascist songs and dances were composed by those who were trained in the camps, and with the formation of the PNM, the organizational structure of the cultural movement in Andhra, based as it was in this form of collectives in camps, was formalized. Sailaja notes that around fifteen such camps were organized at the time when the PNM was formed:

> At these camps Dr Garikapati Raja Rao, Koganti Gopalakrishnayya, Kosuri Punniah, Mikkilineni Radhakrishnamurthy, Machineni Venkateswar Rao, Pattam Setti Uma Maheswar Rao and others were instructors. In such district-level camps held for a period of fifteen days training was given in a number of art forms. The health of the artists attending the camp was taken care by Dr Raja Rao. Everyone used to get up in the morning and start their training under the instructors. Men and women artists who were jointly trained got along like brothers and sisters. Women's squads

> were also prepared. There used to be self-introspection and discipline among the trainees. The expenses of the camp were borne by the respective local squads.[53]

The music that came out of the movement was thematic, dealing with subjects like nationalism, fascism, war and famine on the one hand, and with ordinary life on the other: women's songs about family, childbirth, hygiene and the like. While the former raised broad political issues, the latter educated, caricatured and commented extensively on social life and practices. Moturi Udayam, Josya Bhatla Subbamma, Kondapalli Koteswaramma, Tapi Rajamma, Veera Machineni Sarojini, Chandra Savithri and Kondepudi Radha, prominent members of the Mahila Sangham, were also major cultural activists, singing songs and performing *burrakathas*. Examples of nationalist songs that they sang are: '*Maa Telugu talliki mallepoo danda*' (We salute the mother of Telugus with jasmine flowers), and '*Deshamunu preminchamanna*' (Love your country, my brother).[54]

The Mahila Sanghams also sang about issues that challenged gender discrimination, employing forms that were satirical, humorous and subversive. In the volume *Women Writing in India*, Tharu and Lalita quote Moturi Udayam, who went on to become a senior communist and women's movement leader in Andhra Pradesh:

> We did Lambadi dances and collected subscriptions. We used to sing the songs women sang while pounding grain. One of them went like this:
>
> Plant a seed on barren land
> The couple is cold and there is no fun
> Ah-ha, ah-ha, ah-ha
> Who is there to pick the jasmine in the forest?
> What can a woman do with a weak old man? Ah-ha, ah-ha, ah-ha.
>
> In Tadipatri, ten thousand people had come for a meeting. We had learnt the song and were pounding away and singing it vigorously. Suddenly Hanumatha Rao roared like a lion, 'Stop that song'. We nearly died of fright. 'What is that song you are singing? Get off the stage. An old man is of no use! Is this what your Mahila Sangham is all about?'[55]

There must surely have been many more examples of 'objectionable' songs sung as part of an extensive repertoire, especially when it engaged with traditional forms.

The Andhra tradition of resistance music, exemplified by the repertoire of the PNM in the 1940s and 1950s, contains the following features, as the description above indicates. First, it was a case of extensive revival and representation of indigenous musical forms, involving the identification of various categories of marginalized people, collection of their traditional songs around life and life-events, and bringing them into visibility in rural areas as well as for urban audiences. Second, the mode of engagement was primarily large-scale and collective, organized to a large extent through camps where instruction was given in music, theatre and dance to large numbers of people, generating a mass movement in the cultural field. Third, the stated purpose of such methods of collective formation and instruction was to educate, challenge retrograde social practices, and also artistically forge new solidarities between people who had often never interacted socially outside of caste, gender and class hierarchies. Thus, excavating and representing the cultural forms of those from the lowest castes, making them prominent and getting them performed by those who traditionally might never have had contact with them, was an explicit purpose.

Crafting the Popular Aesthetic: Music in the Representation of the People

The IPTA tradition's music, thus, consisting of hundreds of songs written and performed in different parts of the country during the 1940s and 1950s, played a crucial role in articulating the role of culture, and specifically music, *in* and *as* politics in the historical conjuncture of the country's transition from colonial to post-colonial rule. As is evident, 'people's music' was created out of processes of excavation, preservation, transformation and creation of forms that, in the perceptions of those involved, represented the 'people'. As Dasgupta has argued in a recent contribution, in the case of the visual artists associated with IPTA in the 1940s, the people

> are the main protagonists of a fairly large and wide repertoire of images, produced in multiple forms and techniques: the photographs of Govind Vidyarthi, D.G. Tendulkar and Sunil Janah; the sketches, paintings, engravings, woodcuts and linocuts of Chittoprosad and Somnath Hore; the cartoons of Seethapathi Naidu and Chittoprosad; and works by many more anonymous artists.[56]

The musical representations of the 'people' were propelled by imperatives that were common across regions to the extent of the anti-colonial struggle, decolonization, fascism and imperialism being overarching realities, but also localized and micro-context-driven. In some cases the debates about the appropriate forms of musical representation were explicit, whereas in others they were not, but were expressed through creative work.

At the heart of the varied musical conceptions of the 'people' were the questions of tradition and modernity, and the kinds of realism to be undertaken. The extent and kinds of individual-based or collective music created and the degrees of fidelity to existing forms or transformations therein that musicians were grappling with were also foregrounding the question of representing the 'people'. Engagement with tradition came through exploring classical forms, as well as documenting, giving voice to and performing indigenous music. We have seen the engagement with indigenous elements in the IPTA tradition, ranging from presenting indigenous artists or their music as they were, to using indigenous forms and tunes with political lyrics, to interpreting, mixing and borrowing between different forms, involving substantial aesthetic transformations. In Bengal, this was exemplified by the debates between Paresh Dhar and Salil Chowdhury on the one hand, and Hemanga Biswas and Salil Chowdhury on the other, on the need for and mode of use of indigenous forms and tunes to represent the 'people', based primarily on the supposed dichotomy between rural and urban audiences, with the former being considered more representative of the 'people' and responding more to 'their own music and art'.

In Maharashtra and Andhra, it was indigenous forms that constituted the bulk of the music of the left, and there was a process of revival of subaltern forms with content adapted to the specific political context. Here, the music was true to form and did not involve interpretation that changed form, but used politicized lyrics, like in the first phase in Kerala. In Kerala, as pointed out above, the 1950s saw the coming into existence of the 'crafted' folk idiom, or an aestheticized and crafted language of the people, with strong elements of the indigenous. Here, what was being emphasized was the need for a 'new' art that would allow for the imagination of a new life to be born.

In Bengal, Assam and Bombay, the IPTA repertoire saw the significant emergence of Hindustani classical music-based songs as a conscious contribution to the cultural movement. The idea of the modern was reflected in music in interesting ways as well. Translations and reproductions of French, English and Russian socialist compositions like the 'Internationale' was one way. Also, quite apart from translations, the influence of the western musical idiom was seen strongly in Hindi and Bengali. There emerged a distinct category of western songs adapted to the Indian context, with Indianized inflexions in western tunes, changes in metre or beat patterns to suit Indian tastes. Further, the harmonic tradition of Salil Chowdhury's music marked a complete departure from existing music, even that which already existed in India's 'westernized' tradition and brought in a completely different notion of the modern.

Finally, the multitude of forms and idioms that were produced naturally had an impact beyond the political space, and influenced the popular entertainment forms that emerged in the new nation and its regions. People's music from the various IPTA traditions became one of the key influences on music in cinema, commercial theatre and musical entertainment across the country.

Notes

1 Manuel (1988): 159.

2 Ibid.

3 Ibid.

4 Strophic refers to a verse-repeating or verse–refrain-repeating structure where successive stanzas are repeated in a similar tune or a similar variation of tunes between verse and refrain. A large part of popular Indian music genres use strophic structures along with improvisations to make them open-ended and flexible in terms of timing.

5 Here, 'modern' refers to the shorter structures that became necessary to adopt for various kinds of music with the introduction of recording technology from the early twentieth century.

6 Booth (1993).

7 Jalil (2014); Patel (2002).

8 Naregal (2008).

9 Pradhan (1982): 242.

10 Ibid. (1985): 144.

11 Ibid.: 173.

12 Bardhan (1992): 21.

13 Ibid.: 61.

14 Pradhan (1982): 245.

15 Bardhan (1992): 61.

16 The formal analysis and classification of songs of the IPTA tradition into the sub-genres of classical music-based, folk music-based and western music-based are given in the next chapter. The nationalist song was a kind of song within the classical music-based sub-genre. Here only illustrative examples that buttress descriptions are provided.

17 *Dharti ke Lal* (Children of the Earth) is a Hindi film made in 1946 under the IPTA banner. Scripted by K.A. Abbas and Bijon Bhattacharya and directed by Abbas, it was based on plays by Bijon Bhattacharya and the story '*Annadata*' by Krishan Chander. It is considered a landmark in Indian cinema, along with *Neecha Nagar* (1946) made by Chetan Anand and *Do Bigha Zamin* (1953) by Bimal Roy, for focusing on socially relevant themes and offering a critique of economic and social conditions.

18 This is another category within the sub-genre of classical music-based songs which is described in the next chapter.

19 *Taan* is a vocal technique used in the performance of a *raga* in Hindustani classical music, involving the singing of very rapid melodic passages using vowels during improvisation, resulting in the notes being woven together and sung in a fast tempo.

20 *Mudki* is used to refer to a similar but shorter rapid run between notes, as if the phrase is getting turned and twisted.

21 Reba Roychowdhury and Priti Banerjee emphatically stated their indignation at the communists being considered anti-national in their interviews to me. Their own engagements with the IPTA's project of discovering and critiquing the overarching idea of the nation came through in these interactions.

22 Pradhan (1979), vol. II: 378–80.

[23] Ibid.: 381–83.

[24] This was mentioned to me by Reba Roychowdhuri in an interview, when she was discussing Salil Chowdhury's genius.

[25] Ganguly (2002); Manab Mitra (from www.salilda.com).

[26] *Jeeyan Kanya* was reportedly performed only once in 1946. Much later, some time in the 1960s, it was put together for another performance with different actors, during which the songs were recorded.

[27] The fact of this transition that Dhar made was reported to me by Sima Das, one of the prominent singers of his troupe, in an interview in 2009.

[28] This is dealt with in detail in the next chapter.

[29] The description of this incident, as well as the insight provided above, emerged from a conversation with the scholar Samik Bandyopadhyay when I was collecting material for this project.

[30] Chowdhury (1989), quoted in www.salilda.com.

[31] Ganguly (2002): 3.

[32] Ibid.

[33] Mitra (1980).

[34] Pradhan (1982): 330.

[35] Jussy (2005).

[36] Ibid.

[37] Karat (1973).

[38] Tharamangalam (1981).

[39] One essential difference between the Hindustani and Carnatic traditions is in the rules of *raga* rendering. A *raga*, in its most stripped-down version, can be identified by its ascending (*aaroha* in Hindustani or *aarohanam* in Carnatic) and descending (*avaroha* or *avarohanam*, respectively) note sequences. In the Carnatic tradition, these sequences are required to be rendered in the strict sequence of the *raga* and the freedom to skip particular notes is limited. In the Hindustani tradition, the description of the *raga* by its ascending and descending note sequences is also accompanied by a *pakad* (or a 'holding', or temporary withholding, of particular notes at particular points in the rendering), which is supposed to display the mood of the *raga*. The latter classifies *ragas* into different times of the day and night because of this association with mood. The freedom to skip, hold or withhold notes can result in different combinations being used and with different inflexions, thus creating relatively more flexibility in the Hindustani tradition.

[40] Menon (2001).

[41] The vast region of Assam was geographically divided into the two main valleys, viz. the Brahmaputra and the Surma (now Barak). The Surma Valley Cultural Squad was formed in Srihatta district of undivided Assam in 1942.

[42] Biswas (2002a): 58–59.

[43] Dewri (2012); Hujuri (2014).

[44] Neog (2001).

[45] Dewri (2012): 2.

[46] Ibid.

[47] Ibid.

[48] Ibid.

[49] Dewri (2012) notes that in one of his interviews Hazarika talked about the influence of both

men on his music and said that Rava's consciousness traversed close to the soil, whereas Agarwala's consciousness floated above the soil but never quite lost touch with it.

50 Sailaja (1998): 159–60.

51 Ibid.: 154.

52 Ibid.

53 Ibid.: 164, fn 92.

54 Ibid.

55 Tharu and Lalita (1991): 83.

56 Dasgupta (2014): 445.

4

The IPTA Musical Tradition's Repertoire

One of my objectives in this book has been to present the argument that consciously political music or protest music can be formally considered a kind of popular music in the terms employed by musicologists to understand popular music, and that the IPTA tradition's musical repertoire demonstrates ways in which the radical popular imaginary was constructed in the transitional period between colonialism and independence. Even as popular music traditions are marked out in most analyses by the primacy of commercial valuation and marketing needs, and protest music positions itself in terms of an anti-commercial stance, consciously structured protest music of the IPTA tradition variety marks itself out as popular music by seeking a mediation between musical performers, and potential and actual audiences. Here I present a formal and schematic but historically contextualized classification of the IPTA tradition's musical repertoire, and locate it within the broad or extended conception of the popular that I have delineated at the outset.

The objectives of analysing the IPTA tradition's music through a schematic are two: first, to locate the IPTA tradition's music within categories or genres usually employed to understand diverse musics and to identify the major sub-genres in the music; second, to attempt to understand whether and in what way the rise or prevalence of specific sub-genres is related to the nature and aims of political mobilization. Within the genre of popular music, therefore, the major sub-genres that have been identified are folk music-based, classical music-based and western music-based. The repertoire is limited not only to music that falls into these sub-genres; and to that extent, the identification of the sub-genres is not intended to straitjacket the traditions or to draw boundaries between them. Many songs, even if categorized under a given sub-genre, can fall into more than one category, and there are also songs that fall into none of them. However, the classification, it is hoped, helps make sense of a diversity that is formidable, and explains or points towards the prevalence and persistence or disappearance of one or the other kind of protest song over time. In turn, this also allows for a linking up with politics and underscores many of the debates that occurred explicitly or implicitly about what radical or people's music should be.

The Folk Music-based Sub-Genre: Indigenous Music and the IPTA Tradition

The use of the 'folk' idiom and the need to focus on it, it may be recalled, was the subject of much discussion within the IPTA tradition. It is apparent that preoccupation with the 'indigenous' or 'folk' idiom, particularly in terms of its identification as 'truly people's music', was substantial, despite diverse interpretations. The engagement with the indigenous saw a wide variety, ranging from presenting indigenous artists or their music, to using indigenous forms and tunes with political lyrics, to interpreting, mixing and borrowing between different forms, involving substantial aesthetic transformations.

Folk or indigenous music-based songs that were used extensively in the IPTA tradition can be classified into three types: first, a large number of songs where folk or indigenous forms have been directly used, as they are;[1] second, where very little of the original song is retained except the tune, and where direct protest themes are inserted into these commonly used tunes that can be used flexibly and satirically;[2] and a third category of folk songs as part of composite performance where singing and dancing, or singing, dancing, storytelling and theatre, go together.[3] In fact, different uses of the folk idiom, ranging from direct use of existing and commonly used folk forms to discovering forms that were relatively unknown or had become obscure, and crafting new ways of using the folk idiom were seen with different emphasis in different parts of the country.

The first category, where folk tunes were used as they were, often depicted the conditions of life of ordinary people which, in some cases like the *bhatiali* from Bengal or the *Heer* from Punjab, needed to be sung by expert singers, often from indigenous backgrounds. In many cases the songs were not overtly political, but were effective and popular due to the expressiveness of the forms as well as the fact that the singers were well known. In fact, it was often the left cultural movement that brought these singers into the limelight by having them perform at political events, and the songs acquired political connotations over time. In many parts of the country there was an active effort to bring back forgotten traditions and to support dying forms, especially musical forms that belonged to marginalized sections of society like people from the lower castes. In fact this was often a conscious endeavour, as we saw in the case of Andhra, Assam and Bengal, resulting from an understanding that colonialism had destroyed indigenous folk forms and suppressed spontaneous expression by people, and that it was the left's responsibility to revive this people's music, to 'be a phonograph', to use Guo Moro's expressive phrase.

'*Selam chacha*', a *bhatiali* song recovered and sung by Hemanga Biswas, is an example of what represents this 'documentary aesthetic'. It goes as follows:

selam chacha selam tomar paaye
bodo naaer maajhe banaise allah

koio giya chachir kaache
allai more deen deeyache
oi taanataan ghuicha gaiche
boishe aachi paataye

jokhon aamaar kudin chilo
chachi more shaitha lilo
koio giya chachir kaache
allai more deen deeyache

I salute you, *chacha* (uncle):
Allah has given me my big boat.

Tell *chachi* (aunt) that Allah has bestowed blessings on me
My miseries have abated.
I am seated at the stern of my boat.

When I had fallen upon bad days,
Chachi made me feel welcome.
My miseries have abated.
I am seated at the stern of my boat.

The second category of songs that were satirical, theatrical and simple in terms of tunes, included those that came from traditions of singing praise and depicting glory, mostly of Hindu gods, like the *kirtan*, or imagined dialogues between mythological characters often involving discourses about 'good and bad' deeds, or laments about calamities and times gone bad. These came from devotional song repertoires, which were different, however, from more elaborate and *raga*-based

Selam Chacha

devotional music or traditional satirical folk forms. The song '*Mountbatten mangal kavya*' (In praise of Mountbatten) by Hemanga Biswas demonstrates this.

mountbatten mongol kaabyo
hethaai shaango holo
premaanonde baahutule raamo raamo bolo

deshobaashi gaan gao shoraajo bhojon
raghupati raaghava mountobaton
tata birla tero naam
jai vallabh gopal rajaram
jai jai raghupati raghava mountobaton
raghupati raghava mountobaton

Here begins the Mountbatten praise song,
Raise your arms in salutation and chant Rama Rama!

Countrymen, sing the *swaraj bhajan*
Raghupati Raghava Mountbatten!
Your name is Tata, your name is Birla,
Praise be to Krishna and Lord Rama!

Another example is '*Are bhaago London bhaago*' (Hey, run back to London) by Prem Dhawan, referring to the Cripps Mission's representations, mentioned in chapter 3.

The tunes of songs in these forms are usually repetitive and monotonous, and their popularity is based on familiarity, easy identification and reproducibility. These kinds of songs were written in very large numbers all over the country and because they were able to accommodate all kinds of lyrics, became the kind of songs most often associated with left-wing cultural groups. This form of music can be easily sung by large groups of people at demonstrations, does not require those singing it to be trained and therefore constituted a significant part of the repertoire of political groups attempting to convey a political message.

The third category, of folk forms as part of composite performance, meant that the songs were not spontaneous and needed to be formally 'performed', with the performer being a singer–dancer–actor or singer–storyteller and the success of the performance depending on the effectiveness of the performer. Such songs by themselves rarely work on their own; they have to be powerfully delivered through theatrics. Thus what is remembered, where the traditions survived, are the actors–

Mountbatten Mangal Kavya

singers–dancers without whom the compositions would have fallen flat. Some of the songs in the previous category were performed in this way. Amar Sheikh, for example, was known not just as a powerful singer, but also as someone who exhibited powerful histrionics while performing. Often the theatrics would involve call-and-response mechanisms where the audience would be drawn into the performance, and often the nature of the performance would change depending upon the audience's response. This reciprocal relationship, even while there was a separation, between the performers and the audience also played a major role in the evolution of political plays, like in Malabar in Kerala, especially in the earlier period of the cultural movement. The songs '*Neram poi, neram poi*' (The time is up, time is up) by O.N.V. Kurup from the play *Ningalenne Communistaakki* (You Made Me a Communist) and '*Aapni banchle to*' from *Nobanno* (New Harvest) are examples of this.

As much as there was variety, there were varying interpretations of how the folk idiom needed to be used. Some saw the need for the progressive cultural movement to uncover the *true* music of the people in order to provide the context for ordinary people to express themselves, and to preserve it in precisely that form as a celebration of the 'indigenous'. For them, it was only 'authentic' traditional folk songs that could represent the voice of the people, and merely using the folk form to express political concerns not only 'distorted' indigenous culture, it was unappealing to the people. This point was made extensively by Khaled Chowdhury, the well-known stage set designer who was part of the early IPTA in Calcutta and one of the people interviewed for this research. A large number of activists, however, saw the relevance of the folk idiom as extending beyond its own space, to be performed before national audiences and people to whom the music was not native, especially urban audiences. These questions are explored in depth later in this chapter, where questions of authenticity in the IPTA tradition's music are considered.

There were those who went still further, and used the simplicity and directness of the folk idiom (both in form and content) to express something completely modern and possibly 'displaced' from the original. In Kerala, for example, we saw that activists of the KPAC decided to 'mould' folk tunes and craft a 'new folk' idiom that used simple lyrics and lilting tunes that were soon accepted as the voice of the people. This new idiom consciously worked on the structure of folk music by introducing greater melodic content, as it was felt that the Malayalam folk tradition consisted of forms that were monotonous and repetitive, and that a message to change the world needed to be packaged within a new, more appealing aesthetic. A significant segment of the Kerala song tradition, therefore, used fewer 'authentic' and 'original' traditional songs in their protest song repertoire, and through this also sought to

Pachhapanamtatte

Standard tuning

define an identity of 'Malayaliness' in music and theatre. Two songs, '*Ponnarival ambili*' (Sickle-shaped moon) by O.N.V. Kurup and '*Pachhapanamtatte*' (O green parakeet) by Ponkunnam Damodaran, demonstrate this.

pachhapanamtatte punnara poomutte
poonellin poonkarale
uchhakku neeyente kochhuvaazha toppil
onnuvaa ponnazhake
pachhapanamtatte

teyyannam teyyannam paatana paatattu
neeyonnu paatazhake
koyyunna koittarivalinnu kikkili
kollunna paatupaadu, kollunna paatupaadu
pachhapanamtatte

akkaanum maamala vettivayalaakki
aariyan vitterinju
akkaryam kunhinte anandappattinte
eenamaanen kiliye, eenamaanen kiliye
pachhapanamtatte

My dear green parakeet, my beloved parakeet,
Will you come in the afternoon to my banana grove, my love?

Will you come and sing in the dancing fields?
Will you come and sing a song
That tickles the sickle I hold in my hand?

The hills yonder were flattened,
To make the fields which we sow.
Did you know that every child here
Sings such songs?

The Indian Classical Music-based Sub-Genre

It was in Bengal and Bombay that the IPTA repertoire saw the significant emergence of Hindustani classical music-based songs as a conscious contribution to the cultural movement. By using the term classical music-based in the Indian context, I mean the adoption of an idiom often involving *raga*-based melodies, intricate vocal acrobatics or runs (*taans*) and also some improvisation. In fact, by the 1930s or so, what are referred to as semi-classical forms like the *ghazal* or *thumri* had already 'lightened' the strict rules of rendering and allowed for some meanderings around strictly modal *ragas* and a fixed set of notes, but what remained as an essential feature was the notion of rigour, the need for strong training and an association with tradition. With classically trained musicians such as Ravi Shankar and Jyotirindra Moitra being important members of the IPTA Central Squad, many songs of the Squad had classical *raga*-based tunes, and because many of the members were trained musicians, they were performed extensively. These songs, mostly chorus songs with solo voices singing small parts, involved intricate tunes, modes of rendering and orchestration.

These kinds of songs were written and composed with the explicit recognition that alternative music attempting to convey a message should not be less rigorous in form than music from the mainstream tradition, and that artists performing in the alternative tradition should be as accomplished as mainstream and commercial singers. Here we see a move away from the emphasis on indigenous traditions that allowed for spontaneity, simplicity or reproducibilty to an emphasis on a different type of tradition: that of India's classical music heritage and its associated rigour.

It is necessary here to locate the early-twentieth-century discourse on Indian classical music in the context of a late colonial society's engagement with modernity and the growth of the anti-colonial sentiment. Research by Subramanian and Weidman on south Indian (Carnatic) classical music, and by Bakhle on the north Indian (Hindustani) tradition, point out specific aspects of the development of the genre in India.[4] First, despite the proliferation in India of mass-mediated, commercially profitable forms where borrowings and mixings are celebrated, the clearly demarcated space for art music or classical music marks it out primarily by the stated and celebrated values of purity and fidelity. Second, even when innovations have happened or there have been borrowings, they have to be clothed in this idiom of purity. Third, such 'purity' became a standard for judging music only from the third decade of the twentieth century, as a distinct offshoot of the emergence of an urban patronage structure dominated by a middle class that was engaging with modernity and attempting to create an identity for itself and its 'high cultural standards'. Fourth, traditional forms of music got redefined in terms of performance formats, aims of performance and also in terms of defining 'Indianness'. Thus, as Weidman notes, the music 'academy' of the west absorbed this haloed notion of 'India's age-old classical music tradition' uncritically, as comprising features that were in reality early twentieth-century creations, whereas other kinds of Indian music were subjected to ethnomusicological scrutiny and analysis, including analysis of changes in the forms and the impact of societal changes on them. Fifth, these developments got extensively implicated in the nationalist project, one aim of which was to create a lineage of cultural purity and authenticity.

In the case of the IPTA tradition, as mentioned earlier, the engagement with the Indian classical idiom was because of the involvement of classical musicians like Ravi Shankar and Jyotirindra Moitra with the cultural project of the left.

Here again, as with the category of 'folk', I have used the term 'classical music-based songs' to cover at least three specific types: one, songs in the Indian nationalist tradition; two, a certain kind of music that evolved from the rapidly changing proscenium stage and in turn influenced it; and three, very close to the nationalist tradition, the heroic in the socialist tradition.

The nationalist music tradition was a reasonably well-established one by the first couple of decades of the twentieth century, its hallmark being the upbeat and heroic quality, both of the lyrics, and the structure and orchestration of the tunes. In fact, it had become quite common for classical musicians to include a patriotic song or two in their performances, often composed in *ragas* that conveyed war, valour or victory, and often based on poetry by nationalist poets, or on poetry describing the courage of kings and queens who had fought the British, for example Rani Lakshmi Bai of Jhansi, or on a grand notion of India. In fact, as Ranade argues, in the 'modern' format of Hindustani and Carnatic performances, it had become customary for the second half of a classical music concert to have space for 'folk' and 'devotional' compositions, the latter consisting of characteristics of classical music.[5] Patriotic songs, often composed in *ragas* like Desh or Durbari that were amenable to dramatic crescendos and wide ranges of expression, thus legitimately became 'serious' music, something that classical musicians engaged with without compromising rigour. The patriotic song, two examples of which are '*Jaaga desh hamaara*' by Ravi Shankar and '*Janani janmabhoomi*' by Amar Sheikh, was brought into the left's protest music repertoire by the IPTA, positioned as it was at the peak of the anti-colonial struggle.

jaaga desh hamaara jaaga jaaga desh hamaara
goonj utha hai hark one se azaadi ka naara
yeh sadiyon ka behta paani phoota jal ki dhaara, phoota jal ki dhaara
jaaga desh hamaara jaaga jaaga desh hamaara
maidanon mein jhoom ke nikle laakhon hi mastaane
talwaaron ko choom ke nikle laakhon seens taane
har baghairat peshani pe khoon se yeh likkha hai
woh jeena hi kya jaanega jo na marna jaane, jo na marna jaane
jaaga desh hamaara jaaga jaaga desh hamaara

Jaaga Desh Hamaara

Standard tuning

♩ = 100

Our country has awakened at last.
The call of freedom resounds in every corner.
The waters that have been flowing quietly,
Have burst into strong streams.
Our country has awakened at last.

Lakhs of strong youth throng the battlefield.
Lakhs of people kiss their swords and surge forth resolutely.
Every martyrdom is marked in blood.
Who can know about life if he doesn't know how to die?
Our country has awakened at last.

What I am arguing here is that the musical complexity that came from the classical music tradition, which was first manifest in consciously political music as 'nationalist music' of the kind that I have described above, saw a significant use in left-wing political music represented by the IPTA tradition as well, with nationalist songs on the one hand and two offshoots on the other – rousing music for the proscenium stage and the tradition of socialist heroic music. In form, the nationalist songs typically had uplifting tunes, were sung at high scales and tempos to the accompaniment of large orchestras using instruments like the sitar, veena, violin, tabla and the bugle. Most of these songs were openly mobilizational, exhorting people to rise up against colonialism and oppression.

Use of the classical idiom for the proscenium with substantial singing by trained singers on stage was common in Bengal, Maharashtra and Tamil Nadu by the early part of the twentieth century. In fact, interesting features of traditional Indian classical and folk drama had been combined with European dramaturgy such that even when formal scripts, characterization and dialogue delivery reflected the structure of European proscenium conventions, song and dance formed an integral part of the performances. In classical Sanskrit theatre which drew from local traditions all over the country, songs would punctuate the plays substantially. As seen earlier, the idea of composite performance continued to be relevant even after more 'modern', realist formats had been adopted in theatre, and later in films. Within such music, there were song formats that were highly structured, based on *ragas* that were considered appropriate by the classical system to suit moods and situations in the plays. This was a feature of *nataka sangeetham* in Tamil Nadu and *natya sangeet* in Maharashtra (both meaning theatre music). In Bengal, the *raga*-based music of the proscenium had become more hybrid. Tagore had evolved a complex musical repertoire that was substantially *raga*-based, but also used singing styles of church choirs as well as popular western melodies, and this was used extensively in the performances of his plays.

This stylized or hybridized Indian classical music format was adapted by Ravi Shankar for the IPTA's film *Dharti ke Lal* in the 1940s, and also by Jyotirindra Moitra in '*Nabajeebaner Gaan*', both about the Bengal famine. In the 1940s, the IPTA in Bombay produced several dance dramas or ballets: *Spirit of India, Kashmir, Immortal India*, etc. These ballets combined narrative, songs, movement and mime, again interpreting the composite performance traditions in a new way. This was also put to good use in order to imagine a new nation, to depict variety and syncreticism – one of the chief aims of the 1940s IPTA tradition. The classical idiom, although stylized differently for different theatrical formats, was worked upon extensively in Bengal and Maharashtra. Again, the classical heroic form was used to showcase a diverse India, an imagining of the national, in opposition to imperialism. On stage, the stylized classical form was convenient, facilitating dramatic entries and exits, signifying the curtain call, being able to project a message dramatically. In fact, as noted towards the beginning of this chapter, the structure of traditional theatre performances, where music facilitated the entries and exits of characters, served as incidental fillers and to give relief to actors, was used in music effectively through the classical idiom.

naa, naa, naa, maanbo naa maanbo naa
koti bik kore kine nebo praan pone
bhoyer rajye thaakbo na

obhoy peyechhi nuton diner kaachhe
dike dike taai aashaar potaaka naache
peshite peshite rokter laal aalo
dhue debe omaabaashyar joto kaalo
bhoyer rajye dhukboi more thaambo na

No, no, no, never will we accept this:
We won't inhabit the land of fear.

We found fearlessness in the new dawn.
The flag of hope flutters all around us.
Hues of red blood colour our sinews.
They will wash away the darkness of the moonless night.
We will fearlessly enter the land of darkness:
We cannot be stopped.

Balikudeerangale

Standard tuning

Songs celebrating socialist heroes, common people who gave up their lives fighting for freedom against the British and against exploitation, and songs calling for liberation against an unjust order also used the classical tradition being discussed here. These songs would typically talk about 'fighting to be led out of darkness into light' ('*Esho mukto karo*' in Bengali, the IPTA's anthem), the 'red flag showing the way to freedom, the Himalayas and the oceans celebrating peoples' victories' ('*Balikudeerangale*' in Malayalam), and so on, and would be sung by large choirs at political rallies and meetings. The celebration of heroism in the socialist tradition had a lot in common with the idioms of nationalism in many countries, following from the discussions on music aesthetics in the Soviet Union, and this was seen in Indian music as well.

balikudeerangale, balikudeerangale
smaranakalirambam ranasmaarakangale
ivide janakotikal chaarttunnu ningalil
samara pulakangaltan sindooramalakal
balikudeerangale

himagirimutikal kotikaluyartti
katalukal patahamuyartti

yugangal neendi nadakkum gangayil
virinju taamara mukulangal
bhoopatangalilorindia nivarnnu
jeevitangal tutalooriyerinju
chundil gaathakal karangalilee
poochendukal putiya pauranunarnnu
balikudeerangale

O, memorials for martyrs,
Those which evoke memories of battles,
Countless people honour those who gave up their lives,
They adorn you with red garlands

The Himalayas raise flags high,
The oceans raise banners,
Lotus flowers bloom,
In the Ganga where epochs swim,
India had emerged tall on the world map,
Shackled lives have been freed,
These song-waves signal that
A new Indian is born.

At a basic level, the difference between these three types lay in whether they were responding to certain kinds of audience or were attempting to shape audiences, although structurally they might have had similarities with each other. The 'typical patriotic nationalistic song', like '*Jaaga desh hamaara*', was a part of the IPTA's performances, but it was a response to an idiom that did not necessarily project a political stance that was any more radical than the mainstream nationalist one. The classical music-based theatre song or composition was engaging directly with a discourse that was of the left, of focusing on exploitation, as the example of '*Nabajeebaner gaan*' demonstrates. The classical music-based 'socialist' songs went further, addressing an audience that was of the left, which they desired to expand and hoped to see grow. All these engagements with the classical discourse involved discussions around the relevance of the classical heritage of India and the left's assessment of it, and also the idea of imagining the national in the IPTA tradition's music.

However, from the mid-1950s the production of such protest songs, based strongly in the Indian classical tradition, ceased, possibly because it was difficult for non-classically trained singers to sing them. With independence, the relevance of the nationalist song ebbed for the left-wing; freedom was no longer about celebrating a new nation, and the nationalist, bugle-blowing musical idiom was no longer appropriate. The heroic in the socialist tradition would be addressed more now through the established genre of western compositions, to which I turn below.

The Western Idiom-based Music in the IPTA Tradition

The engagement with the western musical idiom in India and its incorporation into Indian music by the early to mid-twentieth century consisted of several distinct features, relating to the stylizations that arose with the song format. First, popular western melodies were used with lyrics in Indian languages, particularly in Bengali. Often, it was the nature of imitation of exact melodies – and later, the form of the songs written – that sounded 'western'. Second, the primacy of lyrics, a feature borrowed from the European song format, constituted a significant feature of these songs. Third, chordal harmony was introduced in instrumental accompaniments for songs along with the use of European instruments.

One of the distinctive contributions in introducing western elements into Indian music was that of Rabindranath Tagore, through several within the enormous corpus of his songs (about 2,500 of them) called Rabindra Sangeet, in which the first two of the above features were seen. Tagore used a large number of Scottish highland melodies, as documented by Dasgupta, which the poet himself referred to as '*Scotch Bhupali*' in his memoirs (*Chhinno-Potro*) (Despite the reference to the *raga* Bhupali, there is no trace of Bhupali in any of them, strangely.) His dance drama *Kaalmrigayaa*, written in the 1880s, had six songs that have a clear western influence. According to scholarly assessments of Tagore's music,[6] he was a pioneer in his engagement with European music, through conscious imitation of known melodies on the one hand, and incorporating stylistic elements from classical Indian music on the other, resulting in:

> an amalgamation of the principles of the European art song with the traditions of the Indian art of singing. From the standpoint of the European, the Indian elements make the dominating impression, whereas the Indians are more aware of the European model. The novelty in this music is the renunciation of the cramping rules of Indian musical theory. The system of the Ragas and Talas is relinquished; the formal scheme of the Variations-Suite is abandoned in favour of the concise song form; the far too exuberant mannerisms of tonality, rhythm and melismatics make way for a simpler, more popular formation. But the most important innovation is the re-instatement of the words as the decisive element. Whereas in classical Indian art

> music, and in vocal music, too, the text is a characteristic addition to the work of art, the essential elements of which reside in the musical construction, the words of the new popular song composition by the Tagore school command prominent consideration. The poem inspires the composition, which strives to reproduce and emphasize both its emotional content and poetic stature.[7]

Tagore's innovation was based on his assessment and critique of the 'corrupt and ossified' music of Bengal at the time when he started out as a songwriter, the insistence on adhering to the rules of classical music, the decline in the kind of patronage that had supported musicians and singers in the past, and the need for music to change and modernize just as literature and painting had progressed and modernized.[8] He insisted that Indian music would do well to adopt the professionalism of western classical music, learn from the attention that a western singer of art songs pays to interpretation and presentation, and the high standards of musical training and performance. Tagore's pioneering contribution, through introducing specific features in the song format, was very influential in 'westernizing' Indian music and lending a western idiom to Indian music.

The use of chordal harmony in instrumental accompaniment to sung Indian tunes happened around the 1940s, when the IPTA came into existence. A substantial part of this development happened around film music, which was beginning to turn towards sounding western by then. Songs were often written based on a particular classical *raga*, or sometimes a song would resemble a *raga* but contain individual phrases that would be unacceptable in a classical rendition of that *raga*. Given such songs, singers and composers like Pankaj Mullick used chordal harmony widely, with chordal progressions tending to be simple – generally consisting of primary major and minor triads built on the scale tones of the melody. In other words, the harmony embellished the primary melody through the use of the idea of '*samvad*' or natural harmony, even if the notes in the chordal harmony were not present in the main melody. Further, the western influence was also beginning to be seen in the instrumentation, especially for film music. According to Manuel:

> Many songs employ only traditional instruments, and the table and dholak (or nal) remain the most popular percussion instruments. But clarinet, violin, saxophone, xylophone, piano, conga and other instruments are widely used. Moreover, the juxtaposition of sections in contrasting instrumental timbres is clearly a concept imported from the West, as the practice is not characteristic of traditional classical or folk music.[9]

It is possible to postulate here that slowly, the popular music genre was introducing structural changes in music in response to, and perhaps in anticipation of, demands for more 'modern sounding, novel sounding and accessible' music; in other words, it was introducing new kinds of listening without too drastic a structural break. As Manuel argues in the specific case of film music, it is possible to state that the impression of novelty was essential, especially to an urban audience, and at the same time, the traditional element, in the form of principles of melody-making, satisfied a sense of cultural nationalism and allowed familiarity. Like the development of modern realist cinema that employed non-realist song and dance techniques from traditional performance forms, the introduction of limited western elements into Indian-sounding melodies rendered by singers in typically acceptable ways marked a particularly Indian response to modernity.

It was in this overall milieu that the IPTA consciously engaged with the western musical idiom, resulting in a distinct sub-genre that consisted of western music-based songs. The earliest introduction of the western idiom in the IPTA tradition's music was through translations of well-known anti-fascist and socialist anthems. The 'Internationale', written in French by Eugène Poitier, was translated into many Indian languages. There were also direct translations and reproductions of French, English and Russian socialist compositions, mostly anthems ('The Youth International', 'La Marseilles', 'Red Army Song', 'We Shall Overcome'). These were in the nature of direct reproduction of western tunes in Indian languages.

Quite apart from such translations, the influence of the western musical idiom was seen strongly in Hindi and Bengali. There emerged a distinct category of western songs adapted to the Indian context, with Indianized inflexions in western tunes and changes in meter or beat patterns to suit Indian tastes. The first example of this is a song by Bhupen Hazarika in Assamese about the river Loi or the Brahmaputra, and in Bengali about the river Ganga, paralleling Paul Robeson's song 'Ol' Man River' about the Mississippi.

bisteerno dupaare aushonkho maanushe
hahaakaar shuneyo nisshabde neeraube
o ganga tumi ganga boichho kaino

noitikotaar skholon dekhyo
maanobotaar poton dekhyo
nirlojjo aalosh bhaabe boicho kaino
shohosro boroshaar unmaadonaar
montrodiye lokkhojonere

Bisteerno Dupaare

Standard tuning

♩ = 100

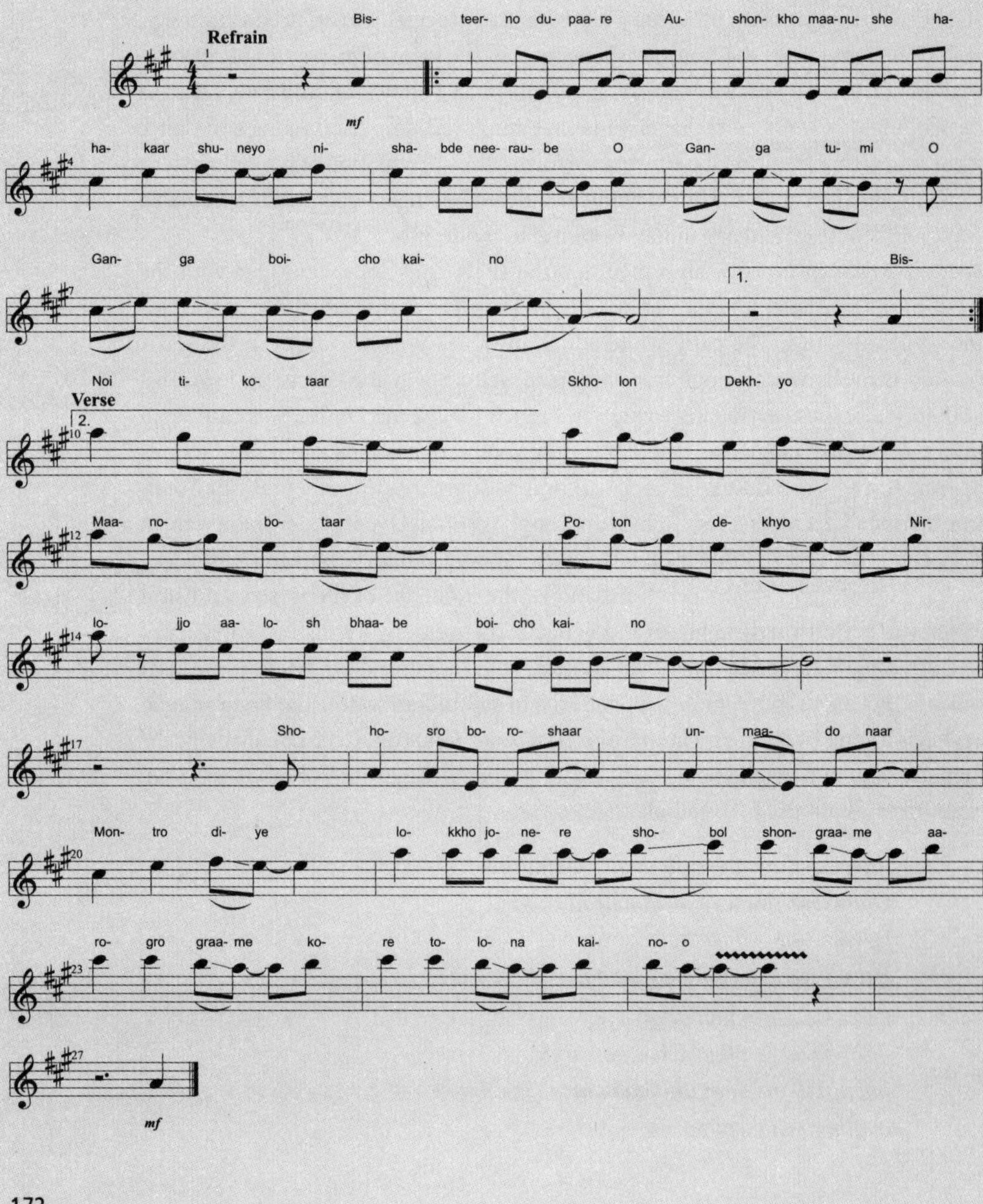

shobol shongraame aarogrograame
koretolona kaino
bisteerno dupaare

gyan biheen nirakkhare
khaddobiheen naagoriker
netribiheenotaaye mouno kaino
unmotto dhoraar kurukkhetre
lokkho koti bharat bashider jagaalena kaino
bisteerno dupaare

With innumerable people on both shores,
How do you flow silently hearing their cries,
O Ganga?

You have seen principles die,
You have seen humanity decline.
How do you still flow along so shamelessly and lazily,
O Ganga?

You have seen citizens,
Letterless and hungry.
Why do you stay silent
To such blindness?
Why don't you rouse millions of Indians,
O Ganga?

A second example comes from Hemanga Biswas's 'John Henry' (an adaptation of a 1930s' trade union song from the United States):

naam taar chhilo john henry
chhilo jaino jeebonto engine
haathudir taale taale gaan gaaye shilpi
khushi mone kaaj kore raat din
ho ho ho ho
khushi mone kaaj kore raat din

kaalo paathore khodaaye john henry
jaanaae te kore beshi jholmol
haathudir gaaye gaaye paathore aagun dhore
haathudi chalano taar shombol

John Henry

♩ = 92
John Hen- ry John Hen- ry Naam taar chhi-lo John Hen- ry
mf
chhi- lo jai- no jee- bon- to eng- ine Haa-thu- dir taa- le taa- le gaa- n gaa-ye shi- l- pi- i
khu- shi mo- ne kaaj ko- re raat din
Ho- O ho- o ho- o ho- o khu- shi mo- ne kaaj ko- re
raat din Ho- o ho- o ho- o ho- o
khu- shi- mo- ne kaaj ko- re raat din kaa- lo paa- tho- re kho- daaye John Hen- ry kaa- lo
paa- tho- re kho- daaye John Hen- ry jaa- naa- e te ko- re be- shi jhol- mol
haa- thu- dir gaa- ye gaa- ye paa- tho- re aa- gun dho- re
haa- thu- di cha- laa- no taa- r shom- bol
ho- o ho- o ho- o ho- o haa- thu- di cha- laa- no taa- r shom- bol

ho ho ho ho
haathudi chalano taar shombol

paschim virginiar rail suronge
pathorer pahaad kete kete
rail line kaata hobe henrir haathudir
ghaaye ghaaye raat jaaye kete
ho ho ho ho
ghaaye ghaaye raat jaaye kete

His name was John Henry.
He was like a live engine.
He sang to the hammer's rhythm.
He sang and worked merrily all day.

He hammered at black rocks, John Henry did.
Sparks flew from the rock as he hammered away.

In the rail tunnels in West Virginia,
He cuts through rocky mountains.
Henry's hammer will lay the railway line.
He will work night after night.

In the Indian context these songs introduced a new idiom for the hard-hitting political song, typically with ominous lyrics that urged people to rise up against their exploiters, musically conveyed through staccato phrases, melodies constructed out of notes that were not close to each other (making for greater drama) and hard drumbeats. This constituted the non-nationalist socialist idiom in Indian music – the left-wing marching song that is also rendered forcefully and dramatically – an idiom that continued to be used extensively in the decades that followed. However, even this sub-genre maintained the formal structure of the typical song, i.e. an established melodic pattern, strict differentiation between refrain and verse components, a constant beat pattern throughout the song, and so on. What changed was the use of voice, the approach to the notes and the use of newer kinds of melodies. With such songs, this kind of western idiom became a typical signifier of revolutionary music.

However, it was with Salil Chowdhury and the corpus of work he created during his association with the IPTA that the idea of the revolutionary song changed completely, and the notion of composition and a larger soundscape emerged – this being the third kind of song where the western idiom formed the basis of revolutionary music.

The harmonic tradition of Salil Chowdhury's music marked a complete departure from existing music, even that which already existed in India's 'westernized' tradition. By the 1940s, as noted above, the use of western tunes as well as western orchestration in dominantly Indian melodies had become common in Bengal, for instance, in Rabindra Sangeet and other music in the Brahmo tradition, compositions by Pankaj Mullick, and so on. However, these innovations continued to retain the 'modal' nature of the Indian musical tradition, where a basic melody uses a certain combination of notes, whether *raga*-based or based on western tunes. When western orchestration was used with the main melody, what made it as pleasing as the original melody was the exploration of chordal harmony in the orchestration, with the instruments exploring notes not contained in the dominant melody but harmonizing with them. As elaborated earlier, this was limited, however, to simple triads around the dominant notes of the *raga* or mode that the melody was based upon. It could not be established whether such chordal harmony was intended to challenge or disturb the fundamental consonances or dissonances inherent in the melody, or whether it merely served as a kind of embellishment that lent variety and newness. In other words, the change in grammar was probably merely echoing the need for variety and not fundamentally making an aesthetic point of challenging existing grammars of music as a symbol of protest. This was probably in keeping with the trends in urban popular music where variety allowed transmission to larger audiences.

Salil Chowdhury's compositions for the IPTA, exemplified by '*Dheu Utchhe*' on the Naval Mutiny of 1946, moved away from the modal structure of a standard melody based on a given pattern of notes at a given tonic scale throughout the song. He converted the relatively uniform song format into the western classical composition format by using a series of modal melodies, each with its own given combination of notes and accompanied by harmonic orchestration, but such that each of the pieces of the song sounded very different from the other. What was interesting is that very often, the melodies that were strung together came from the folk traditions of Bengal and other parts of the country. Salil Chowdhury broke away from the strict refrain–verse–refrain or *sthayi–antara* structure of Indian songwriting, in that sense introducing the notion of the composition, and a wider idea of a soundscape using voice and instruments rather than just voice and musical accompaniment. He also introduced significant silences, varying speeds and scales in the different sub-melodies, harmonies in singing, and superimposition of one scale upon another, which went on to become a hallmark of the Indian choir tradition, first in Calcutta and later in Bombay and Madras. For him, thus, the creation of the new aesthetic involved innovation not only in the poetic content of the composition, but also in form.

dheu uthchhe kaara tutchhe
aalo phutchhe praan jaagchhe jaagchhe jaagchhe

guru guru guru guru dam maro pinakir
jegechhe jegechhe jegechhe
maya bondore aaj jowar jaagaano aaj
toraano paataano dheu uthchhe

shoshoner chaaka aaj ghurbe na ghurbe na
chimnite dhnuaa aar uthbe na uthbe na
chita aaj jolbe na jolbe na
chaaka ghurbe na dhnuaa uthbe na
chita jolbe na
aaj hartal, aaj chaaka band

The waves are rising, the prisons are breaking,
The lights are shining, the soul is awakening.

We can hear the sounds of Pinaki's bow being strung,
As the tide rises in the magical harbour.

The wheels of oppression will no longer turn,
Chimney fires will no longer rise,
No funeral pyres will be lit.
The wheels will not turn, smoke will not rise,
No funeral pyres will be lit.
Today we are on strike,
Today the wheels will not turn.

To summarize, the western idiom in protest music in India worked with two principles that came from the westernization imperatives prevalent in popular music in the first four decades of the twentieth century. The first of these was the Tagorean kind of attempt at making Indian music more formal and structured, open to outside influences and less constrained by classical rules. The second was the introduction of variety through the use of western instruments and principles of chordal harmony that allowed for a different kind of sound from that which was traditionally available or admissible. In both these, the modal principles of melody-making and songwriting were adhered to, as also the primacy given to the conventional

Dheu Uthchhe

Male 2
Choir
Keys
7
chhe jaa- g chhe
9
B
11
Gu- ru gu- ru gu- ru gu- ru dam maro pi- na- ki- r
je- ge- chhe je- ge- chhe je- ge- chhe
mf
mf
13
mo- ra bon- do re aaj jo- wa- r jaa- gaa- no aa- j

Male 2
Choir
Keys
14
to- raa-no paa-taa- no dhe-u uth chhe
mf
16
18

Male 2
Choir
Keys
21
25
Sho- sho- ne- r chaa- ka aaj ghu- r- be na ghu- r- be na
mf
mf
26
chi- m- ni- te dhnu- aa aar u- th- be na u- th- be na
27
chi- ta aa- r jo- l- be na jo- l- be na

Male 2
Choir
Keys
Chaa- ka jo- l- be na dhnu- aa
u- th- be na chi- ta jo- l- be na chi- ta jo- l- be na
1.
ha- r- taal ha- r- taal har- taal
2.
ha- r- taal ha- r- taal har- taal aa- j har- taal aa- j chaaka band aa- j

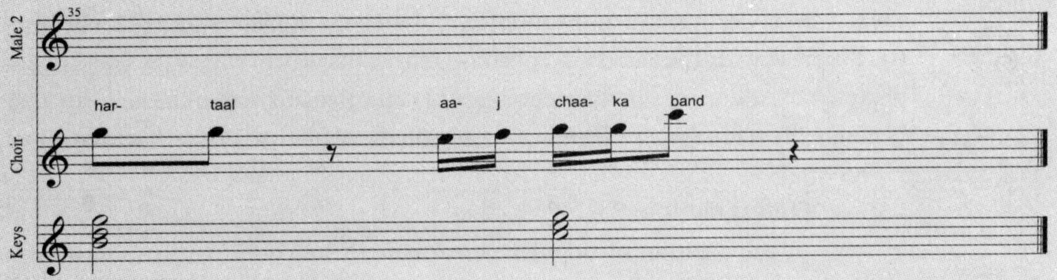

verse–refrain structure of the song, with instrumental accompaniment allowing for greater variety but nevertheless only serving as accompaniment to embellish the basic melody. These kinds of western influences were to influence the trajectory of popular music in India for decades to come, and many of the musicians who took this up seriously were associated with the IPTA. The fundamental departure from existing ways of introducing western elements into Indian popular music came from the music of Salil Chowdhury, which not only established the harmonic tradition, but also fundamentally altered the principles of songwriting, brought in the notion of western-type multi-modal compositions, and the idea of a soundscape involving instruments and voice. This need to break away from structures that might be considered constraining while maintaining a strong connection with indigenous traditions came, I believe, from the idea that music of protest should also question musical grammar or fundamental structures of music-making.

The music that is being analysed here was created to respond to key political issues of the transitionary period from colonialism to independence, and in the process it created a landscape of the radical–popular imaginary in different parts of the country. A critical component of this imaginary was the idea of the collective of the 'real' people of the country because the radical cultural project was fundamentally about creating a new 'popular' based on old and newly imagined collectivities or solidarities. Expressed in a variety of ways musically, this popular imaginary involved questions of the individual in the collective, of authorship in a collective movement and of multiple representations of the collective. These issues became the basis for important debates and fundamental disagreements both within the left movement and outside it, in assessments of the left movement's cultural project, as we saw above.

I turn now to the facets of visualizing and performing the collective through music in the IPTA tradition. The idea of the collective was shaped in and through this music as a pivotal concept that foregrounded and expressed new solidarities, new spaces and new politics. The popular imaginary was shaped fundamentally by the way the collective, and the relationship between the individual and the collective, were represented. The variety in collective music, the way in which the collective is depicted or interpreted in different kinds of collective music and the contexts that generate them are reviewed while focusing on the analytical issues that arise.

Protest Music and the Collective

In the creation of popular performance, the collective that constitutes the audience as well as that which constitutes the performers, both are important. The image that comes up is of a quintessentially collective political performance performed to a mass gathering, where audiences are expected to be shaped by the performance, to be tailored to its needs and expectations and those of the political movement. The idea of the collective is inherent to the mass gathering and, typically, forms that are collective are used and reworked for the gathering. Over the course of the twentieth century radical cultural movements used a range of collective forms, from ritual- and tradition-based, to the work of artist collectives involving reproductions or transformations of forms from familiar contexts, with a wide variety in between.

The collective song, in itself, can carry the image of collective identities and struggles, and thus becomes a natural form of cultural representation at mass gatherings. Different kinds of collective music that get harnessed and are performed are inscribed with varying levels of participation, different kinds of audience–performer interaction and requirement of skills. For the collective performance, therefore, either the established signalling systems or routines of traditional performances (which ensure the coherence and meaning that comes from traditional collectivities), or actively conceived, constructed and executed collective processes and idioms that fall outside the realm of the familiar, are necessary. What I seek to emphasize here is that the actual range of collective music that is revealed depends on the traditions that are available, the extent to which they are used and the transformations that are considered necessary in communicating a radical politics.

While the image of rousing collective songs from the Russian Revolution, post-revolutionary Soviet Union, China, the Spanish Civil War and elsewhere are well known and also well documented as classic radical cultural creations, little has been written about the processes that animate the use of traditional collective forms in radical cultural movements. I argue here that these are important to understand because often the collectivities originally represented in the traditional forms and those that the latter were deployed in were totally removed from each other. Yet, the codes that signified meaning in the former would often be used in the latter, making the job of conveying the message simpler. The modes of rendering and the communicable nature of the forms could be used to invert meanings and subvert structures, making such ritual–collective forms powerful aesthetic devices in articulating the radical collective. The characteristics of the music that engaged with traditional collective forms are important as they underscore the IPTA tradition's music in aesthetic as well as political terms, and this marks a significant contribution to the evolution of a radical–popular aesthetic.

In typical cultural forms attributed to left cultural practice, simplicity, reproduceability and repeatability are important criteria determining the suitability of forms, and thus arguments and creations such as Eisler's constituted a major sub-genre of collective music in the radical tradition. In India, a substantial, in fact dominant, part of the repertoire was formed by collective music, the different types of which have been described earlier. One such type consisted of the western-style, message-giving collective song with both simple as well as complex 'compositions' that brought forth images of rousing choruses, a multitude of voices and hard-hitting rhythms in anthem-like songs. While this Eisler-type collective song constituted a distinct sub-category within the collective music repertoire, the IPTA tradition also engaged substantially with traditional modes of collective singing. The performance venues or contexts varied from processions and marches that would culminate in a public meeting or gathering, to formal performances in auditoria and even feature films, with the former involving high levels of performer–audience interaction and the latter coming the closest to passive listening or viewing. In all the regions that the IPTA tradition came into existence, traditional forms of collective singing were employed extensively, whether it was harvest songs, boatmen's songs, laments or stylized devotional music. These songs, as quintessential 'music of the people', were attractive because of their open-endedness, familiarity and repeatability, and also because they represented traditional solidarities of various kinds and possessed features that allowed the collective to express itself through them. They were used in processions and gatherings, as well as in proscenium plays like that of the KPAC's and films like *Dharti ke Lal*. In the latter, i.e. large proscenium plays and films where the audience response was not direct, the songs were reproduced as they were, in the traditional way. A traditional collective song thus was part of a larger realist narrative, with the song serving as illustration, embellishment or elaboration of situation, providing an overall realist landscape. In such cases, often, the songs were transformed from open-ended, monotonous, repetitive entities into timed, song-format, 'performed' music. These would be in keeping with the larger context of realist narratives also being interrupted by song and dance, like in the popular entertainment genres of commercial cinema and theatre. Often, a cathartic moment in the play would require an individual singer to perform in a way that would touch emotive registers, making the job of message-giving easier. These could be considered examples of the cathartic or entertainment mode being employed extensively; this in turn being more effective if performed by individual performers.

However, the same traditional forms would be 'worked upon' for a mass political gathering. For the gathering, those elements of the forms that involved reciprocity and responses were considered more appropriate to articulate the political explicitly, i.e. invoke the cognitive mode. In such cases, often traditional solidarities could be converted into new solidarities by the reworked songs which retained the qualities of allowing for the collective joining in, of singing along with familiar tunes. Such collective music continues to be a part of the repertoire of left-wing music groups in different parts of the country. Their attraction comes from their spontaneity, their closeness to the daily lives of ordinary people, and hence the possibility of shifting between such music as spontaneous collective expression, on the one hand, and as transformed, consciously 'performed' versions that can project new ideas through the same expressions of solidarity, on the other. However, the efficacy of this also depends on the virtuosity of the performer(s), especially the 'star performer' who is the lead. This often also involves theatricality, dance and spectacle, and attention being drawn to a few talented artists, potentially creating tension.

These modes are analytically important for several reasons. In this discussion, I draw from work on the use of theatre, poetry and performance in political mobilization in South Africa, to bring out aspects of the use of ritual and traditional forms in political mobilization.[10] Used extensively in theatre in the trade union movement in South Africa, for instance, where 'in traveling from union halls to community venues, from church halls to schools, from backyards, to hostels . . . has been seen by tens of thousands of people from all walks of life, classes or "colours"', the various cultural events that were performed at mass gatherings, result in a unique communion between audience and performers that 'goes beyond the "staid" relationship between stage and gallery, musicians and listeners, producers and private consumers'.[11]

First, an important consequence of understanding the engagement with traditional forms is that it enables understanding the signalling systems inherent in their use, which imply use of aesthetic devices that come from non-western contexts. Second, traditional song-performance techniques which consist of 'finely tuned techniques of rhetoric, gesture and sound' are natural bearers of collective processes that affirm and manufacture identities and comradeship.[12] Such collective processes that are important for political mobilization create a sense of belonging, and ritually demonstrate resistance and defiance. Third, various aspects of the ideas around the artistic collective, and, more importantly, around the relationship between the individual and the collective, surface in the process. For example, even if the emphasis in political mobilization is on the 'cognitive', on a more defiant and heroic mode or a 'mode where rational as opposed to symbolic capital is being exchanged', where the political situation can be understood rationally, it can be seen, as Sitas argues, that the use of traditional genres and expressions relies also on the festive or more 'carnivalesque' or 'entertainment' mode where the collective identification happens through enjoyment of traditional depictions that are already a part of popular culture.

Further, while the cognitive mode of generating collectivities requires the expression and reiteration through performance forms that are collective, and thus work against individual characterization or a focus on individual performers, a lot of traditional performance forms involve precisely such characterization. Also, for successful reception, performance often has to be 'magical' or 'brilliant' with a degree of exhibitionism which again allows for the use of traditional forms that are exaggerated and larger than life. Or, the cognitive mode gets ignited only in the instance of the unfolding of 'cathartic' moments in performance, but which again brings focus on to an individual 'star' performer, working against the collective symbolism.

Finally, for cultural activists, the challenge is to capture the interest and imagination of the people through a combination of forms that involve the different modes, or through creating new forms or genres where the different modes can be employed, so that although the ultimate intention might be to convey messages employing the 'cognitive mode', the performances themselves borrow from each other and transform and meld into other modes. Thus, the success of the gathering depends on the combination of the cognitive mode with the cathartic and entertainment modes.

The IPTA tradition's music also brought in completely new formats for collective music. The first of these, collective music of the 'socialist' variety, exhibited three types: translations and adaptations from popular socialist songs, such as the 'Internationale', the 'Youth International', the 'Red Army Song', and so on; agitprop sing-along songs that were pamphlet-like, exhorting to action; and crafted, collective songs by artists like Hemanga Biswas that reflected moods and markers of socialist music of the time. This category has already been mentioned earlier as the Eisler kind of music. This category of music could somewhat be contrasted to the upbeat, major note-based nationalist songs; in fact, they consisted of varying tempos, a significant use of minor notes, notes with large distances between them being used consecutively to convey drama and grimness, and so on.

The second of the 'new' collective formats, we saw, was represented by Salil Chowdhury's harmonic tradition, which completely transformed the dominant style of composition and singing in India. The third of the new collective formats was the unique use of 'disembodied voice' choruses that originated in theatre and were also used in films made by directors such as Ritwik Ghatak. This unique use of voice, which was new in the Indian context, used western voice technique, often with Indian instruments, to draw attention to the 'street' or to social situations in general, using atonal phrases and enhanced emotive voice techniques that also often employed the theatrics inherent in the mood-making capacity of *ragas* rendered and interpreted in the north Indian style.

What was being reflected in and through these different idioms? First of all, there was always an underlying notion of the greater normative ability of the collective song to arouse, mobilize and exhort to action. In this sense, the solo song was often less preferred to the group song, this tendency getting accentuated in later decades. The relative marginalization of solo songs, especially those that were evocative and involved substantial skill, could also be justified through the stated objective of subjugation of the individual to the collective.

Second, the ideas around the necessity and effectiveness of the collective song over the solo one varied, depending on whether it was considered the voice *of* the collective or *for* the collective. If it was *of* the collective, the emphasis was on simplicity, familiarity and sing-along ability. If it was *for* the collective, whether or not simplicity and accessibility were important depended on whether the musical ear and level of understanding of those for whom the song was being sung were sophisticated enough. This determined, for example, the judgement about a collective 'composition' vis-à-vis a mere collective song, or the relative importance of the 'mass song' vis-à-vis a 'composition'. When Salil Chowdhury's complex harmonic compositions became extremely popular in Bengal and elsewhere, it was held as testimony to the high level of aesthetic sensibility of working-class audiences. In the same period, the aesthetic value of such compositions was understood in some quarters as being elitist, limited only to upper-class urban audiences and hence not truly representative of the collective – a position argued persuasively by Paresh Dhar and Hemanga Biswas, and often finding reflection in IPTA documents, as we have seen in an earlier chapter.

Third, a significant dimension of the debate on the collective in India, which spilled over possibly from theatre, is the idea of authorship, about who owns the progressive song. This is something that was never consciously discussed, but came up when songs or musical productions had to be identified with particular people, especially when the same tune or lyric was used more than once in different ways, when there were 'distortions' of original compositions, and so on.

In the period under study here, I argue, ideas of collective art production and underplaying of individual talent did not undermine the prominence of the composers or singers; in fact, they made authorship wonderfully ambiguous and unleashed tremendous creativity. Two examples illustrate this. '*Jaane waale sipahi se poochho*', the Second World War song written by Makhdoom Mohiuddin, disappeared from public memory after the 1940s, until it was used in a Hindi film in Bombay in the 1950s by Salil Chowdhury, but with altered lyrics and with the revolutionary content of the last stanza not being sung. Thus, it was generally remembered as a Salil Chowdhury song (although somewhat nondescript) because of the natural prominence that film music from Bombay acquired, although neither Salil Chowdhury nor Makhdoom himself emphasized authorship. It was with the publication of Makhdoom's poetry years later, and the revival of the song in its original form in 1984 by the protest song group Parcham in Delhi, that Makhdoom's name came to be indelibly marked on the song.

jaane waale sipahi se poochho
woh kahaan ja raha hai (2)

kaun dukhiya hai jo gaa rahi hai
bhookhe bachchon ko behla rahi hai
laash jalne ki boo aa rahi hai
zindagi hai ki chilla rahi hai

jaane waale sipahi se poochho
woh kahaan jaa raha hai

kaise sehme hue hai nazaare
kaise dar dar ke jalte hain taare
kya jawaani ka khoon ho raha hai
surkh hain aanchalon ke kinaare

jaane waale sipahi se poochho
woh kahaan jaa raha hai

gir rahaa hai siyaahi ka dera
ho raha hai meri jaan savera

ai watan chhod kar jaane waale
khul gaya inkalaabi pharera

jaane waale sipahi se poochho
woh kahaan jaa raha hai

Ask the departing soldier,
Where is he headed, where is he going?

Who is that woman who cries,
Soothing her hungry children?
Can you hear life cry out amidst the stench of burnt bodies?

Ask the departing soldier,
Where is he headed?

The surrounding scenes are grim,
Even the stars are afraid to twinkle.
Is youth being killed forever?
The edges of our garments are bloodstained.
Where are you headed, o soldier?

As dusk descends and dawn approaches,
Those who leave the country behind
Wait for the revolutionary dawn.

Similarly, in the days of the Bombay Central Squad, Benoy Roy wrote '*Suno Hind ke rehne waalon*' about the Bengal famine, which was sung extensively in the early 1940s by his sister Reba Roychowdhury. In 1947, during the partition, Prem Dhawan wrote a song set to the same tune and using the same refrain, although with a substantially altered mood towards the end of the song. Interestingly, neither of them claimed authorship of the song, which was created when both songwriters were living in artists' communes where the emphasis on collective production was strong. In recent years, the question of ownership came up strongly when material was being collected for this book; it was asserted that Reba Roychowdhury was falsely claiming that her brother was the author of the song, whereas what had been found in recorded form by a collector was the Prem Dhawan version.

What is evident from both these examples is that the connectedness of the music to 'the collective' was undisputed, and the consequently reduced emphasis on authorship did not affect creativity in any substantial way. In fact, often authorship was apparent through style and probably did not need to be asserted as a right.

Notes

1 This understanding of folk music meant that it was necessary to collect such music in whatever form it existed and bring it to the radical platform provided by the IPTA, where, it was understood, it would not be unfairly used for commercial gain, or colonial exoticization and manipulation. In Bengal, it may be recalled, the IPTA organized district-level festivals of relatively unknown or underperformed forms such as the *gaajan* and *gambhira*, bringing the traditional artists into the political fold but not interfering with the forms in any way. This was a convention that continued with the left cultural movement in Tripura well into the 1980s and perhaps even later, whereby musicians and dancers from remote villages or those living in obscurity in urban areas would be provided a living by the CPI and were actively involved in the cultural activities of the Party. Hemanga Biswas, Bijon Bhattacharya and Nibaran Pandit toured Assam and Bengal extensively to collect less known songs – underscoring the important role ascribed to the song collector – to be performed as they were and prior to considerations of how some of these would be interpreted later.

2 Examples of this are '*Mountbatten mangal kavya*' written by Hemanga Biswas, composed in a *kirtan* style; *gaajan* singing about the Bengal famine; a large number of songs using the *aalha* or *sapri* from Uttar Pradesh; and the *vallamkali* or boatmen's songs in Malayalam.

3 Examples of this are the *Burrakatha* in Andhra, the *Harikatha* in Kerala which would later transform into the *Kathaprasangam* (or story-speech), the *Sukh-Sharee Samvad*, *Panchali* and *Tarja* in Bengal.

4 Subramanian (2006); Weidman (2006); Bakhle (2005).

5 Ranade (2002).

6 Fritz Bose (1959); Radice (2008).

7 Bose (1959): 47.

8 Radice (2008).

9 Manuel (1988): 168.

10 Sitas (1987).

11 Sitas describes the processes and contradictions involved in the creation of 'popular class theatre', referring to its various kinds in South Africa, from the Junction Avenue Theatre Company's work to the making of workers' plays. 'The oral and committed communication involved is seen to differ in form and substance', referring to powerful renderings of oral genres such as prayers, militant and defiant songs, call-and-response chants, and poetic reveries in the mass gatherings.

12 Sitas (1987).

5

The Nation, Nationalism, Tradition and the 'Authentic'

Authenticity is an important trope around which radical left-wing cultural practice has unfolded. It was also critiqued in the Indian context, as some of the debates foregrounded in Chapter 1 demonstrate. With cultural formations such as the IPTA's tradition interrogating the idea of the 'national' and its representational modes, along with a decisive internationalism, it was engaging with various ideas of the people that represented the nation. From the use of what came to be characterized as elitist classical traditions to marginalized indigenous ones, as well as the location of the performers, the political legitimacy or illegitimacy of movements such as the IPTA was sought to be established around questions of authenticity. Here, I examine how such questions of authenticity link up with more contemporary debates on nation, nationalism and nationalities, and their cultural representation. In doing this, I attempt to bring out the relationship between the working out of the national–popular and the radical–popular in artistic production, or, more specifically, to draw out a crucial element of the radical impulse.

Nation, Identity and Politics: Constructing an Authentic Culture

Ever since Benedict Anderson's influential idea of discrete forms of nationalism involving 'imagined communities', there have been diverse lines of enquiry into the various constructions of large and small cultural identities among people in different parts of the world. Despite critiques, such as by Partha Chatterjee, Anderson's contribution opened up a new space for understanding the feelings of national comradeship and identifications by people in ex-colonial countries as well, but often, the discussion on construction and imaginings has been counterposed with the question of authenticity too: i.e. whether such constructions involve an obscuring of 'real' cultural identities or, in fact, a marginalization of specific groups of people because of the nature of identity formation. In fact, a substantial part of contemporary discussions on the relationship between nation, ethnicity and culture has been dominated by the idea that cultural constructions of the nation, of regions and of new identities, such as that of the working class, characterized both nationalist and left-wing politics in the twentieth century, and both are marked by serious marginalizations and the persistence of social hierarchies.

For example, Dilip Menon's study, an important example of scholarship that attributes inauthenticity to left cultural practice, projects the post-independence decade of the 1950s as one of political and aesthetic closure in India, with the nationalist state-building project seeing its apogee, and the cultural role of the left movement being one where 'radical regional cultural practice came to share in the discourse of modernization envisaged by the post colonial state', thus shedding its radical role and potential.[1] Parliamentary communism, linguistic statehood and the coming into existence of a Communist Party ministry in the state of Kerala, for example, transformed communist cultural expression towards conservative practice geared in favour of the state. This, according to Menon, resulted in a closure of the caste question and of lower-caste radicalism that had been initiated through militant peasant movements under the left, in turn getting reflected in theatre and music that served the interests of statehood on the one hand, and entrenched caste inequalities on the other. Thus, plays from the 1940s were 'localized people's art merging folk traditions with the exigencies of a contemporary politics',[2] where there was less concern with aesthetic form than with the political present and its transformation, where theatre was understood 'as political practice, rather than creation or tinkering with a canon'.[3] Such an analysis, it is obvious, considers participation in electoral politics and struggles based on linguistic identity as attempts to forcibly homogenize and obfuscate hierarchies in class and caste positions, on the one hand, and to institutionalize and in the process suppress resistances to hierarchies, on the other, with cultural interventions playing a critical role in furthering these processes. It is also argued that concern with aesthetic form is antithetical to theatre as 'political practice', implying a necessary opposition between aesthetic concerns and the imperatives of political transformation. Further, though not explicitly stated as such, Menon's analysis implies a necessary divergence between cultural forms that represent the nation, modernization and statehood at one end of the spectrum, and those that project fundamental caste and agrarian conflicts and popular struggles at the other end.

The left movement's cultural interventions are thus criticized as uncritically modernist and supportive of a statist project that consciously attempts to obliterate and obfuscate multiple identities. Rustom Bharucha's critique of the post-independent state's cultural preservation project is an example of the latter, which addresses the questions raised by the well-known 'Drama Seminar' organized by the newly established performing arts academy (Sangeet Natak Akademi) in 1956.[4] As seen in an earlier chapter, one of the ways of conceptualizing different elements of 'national culture' that included the indigenous, which arose to a large extent from questions that the IPTA raised, took the shape of setting up national institutions for promoting culture as part of the Nehruvian government's vision. Bharucha refers to an animated discussion that took place in the 1956 seminar around the Gujarati form *bhavai*, initiated by Dina Gandhi who had been a prominent activist of the IPTA's Central Squad. Her argument for preserving, researching and showcasing *bhavai* was based on the fear that it was getting destroyed because of the deteriorating economic conditions of the performing artists. Her suggestion for studying the form through research and documentation, and trying to ensure its survival and in its true essence, without contamination, is dismissed by Bharucha as revealing some of the deeply entrenched premises and problems underlying the urban construction and use of 'folk theatre' in India. He writes, 'Part of the problem with her suggestions, as with most urban recommendations for the "folk arts" is that she assumed an empathy with the folk artists, and then proceeded to represent them as if she were speaking on their behalf.'[5] By this logic, Gandhi's assumption that there is a serious cultural and social distance between the 'urban' and the 'folk' artist, and that this can be bridged, can 'scarcely be seen as altruistic'; it involves an instrumentalism, just as Bharucha implies was the case with Dina Gandhi – to further her own theatre practice. An urban, middle-class artist can at best help 'indigenize' urban theatre to win the approval of urban audiences and cannot claim to be authentic in terms of the indigenous, according to this analysis.

Specific ideas of what constitutes the 'people' and their identities as part of left cultural practice have also been critiqued as inauthentic. In an analysis of patronage from the left for subaltern performance forms such as the *lavni* and *tamasha* in Maharashtra, Veena Naregal argues that the Communist Party leadership sought to balance the innovative possibilities, popular appeal and democratizing potential of these forms within the Party's political framework, and in the process ignored and in fact marginalized the self-conscious positioning of an artist like Annabhau Sathe as Dalit. She writes:

> Consider, for instance, the interesting contrast that emerges even through briefly juxtaposing Dange's Introduction to the anthology of Annabhau Sathe's work issued in 1952 with an address that Annabhau made to a Dalit Sahitya Sammelan held in Mumbai in 1958. Both these texts share an implicit understanding about the economic basis of dominance, exploitation and marginality. It is significant, however, that the term 'Dalit' figures only once in Dange's essay, and that too to reiterate what he terms the 'internationalist' dimension of contemporary Dalit consciousness, by which Dange means the ability of the working class to seek out international allies, ostensibly the distinguishing hallmark of the Communist poet. Dange draws on his considerable knowledge of Marathi literary history to argue that true art and dissent have always gone hand in hand, and to specifically commend Annabhau's 'Mumbaichi lavani' as a powerful example of how class politics can inform poetry, and praise Annabhau's povada, 'Maharashtrachi parampara' for its celebration of the cultural and political ethos of the Maharashtrian people. And yet, oddly, each laudatory remark is immediately checked with qualifying comments about the need for further improvement: Annabhau is even peremptorily taken to task for not delving beyond conventional interpretations of Marathi history. Dange concludes with the unabashed hope that the Introduction will guide Annabhau and his colleagues in their future work. Seemingly, as reiterated by other testimonies, even within the leftist trade union movement, low caste subaltern activists like Annabhau could not hope to be seen as providing anything more than mere cultural labour that would need to fit pre-given moulds determined by a theoretical elite. No wonder, then, that Annabhau should have felt marginalized within IPTA circles![6]

The different arguments around authenticity, threads of which have been drawn from diverse scholars, including those whose work is mentioned above but which connect with each other intrinsically, can be summarized as follows.

1. In countries like India, the construction of a national identity hinged on a process of 'classicization' through the middle class and the state under a nationalist project, an attempt at creating a 'national, immutable, distinct' identity. This identity, while it is distinct, not 'modular'[7] or formulaic, as Partha Chatterjee emphasizes,[8] also defines itself as 'modern' and, in fact, as 'advanced' as hegemonic nationalisms elsewhere. Contrary to Benedict Anderson's initial argument that there was modularity in the ways in which cultural nationalisms emerged, Chatterjee emphasizes the distinctiveness of this classicization and looks at it in terms of 'points of departure'. He distinguishes between the three stages of nationalist thought, and discusses

the first stage, the moment of departure, as involving the recognition of an 'essential cultural difference between East and West' with the east being 'superior in the spiritual aspects of culture' in comparison to the west's material culture and its commitment to progress. The second stage, the moment of manoeuvre, 'consists in the historical consolidation of the "national" by decrying the "modern"'. And the final stage, the moment of arrival, occurs when the discourse is 'conducted in a single, consistent, unambiguous voice', at which point it 'succeeds in glossing over all earlier contradictions, divergences and differences'.[9]

2. The distinctiveness of this classical or classicized identity uses elements from a constructed past that, in the Indian case, is exclusionary (glorifying a Hindu past, decrying Muslim rule and hence excluding Muslims, for example), culturally distinct (spiritual, in the Indian case) and hence not standardized. In this way, despite the localized and specific characteristics of the cultural nationalism, it shares the impulse to construct symbols of glory with hegemonic nationalisms and is hence artificially constructed. This construction of the national thus involves homogenization and obscuring of difference and of the existence of sub-nationalisms or 'other' identities.[10]
3. This critique of the 'nationalist' project is extended to the vision of the left as an attempt to create grand identities that end up obliterating differences between identities and hence are inauthentic.[11] This is argued in the following way: like with the nationalist project that created overarching and often artificial identities around the territorial idea of the nation, the concept of class, brought in by the left, is an artificially constructed and overarching identity that is forced and inauthentic.
4. The critique detailing the inauthenticity of left cultural practice and experience, based on an ideology of sub-national, sub-regional or ethnic identity, extends in three directions. (a) It results in a questioning of identity formation based on left ideology and politics – for example, of whether class-based identities on the one hand, and internationalist and nationalist politics on the other, are overarching and artificially constructed, in Chatterjee's sense. The argument in fact goes further – that class-based politics, by underplaying identities of origin such as caste, reassert dominant non-class hierarchies and inequalities. (b) In terms of cultural interventions, it introduces the idea of the inauthentic artist, the 'middle-class' or 'upper-caste' artist–activist who reproduces the ideology of his origins, and the authentic marginalized or lower-caste artist–activist who is uncomfortable with the

non-acknowledgement of subaltern or caste identities. (c) It questions the authenticity of the aesthetic creations of the left and conflates this critique with the critique of homogenizing nationalisms. Clearly, the notions of authenticity encompass identity (what kind), the people (who) and the cultural output itself.

Nationalism, Classicization and the Radical Imaginary

I first take up the question of classicization and its reflection in the music of nationalism, both mainstream as well as the alternative nationalism that movements like the IPTA were projecting. I argue as follows. (a) The cultural constructions of mainstream nationalism involved, to different degrees in different countries, processes of classicization as well as folklorization, as part of a 'nationalism from above' or a marking out of national identity that was territorially defined. (b) Both these processes engaged in different ways with local indigenous traditions, and were determined in some cases by the desire to create exclusive and overarching national identities (like in Turkey), or in other cases by an inclusionary impulse (like in Latin America), in a context of populist politics.[12] (c) There was also, in the same period, a tremendous nationalist impulse 'from below' that was fuelled by a radical emancipatory politics and where hitherto unexplored solidarities were being expressed in terms of different kinds of identities. This expression engaged in a variety of ways with the 'indigenous', was influenced by existing nationalist discourses and at the same time sought to challenge them. (d) In the process of such horizontal imaginings, indigenous traditions were recovered, reproduced and transformed in terms of form, space and kinds of audience. (e) In the post-colonial period, some of these inclusive processes and experiments were appropriated and also standardized, emerging as blueprints for the representation of diverse identities in the context of the nation and also as forms representing popular culture, mediated through state patronage and the market.

With respect to the 'classicization' processes in India, Thailand and Java, Moro argues:

> In the case of the Asian musics we call 'classical', such music 'goes with' the nation in a convenient homology so that, for example, classical Thai music is 'the' music generally associated with Thailand, while the court gamelan traditions of Bali and central Java often represent 'the' music of Indonesia. Such homologies are not limited to the views of outsiders – be they scholars, adventurous listeners or other consumers of music – but derive in part from the elevation and wide dissemination

> of particular elite musics within nations over the last century or more. Elite musics became classical, their distribution congruent with the boundaries of nation-states (at least in theory) and their status as high culture deceptively natural. . . . A number of prominent music scholars and teachers of the late nineteenth century set out to revitalize what they felt had become a neglected and tarnished musical tradition.[13]

This revitalization took place through efforts to classicize, in Chatterjee's sense of the term – for example, by inventing notation systems, founding schools, generating the principles for organized music scholarship and historiography (based on the study of Sanskrit treatises and intended to establish norms for performance), organizing music conferences and instituting the public concert.

However, nationalism from the early twentieth century was being explored in musical terms not only with respect to classical music, but also in terms of various ideas of the 'indigenous', in an attempt to understand the relationship between newly emergent nation-states, the cultures of the people that inhabited them, and the modes of their representation and expression. Mainstream nationalism or nationalism from 'above', thus, was dealing in different ways with traditions, whether classical or indigenous, and this was to impact significantly on the alternative nationalisms that were expressed in music by radical activists. The cases of Latin America and Turkey are interesting to compare for a delineation of the imperatives involved as well as to provide the background against which the radical imaginary engaged with nationalism in a country like India. These are both examples where creating a 'national' music was an important part of the political project of mainstream nationalism and they demonstrate the nature of the questions that were raised.

The imperatives of classicization were different in Turkey from, say, India, because western classical music emerged as an important element in the construction of national music. After the establishment of the Turkish Republic in 1923 under Kemal Atatürk, the creation of a 'national music' that represented the 'essence' of the Republic was considered essential for the cultural unification of diverse peoples of different nationalities under a single Turkish identity. The idea of national music, which was theorized and constructed consciously out of specific elements that were taken to constitute the Turkish heritage, involved a process of assessment, negation, unearthing and reprocessing of particular elements of the heritage that the Republic inherited, and an attempt to define national music with elements from 'healthy, genuine music that can be heard among the Anatolian people'.[14] The specific history of the establishment of the Turkish Republic under Atatürk needs to be kept in mind here, involving the rejection of 'Ottoman' symbols and the creation of 'Turkish' music. The authenticity of each type of music that was seen to be prevailing in different parts of the country needed to be established, and the identity also needed to celebrate the spirit of progress and reject ideas of 'backwardness' in music. Progress, it was argued, was associated with western music, which over centuries replaced what were stated to be dull and boring quartertones in 'Eastern' music (derived from Greek music) with harmony. Ottoman music, on the other hand, was primarily eastern, based on quartertones and assessed to be 'primitive'.

According to Gokalp, an influential theoretician of the new nation, the new music of the Turkish nation needed to emerge from the synthesis of folk music and western music, the former being termed the music of the new culture and the latter the music of the new civilization. Further, since it was stated that Turkish people did not have time to wait for their music to reach the level of western music, it needed to be done by the new state. In order to create a national music, and to get rid of Ottoman institutions and replace them with their Republican equivalents, the Turkish Republic transformed or closed down various musical institutions. Monophonic music education (Ottoman music) was banned in public and private schools, and centres of *tekke* (Sufi) music were abolished. Gokalp stressed the importance of collecting folk songs to create a national music culture, and he carried out ethnographic research among Arabs and the Kurdish and Turkish tribes. Béla Bartók, the Hungarian composer, was invited to Turkey to carry out a field trip to collect folk songs.

In the colonial countries of Latin America, nationalism in music from the early to the middle decades of the twentieth century was different from the Turkish example in that it involved more inclusive, culturally-based conceptions of the nation, often within the politics of populist movements, especially when efforts to link formerly disenfranchised populations to the state got under way.[15] This involved, in a variation of the state-sponsored 'nationalism from above', a process of 'folkorization', or a showcasing, exhibiting and reform of indigenous customary and ritual art forms. 'Folklore' festivals and contests in Latin America involving a recognition and celebration of the *indigenista* are examples of this sort of engagement with the indigenous. Turino and Miller (2003) argue that by providing incentives such as monetary rewards and prizes, these contests attracted people who did not normally perform on stage, or in formal presentations, or as codified ensembles.[16] The contests thus worked as mechanisms for bringing marginal participatory traditions into formal performance contexts, 'often initiating the profound conceptual shift of music-dance as play or ceremonial interaction' to 'music-dance as art product'. They also shaped indigenous and regional styles to conform to dominant performance formats; thus 'contests are a key mechanism in the process of cultural reformism –

the transformation of localist traditions according to dominant, typically "modern", cosmopolitan aesthetics and contexts'.[17]

In India, too, the classicization process took place – and has been documented in detail – involving both north Indian (Hindustani) and south Indian (Carnatic) classical music. This process unfolded as a response to colonialism and the idea of the 'modern', but also to the development of technology, large-scale migrations, and urbanization and commercialization processes of the early twentieth century.[18] This was seen in the cultural representations of the mainstream of the national movement for independence with various classical musicians emerging as symbols of Indian nationhood, as well as the idea of the two classical traditions as immutable and 'pure'.

However, there were various sub-regional and regional 'imaginings' from below that were spontaneously harnessed, as this book attempts to demonstrate. By the time the IPTA was formed, these localized mobilizations had established connections across regions, and were also expressing solidarities at the level of 'India' and, in fact, beyond national boundaries as well. As Priyamvada Gopal has convincingly argued in her work on four writers of the PWA, those engaged in the progressive cultural movement from the 1930s onwards had a 'shared, however differently articulated commitment' to emancipatory politics and socialism, a commitment that was located firmly in the terrain of the nation even as it critiqued and 'restlessly inhabited' it.[19] This restlessness that resulted in a wide variety of imaginings from below engaged in different ways with the idea of the 'folk' or the 'indigenous', as we have seen, and thus the nationalism that was explored, while engaging with the classical, was not just of the 'classicization' kind. In fact, with classical musicians of note (Ravi Shankar and Ali Akbar Khan, for example) being part of this alternative nationalism, and also being part of the post-independence dispensation, even the cultural symbols that were adopted by the Indian state were influenced by these processes. Thus, in India, a nationalism where diversity in musical cultures was beginning to be celebrated in many ways was pioneered by the IPTA. So, even as mainstream nationalist idioms in the pre-independence period and 'state-sponsored' symbols of nationalism were being developed, this was not happening independently of the alternative nationalist imaginings of the radical fraction. Nationalists like Jawaharlal Nehru, Sarojini Naidu and others were influenced by the IPTA's activities and its vision, even as the IPTA functioned in tension with them.

Various dimensions of the national–cultural, whether classical or folk/indigenous, were also significantly to shape the popular culture that emerged in the 1940s and took shape substantially in the 1950s. One of the realms in which this was seen was in the cinema, where it might be argued that the Gramscian notion of the 'national–popular' that was being shaped was intensely influenced by the 'radical–popular', where 'people', defined in different ways, were at the centre and constituted the subject of cultural expression. This radical–popular, with its various dimensions, thus influenced and, at the same time, was in tension with the mainstream. Situated in a position of imagining the post-colonial from the immediate pre-independence years, in shaping it critically and then defining its distance from the mainstream post-colonial, the radical–popular tradition was thus constantly engaging with different ideas of the 'people'.

The Authentic Artist

The supposed marginalization of issues of caste identity in the left movement forms a significant part of contemporary critiques, as summarized earlier. In contrasting Dange's position with Annabhau Sathe's, Naregal states:

> Annabhau's forceful foregrounding of caste as class in his opening remarks to the Dalit Sahitya Sammelan provides an interesting counterpoint. It is true that none of what he says deviates explicitly from the underlying assumptions of the party position, and could even lend itself as a useful corollary to the official line. However, Annabhau's speech does point in directions that Communists were clearly not prepared to go, at least in the 1950s. He points out that a separate Dalit literary meeting was necessitated precisely on account of the widespread tendency to disavow caste as a category of marginality and the implicit refusal to recognize Dalits as a large and distinct class whose cumulative experience and labour in fact constitute the social and cultural foundations of the nation, but even now remain marginalized and invisible within mainstream regional literatures. As a Dalit intellectual, Annabhau was to later clearly acknowledge his debt to Ambedkar, even as his work seems to strike a perceptibly distinct note from the emphasis on Dalit 'victimhood' that formed part of the dominant rhetorical strategies of later Marathi Dalit writers. A brief mention of Annabhau's best-known novel *Fakira* will show this. First published in 1960, and currently in its 19th edition, it is an account of *mang* valour set in the early 20th century, depicting the principled resistance offered by its young hero, Fakira, who dies fighting against unjust colonial laws seeking to criminalize his community. The novel, valorizing pride in being a *mang*, is dedicated to Ambedkar with the lines: *jag badali ghaluni ghav / sangun gele mala Bhimrao* (Rupture and change the world / Was Bhimrao's message to me). From all this, it seems that Annabhau found it difficult to accommodate his great need to

> write about caste within the possibilities opened up by his progressive experiments with the *tamasha/lavani* forms during his long association with Bombay left circles.[20]

Naregal's characterization of Annabhau's Dalit self-positioning as authentic because of his Dalit origins, resulting in the legitimacy of his art, is clearly pitted against the conceptualizations of the 'progressive experiments in Bombay left circles', where 'cultural labour would need to fit pre-given moulds determined by a theoretical elite', represented by leaders like Dange who are seen as belonging to the upper castes and hence incapable of understanding the Dalit aesthetic intrinsic to Annabhau's work.

For Annabhau Sathe or, in fact, Amar Sheikh, the other working-class Dalit poet and performer from Maharashtra, a sense of belonging based on being Dalit and expressions of cultural autonomy through Dalit symbols might not have contradicted their engagement with creating working-class solidarities in the trade union movement in Bombay in the 1940s and 1950s. In fact, oral accounts from their co-performers within the left movement as well as work by chroniclers of the Dalit movement suggest that both of them were engaging continuously with multiple solidarities that were being forged, where identification with being Dalit and being at the bottom of the exploitation pyramid was not considered contradictory to other kinds of solidarities within the left. In fact, to derive dignity, pride and coherence out of a Dalit identity does not suggest that this was a belief in an immutable subaltern identity that would necessarily get overshadowed by other identifications. As activists who were attracted to and extremely active in the left movement, which asserted class solidarity and the forging of such solidarity across caste, religious or ethnic divides, they were also involved in the active appropriation and interpretation of their ethnic traditions as self-conscioulsy ethnic subjects. Especially in the context of India where the left movement was influenced strongly by social reform movements that addressed caste exploitation, a denouncement of one's own caste identity if from the upper castes and an identification with one's caste origins if Dalit, and the politicization as well as cultural expression as an 'exploited' and hence resistant subject, should not come as a surprise. So, while it is important to resist interpretations of 'being Dalit' as standing in contradiction to the working-class identity by believing somehow that such cultural identifications are non-revolutionary and inscribed from above, it is necessary to point out that such identities are negotiated through the symbols of everyday life, and of imaginings and political ideologies that seek to mobilize them, in ways that go beyond the everyday and the immediate local context. Thus, the tremendous popularity of an

Annabhau Sathe and an Amar Sheikh lay in their ability to actively mobilize and utilize various non-class cultural elements to focus on Dalit-ness, and at the same time project the common experiences of an oppressed and poor working-class majority. To reduce their engagement with the cultural movement of the left and to debunk the movement as merely needing Annabhau's 'cultural labour', as Naregal does, is to view such powerful activists as only 'victims' of overarching ideologies that are inscribed from above. An examination of their corpus in aesthetic terms, in fact, reveals anything but such victimhood.

A similar critique of the left's theatre movement of the 1950s in Kerala by Dilip Menon, mentioned earlier, accuses the cultural movement represented by the KPAC of not being capable of representing the art of the people because of the upper-class and caste backgrounds of the activists.[21] Authenticity of representation of the indigenous, the true culture of the people, according to Menon, comes into play only with personal experience, and only if such initiatives happen within the indigenous communities or when it is people from these communities who assume the leadership of political cultural movements. In an analysis of one of the most prominent and popular plays of the KPAC, *Ningalenne Communistaakki* (You Made Me a Communist), he argues that the upper-caste ideology that gets reflected in the script is attributable to the caste identity of the playwright. His political critique goes further, arguing that this tendency that represented the left movement's nature and activities in Travancore, where the KPAC came into existence, overshadowed the 'truly radical' culture that came out of the peasant movements in Malabar. The CPI's projection of the success of the KPAC's cultural intervention involved a relative obscuring of the engagement with the indigenous and the authentic that characterized the Malabar movement. What is critical to note is that Menon's aesthetic critique and analysis of content in the theatre of the KPAC rely heavily on the personal background of the activists involved, which is then extended into a critique of the movement and its politics, attributing a lack of genuineness to it. His argument is that despite the left's engagement with exploitation and the marginalized, as in the case of the Malabar peasants' movement, it failed to engage with the marginalized as 'subject', from the marginalized person's own subject position which, in this case, is from the lower castes.

About the music of the left cultural movement, Menon states that the songs were 'exhortatory political songs speaking of a redemptive future, with the majority of them being based on folk tunes and rhythms, a veritable invention of a tradition of *naadan paattu* (used to refer to folk songs), a romantic recovery, representing a nostalgia for a rural idyll of a happy peasant'. The problem here, according to Menon,

> is of carrying the peasant into modernity while retaining the structures of deference as well as a culture centred around lost routines of work in the fields . . . a sentimental rendering of labour as a site for production of folk culture rather than as demeaning or back breaking . . . politics is rendered as affect, social stasis, decay and inequality are captured and represented in the impossibility of love in a space yet to become modern.[22]

How can this argument be read in terms of the music that emerged out of Kerala, both the spontaneous music of the 1940s and the 'crafted' folk music of the 1950s? Obviously, the former would be considered more authentic than the latter because it came out of peasant movements, whereas the latter was crafted and aestheticized by middle-class and upper-caste activists. What would be under the scanner in Menon's scheme are songs written for the theatre that involved the creation of a new grammar of form as well as lyrics that attempted to create a new language of the people. This would be considered an inauthentic intervention imposed by upper-caste activists, for whom aestheticization in the creative process stems from their 'refined' caste backgrounds, far away from the ruggedness and non-refinement that characterizes the 'true people'. This kind of position stands very close to that put forward by the Dravida Munnetra Kazhagam (DMK) in Tamil Nadu, the organization representing the non-Aryan, Dravidian identity, and the Dalit cultural movement typified by artists like Sambhaji Bhagat in Maharashtra much later,[23] which actively denounced classical music for being non-popular, too refined and non-representative. As I have pointed out earlier, this argument was an intrinsic part of a debate within the IPTA tradition and could be seen in different kinds of songs as demonstrative of that debate, a fact never acknowledged or even investigated seriously by the critiques around authenticity being taken up here. Further, while an aesthetic argument based on the kinds of music that are produced by 'the true people' is a part of these critiques, a major purpose is to attribute inauthenticity to those from middle-class and upper-caste backgrounds as representers of various indigenous musics from their contexts, fundamentally because of their lives and backgrounds. In other words, it is the authenticity of the artists that is considered crucial.

Thus, questions about whether the people associated with specific interventions were eligible to do so or not, primarily due to their origins in terms of caste, class or location, have been significant in debating issues of authenticity. The legitimacy of the people, in turn, has spilled over into questioning and establishing genuineness in these people's intentions to represent the indigenous, where the distance between them and such sources of the indigenous is considered to be obvious and apparent. Further, it has also spilled over into questioning the legitimacy of the politics they represented, with such political movements being accused of *de facto* encouraging practices that discriminate against genuine practitioners of the indigenous, and thus at best serving a reformist and paternalistic agenda.

In assessing strident critiques such as these, which assert the inauthenticity of representation as well as of the politics that such representation attempts to convey, the following points are necessary to note. First, that it brings out the construction of the radical aesthetic straddling issues of class, nation and ethnicity, and the factors that influence their multiple cultural imaginings. Second, that the cultural energies unleashed in radical moments like the 1940s and 1950s, which this book is about, resulted in multiple interpretations and explorations, often contradictory to each other, and need to be understood as such, not just in terms of deterministic conclusions. The critiques outlined above, both from within the IPTA that hinged on class as well as the subaltern identity-based ones, tend to be deterministic, in the process denouncing or caricaturing the political legitimacy of particular people or politics. By failing to notice the multiple interpretations or the debates that took place, the critiques ignore very crucial dimensions of the art–politics relationship.

Third, one of the points that emerges from available evidence is that across diverse regions, the cultural productions of the IPTA in the 1940s and 1950s were hugely popular, and played a mobilizational and political role that has not been paralleled in other periods. For example, the play *Ningalenne Communistaakki* had over 5,000 shows in just a couple of years in the mid-1950s. The crafting of the new popular imaginary that attempted to project, through music, the ideas of an emancipatory future, involved great variations in the kinds of songs that were written and sung. Both aesthetics and politics get reduced to a limited functionalism if it is argued, as Menon does, for example, that the songs were sentimental renderings of labour in the march towards a redemptive future. Further, it is ahistorical to state that the artists, operating in completely non-commercial contexts, often facing great repression and having to deal with wide variations in experience and talent, received the responses they did by merely reproducing existing hierarchies in productions, particularly in seeking to convey an alternative emancipatory politics.

Fourth, given the objective conditions under which the plays and music were performed, a sense that the aesthetic representations were likely to have been far from perfect and that this would have to be pointed out from within the movement itself was not absent. The examples, within music, of debates between artists regarding appropriate forms of representation of the people are numerous, as we have seen at different points in this book. E.M.S. Namboodiripad and S.A. Dange wrote extensively about such issues, where the characterization of those being represented in productions came up for criticism from within the communist movement itself, because it was understood that it was but one part of an experiment that was attempting to create a new aesthetic, even as it was firmly located within a specific cultural context.

Finally, to attribute primariness to identities based on birth or ethnic origins to an extent that suggests an artificiality of new imaginings and solidarities grounded in region, nation or the international, and which makes activists and leaders from the upper castes incapable of or unwilling to understand subaltern identities, or even active agents in promoting the reproduction of caste inequalities, trivializes the politics of emancipation that is being discussed here.

A final dimension of the authenticity question that I now turn to is, what constitutes the authentic and legitimate aesthetic transformation of indigenous forms.

Transformations in/of the Indigenous: The Question of Legitimacy

Different kinds of transformation that were undergone by indigenous forms in the process of their discovery or the invention of new versions are discussed below. The engagement of the IPTA tradition with indigenous music, we have seen, occurred through new discoveries as well as through adaptation to context, interpretation and crafting. The processes of discovery involved unearthing obscure and dying traditions as well as showcasing lesser-known traditions, as happened in Bengal through music festivals, in Andhra through the systematic collection of such traditions by activists, and in Maharashtra through the revival of the *lavnis* and *tamashas*. The interpretation and crafting of newer folk traditions based on indigenous forms took place in Bengal and Kerala, where this rearticulation was a perceived need keeping in view specific audiences and definite political aims. In both cases, whether indigenous or folk traditions were 'discovered' or 'invented', they underwent changes and transformation of form, location, mode of communication and of the artists themselves, which are analysed here.

One of the considerations that determine whether such transformations are authentic and hence legitimate stems from a distinction between endogenous or organic transformations, and exogenous or externally imposed ones. Bharucha compares the transformations involving a *theyyam* performer from Kerala, who on his own introduced a flashing electric bulb into his headgear to enhance his sense of the demoniac, and the transportation of a traditional performance from its own environment to a proscenium-bound, air-conditioned theatre in New Delhi or a *mela* in Paris. In the first case, he argues that 'one cannot but appreciate the sheer ingenuity of the performer in incorporating a historical change (electricity) within the framework of his costume. Here one senses an organic relationship between the environment and the performer.'[24] With regard to the second, Bharucha's position is that:

> In the case of the altered environments provided by proscenium theatres and spectacles, it is difficult to accept their impositions on the choices of the performers. Inadequate exposure to these spaces, and more specifically, to the power relationships embodied in them, create an imbalance between what the performers are ready to give and what is expected of them from a foreign clientele. In such spaces, the performers invariably fail to represent themselves. Rather, they are represented by the environments themselves, and by all the values – political, social, commercial – embodied in them. This environmental change alters the very context of the performance. In some extravaganzas, the performers are merely 'slotted' into a spectacle over which they have no control. Reduced to exotica, they resemble spots of colour without mind, body, or soul.[25]

In other words, according to assessments such as this, if change comes from within performative contexts with some notion of an 'original' context, it can be considered authentic, whereas 'external' influences that cause the performances and performers to undergo transformation of location and in the mode of audience–performer interaction can be considered inauthentic and hence forced. In the second case, it would be a matter of 'using' tradition and imposing changes on it through external interventions, whereas an authentic change would make it a question of 'living tradition' and of making the necessary adjustments to keep it going – which are intrinsic to the growth of a traditional performance.

While such a distinction can be useful in unpacking the analytical dimensions of performance traditions, the relationship between the performer and the audience, and innovations in performance genres in response to societal changes, what are the implications of using such a distinction to normatively judge movements and their legitimacy? Where does the above argument fit in with the historical experiences and debates on the authenticity of form? Are cultural political interventions and the accompanying transformations that occur exogenous or endogenous?

Two examples, from Latin America and South Africa, are discussed here to illustrate the different contexts in which such questions can be addressed. In the case of the transformations or 'reform' of indigenous musical traditions, Turino relates examples of 'flattening' transformations that occur with indigenous forms:

> In a contest performance I witnessed in Puno (Peru) during the 1980s, I saw a formalized indigenous ensemble imitate, in great detail, a *mestizo-indigenista* stylization of these peasants' own participatory courting dance, the *kh'ajelo*. What was striking here was that the *indigenistas'* stylization included a parody of silly, drunken, emasculated indigenous men being led off by their domineering women at the end of the dance; the indigenous contest performers reproduced these unflattering stereotypes of themselves. It remains to be said that the *kh'ajelo* continued to be danced in its normal participatory way by young people in usual semi-private courting contexts at the same time that an increasingly standardized presentational version was being diffused throughout the country in 'folkloric' stage shows and contests. Nonetheless, the young peasants knew what was expected of them, at least in presentational 'folkloric' events – indicating the penetration of the *mestizo-indigenista* version.[26]

To argue that this phenomenon is particularly troubling when performed by indigenous people themselves is to miss the fact that this kind of parody does not necessarily happen always. For example, with the *samba* in Brazil or *Jarocho* music in Mexico the parody effect might be less obvious, but the transformation that happens is one of signification, of local or regional forms getting identified with national identity, but where the original 'folk'/regional resonance remains important for the purposes of grounding and 'authenticity'.[27] These are examples of nationalism from above that this chapter has discussed earlier, the inclusive variety of nationalism that resulted in various indigenous forms being brought out into the public sphere, sometimes 'showcased', sometimes standardized, often caricatured and sometimes diverse. In fact, with the *samba* in Brazil, it has been argued that its representation of resistance, an expression of the emergent identity of poor, urbanized blacks following the abolition of slavery, was in fact not dampened down in the populist period (1920s) in Brazil.[28] Later, the resistance aspect of forms like the *samba* was expressed in the radical protest song movement that consciously drew upon the traditions and experiences of sections of the population severely affected by the country's industrial revolution and, later on, by the dictatorship.

> Urban and rural musical traditions such as *samba*, the rural folk ballad, *berimbau* (the accompaniment to a form of choreographic martial combat) and the *samba de roda* (circle-dance), were to restore a national-popular authenticity to the song of political protest, against the imported, 'Americanized' culture which *bossa nova*, and increasingly rock, were held to represent.[29]

In a fascinating account of the development of oral performances in mass gatherings in Natal, South Africa during the anti-apartheid struggle, Sitas describes the transformation that occurred in such performances, and the differing degrees and modes of performer–audience interaction. He describes these gatherings 'as not some pristine traditional form of mass communication; rather they are organized and patterned events proscribed by goals and agendas', and as consisting of the recital by people from traditional backgrounds of 'oral genres such as praise poetry, propaganda poems in English punctuated with chants, *toyi-toyi* sequences with quasi-poetic call and response vocalizing and struggle songs'. He traces the ways in which, through these performances, traditional rituals of affirmation of identity, comradeship and defiance took place in the gatherings, in contexts that were removed from their original ones.[30] Also, the introduction of plays about working-class struggles, involving workers from indigenous backgrounds, into the gatherings resulted in a further transformation which reflected political goals and agendas more explicitly. Interestingly, the ritual aspect of the performance genres and the cognitive aspect of the plays started borrowing from each other, and new styles evolved which, when they succeeded, resulted in 'an entertaining combination of genres . . . creating a vibrant rapport with spectators and eliciting popular participation'.

This example, like that of call-and-response music from Bengal, *burrakatha* performances from Andhra, the Malabar performance genres and numerous others from the IPTA's repertoire, brings out the contradictions inherent to the exogenous–endogenous and organic–external binaries that analyses such as Bharucha's bring up. In all these instances, it is cultural political intervention that is the basic principle of organization of the performance, and hence would be considered an 'external' agent. The people involved in the performance would in most cases be from indigenous backgrounds with traditional forms of training and conversant with traditional performance contexts. As initiators in the performances of changes in form or in lyrics, they would qualify as organic performers and hence the transformations would be justified. However, given that the performance contexts themselves were very often altered from village to street to stage, would not the political and social values embodied in these different contexts render such performers mere tools in the hands of external agents, in this case the political movements? In cases where such endogenous performances also involved spectacle and pure entertainment, in contrast to original contexts, would that not reduce organic performance to mechanical reproduction without body and soul? Finally, when there is a transformation from the participatory performance mode to a more formal, proscenium or stage mode, or even a mode that decidedly relies on the cognitive abilities of audiences, does the change from an active to a passive audience reduce the legitimacy of the message that is being conveyed? Does it necessarily have to imply less popularity and lower audience response?

A few years ago, Reba Roychowdhury recounted how IPTA artists would sing tunes from their respective regions to each other, and often spontaneous 'mixings' or 'borrowings' would occur as something new would be created, often obscuring the original nuances. While some of this would be done consciously, out of a desire to display and expose local traditions from different corners of the country to those outside them, often it was done for the sheer pleasure derived from exploring similaritie or even marking out differences in tonalities and rhythms. That these aesthetic explorations were underpinned by the emerging 'horizontal comradeships' that came out of a particular politics, and perhaps led to particular transformations that were mediated by that politics, is obvious.

Further, the people involved in these explorations came from diverse backgrounds, as earlier chapters in this book have described, and irrespective of class or caste backgrounds, they were active participants in the 'mixing and borrowing' exercises, even as some chose to work extensively with musical traditions of their 'origins'. Thus, Amar Sheikh performed and wrote *lavnis* and *powadas* even as he negotiated the complexities of classical music-based, nationalist styles of singing in his songs '*Janani janmabhoomi*' and '*Balidaan*', or the newly constructed, rousing 'socialist' songs that have been analysed earlier. Even as he became famous for his indigenous songs, the stories of his performances of the 'socialist' song '*Nayaa taraana gaaein, jag mein dhoom machaein*' (Let us sing a new tune, let us fill the world with cheer and celebration) in Hindi are testimony to his tremendous popularity with audiences outside the context of his origins, owing to his working with and comfort in styles outside his indigenous ones.[31]

Here, three points need to be noted if we want to make sense of the relevance of these kinds of authenticity questions. First, it needs to be emphasized that it is trivial to go into questions of exogenous or endogenous changes in indigenous performance genres to bring out the difference between organic and mechanical transformations that occur over time. It is a fact that continuous change has characterized all creative forms, mediated by specific histories, technology and the needs of audiences. These mediations, which involve change of location, timing and length of performances, and responses to specific audiences, make it difficult to imagine a 'pristine folk' that is devoid of such influences. Thus, traditions are constantly changing within their own performative and cultural contexts, often in deference to the needs and demands of the communities themselves. Losing sight of this and searching for the pristine folk or the truly authentic runs the risk of putting forth an antiquarian and sometimes even right-wing standpoint which, at the least, tends to be ahistorical and frozen in time.

Second, given that all of what might appear to be 'authentic' may be said to be crafted by time, history, technology and politics, what is perhaps of greater importance, and certainly of greater relevance for our purpose, is to understand what specific interventions such as the IPTA tradition were trying to do and what they achieved in terms of what they set out to do. So, as mentioned earlier, while concerns of who was involved in engagements with indigenous and folk forms, how that manner of engagement unfolded, and what transformations occurred to the forms as a result are important to understand the aesthetic dimensions and the political dynamics of movements such as the IPTA, what is very necessary to understand is how they were received and whether the projected impact was achieved or not.

Third, it is appropriate to interpret engagement with tradition such as that of the IPTA in the manner of Raymond Williams: in other words, to see how it represents 'a selection and reselection of those significant received and recovered elements of the past which represent not a necessary but a desired continuity'.[32] Here, in the consideration of various elements of the indigenous, it is obvious that all transformations in form and content are manifestations of such 'desired continuity', to see tradition within the limits of a vision – in this case fundamentally political.

To sum up, the musicians of the IPTA tradition were interrogating and creating musical ideas around various notions of the 'people' that came from specific local histories, as well as nationalist and internationalist imaginings. What is interesting is that it was precisely the dynamic created by these complex ideas, often contradictory to each other, that made musicians attempt to stretch the boundaries of their craft, even as they were strongly located within their specific social and cultural locations and traditions of training. It is clear from the repertoire that exists that a critical spirit was continuously employed in processes of song-writing and music-making, this spirit both allowing for the invoking of traditional 'nationalism' and at the same time questioning it. What is important to note is that in historical terms, it was for the first time that such a project was being undertaken at such a scale, and for this reason it played a profound role in laying the basis for all that was to emerge in the realm of the popular culture in the years to come.

Notes

1 Menon (2001): 264.

2 Ibid.: 262.

[3] Ibid.
[4] Bharucha (1990).
[5] Ibid.: 200.
[6] Naregal (2008): 6.
[7] Modular nationalisms is an idea put forward by Benedict Andersen to denote typologies of nationalism, defined by typical characteristics and seen across a long number of countries.
[8] Chatterjee (1986).
[9] Ibid.: 51.
[10] Ibid.; Bakhle (2005).
[11] Menon (2001); Naregal (2008).
[12] Turino (2003).
[13] Moro (2004): 189–90.
[14] Degirmenci (2006): 56.
[15] Turino (2003). Examples of this include Mexico in the context of and following the 1910 revolution; Peru with President Leguía (1919–30) and ,more markedly, with President Velasco (1968–75); Brazil with Getúlio Vargas in 1930–45; Argentina with the Radical Civic Union in 1916–30 and Perón (1946–55); and Bolivia beginning with the Movimiento Nacional Revolucionario in 1952.
[16] Turino (2003).
[17] Ibid.: 185.
[18] Subramanian (2006); Weidman (2006).
[19] Gopal (2005): 4.
[20] Naregal (2008): 7.
[21] Menon (2001): 19.
[22] Ibid.: 19.
[23] Sambhaji Bhagat, in music performances, argues that 'upper-caste' music, especially classical music, is too 'smooth and sanitized', in contrast to the loud and harsh Dalit music that he performs.
[24] Bharucha (1990): 197.
[25] Ibid.
[26] Turino (2003): 185–86.
[27] Ibid.: 196.
[28] Treece (1997): 1.
[29] Ibid.: 4.
[30] Sitas (1990).
[31] There are almost no known recordings available of Amar Sheikh singing the said song. The one that is available is by Montu Ghosh from Bengal in an IPTA collection and from a personal interview given to me by Ghosh in 2009.
[32] Williams (1981): 187.

Conclusion

I have tried to argue in this book that the IPTA tradition's musical repertoire, wide in its range of styles, forms and languages, played an important role in creating a radical imaginary in the arts in India. This imaginary was part of a radical impulse that unfolded in response to particular historical circumstances in the first half of the twentieth century in different parts of the world, fuelled by a politics of emancipatory humanism and the desire for socialism. Despite it being historically specific, I call this impulse 'radical' because as part of it, pushing the boundaries of existing art forms became like a natural tendency, and hence an impulse. Artists were not mimicking, neither was their art derived from external contexts; the impulse was driven by processes of art creation that were grounded in the international politics of the time, and informed strongly by specific histories and traditions. Even if it was a small 'fraction' that pushed the boundaries, what was remarkable, as is evident from the variety and range of cultural output produced by formations like the IPTA tradition, was the numerous smaller impulses that were unleashed and that are inherent to the process of art-making, where artists become the bearers of processes that interrogate, unearth, interpret and transform existing forms and traditions.

Drawing from the Gramscian idea of 'popular culture' as representing the 'culture of the popular classes', I have attempted to demonstrate that the IPTA tradition's musical forays resulted in the retrieval and reproduction of existing musical traditions, crafted new sounds, styles and musical structures, affected a variety of institutions, and performed an important function in 'voicing the popular'. One of the aspects that I am choosing to bring out is the uniqueness of the IPTA tradition's intervention, even if it was profoundly influenced by debates that were animating the creation of radical music in other parts of the world. The uniqueness lay in being located in and responding through its immersion in performative traditions that were composite, where sound, voice or the aural sensibility is developed and demonstrated as part of several other sensorial registers. At the same time, the music created was such that it stands on its own as a repertoire that has a very specific identity as music, and also as one whose analysis brings forth a range of conceptual issues that arise in the creation of protest music. As stated in the introduction, the repertoire helps reconfigure and reconstellate the relationship between music and politics.

From the standpoint of contemporary times, this reconstellation is important for two reasons. One, because the creation as well as reception of the music of protest, as in this repertoire, is inscribed by history and context as much as by political function, and that this is important to point out for the sake of political praxis as well as for understanding the music itself. The Indian case is particularly useful in demonstrating nuances of the relationship between music and politics that are relevant in the contemporary period as well.

Second, due to musical traditions being largely orally or aurally handed down, and also being part of composite performative traditions, understanding such music becomes an exemplary methodological exercise to understand creative processes in a post-colonial society that is engaging with modernity in multiple ways. A key aspect of this is the importance of the IPTA tradition's music in creating a popular imaginary in the country that moved from the realm of political practice into public entertainment genres. Unlike in the west where understanding and analysing different performing arts take place, to a large extent, in clearly demarcated disciplinary silos, music in cases like the IPTA tradition becomes an interesting vehicle through which performance in general can be understood even as it maintains a distinct identity of its own, as I have tried to demonstrate.

An important constituent of 'voicing the popular' by the IPTA's songwriters and musicians was cinema. The 1940s had seen the production of *Dharti ke Lal* and *Neecha Nagar* in Hindi as explicitly political films, the first directly under the IPTA's banner and the second by Chetan Anand, an IPTA activist. In 1944, a Bengali film, *Udayer Pathe* (Awakening), made by Bimal Roy, had brought in cadences of everyday life and speech into film dialogues, marking it out as a milestone in realist cinema. But it was in the post-independence period that the IPTA's aesthetic was incorporated into popular cinema in different languages, with music playing a very important role. In 1954, *Neelakkuyil*, a film considered a landmark in Malayalam cinema, created a new musical idiom that reflected strongly the influence of the left cultural movement's deliberations on radical music. Working with colloquial usages in language and folk tunes that stemmed from the lives of ordinary people, it inaugurated an era of socially relevant, yet commercial cinema, to be followed by *Newspaper Boy* in 1955, *Odayil Ninnu* (From the Gutter) in 1965 and *Iruttinte Aatmaavu* (The Soul of Darkness) in 1967. In Bombay, similarly, films like *Shri 420* (*Mr 420*, 1955) and *Pyaasa* (*The Thirsty One*, 1957), to name two, established the ordinary person as the critical protagonist in a newly independent nation that had achieved the desired transition from colonialism but was fast reneging on the radical agenda of independence. From Sahir Ludhianvi's poignant lyrics in the song '*Jinhe naaz hai hind par woh kahaan hain*' (Where are those who are proud of India?) in *Pyaasa*, to the scathing statement of want and misery in '*Cheen-o-arab hamaara, hindostan hamaara, rehne ko ghar nahin hai, saara jahan hamaara*' (China and Arabia belong to us, Hindustan belongs to us, we don't have a house to live in, but the world belongs to us), there were innumerable examples of music that reflected the IPTA tradition's critical spirit and musical idioms.

ye kuche, ye nilam ghar dilkashi ke
ye lutte hue karvan zindagi ke
kahan hain, kahan hain, muhafiz khudi ke?
jinhen naaz hain hind par, woh kahan hain?

These streets, these auction houses of pleasure,
These looted caravans of life,
Where are they, the guardians of selfhood?
Those who are proud of India, where are they?

The persona of the ordinary man was conveyed to mainstream audiences through a realist acting format punctuated with song-and-movement sequences that drew from particular performance traditions in many of these films that were produced under commercial banners. Many of the songwriters and musicians from the IPTA tradition who were involved with commercial cinema were accused of being careerist and having 'sold out' to commercial pressures. Often the songs that were written would have two versions: one for direct political use in meetings and campaigns, and another for the silver screen. Elements of strong social critique in the former would be toned down for the latter, ostensibly to ensure commercial acceptance. For example, Makhdoom Mohiuddin's '*Jaane waale sipahi se poochho*' (Ask the departing soldier) was sung, under the music direction of Salil Chowdhury, by the singers Sabita Chowdhury and Manna Dey in *Usne Kaha Tha* (1960), with the last stanza that contained a call for revolution omitted. In the original version, the last stanza went thus:

gir rahaa hai siyaahi ka dera
ho raha hai meri jaan savera
ai watan chhod kar jaane waale
khul gaya inqilabi pharera
jaane waale sipahi se poochho
woh kahaan jaa raha hai

As dusk descends and dawn approaches,
Those who leave the country behind
Wait for the revolutionary dawn.

Similarly, Prem Dhawan's '*Jhoom jhoom ke naacho aaj, naacho aaj, gao khushi ke geet*', written on the occasion of independence, which contained a stanza expressing the hope that hunger and unemployment would end with national independence, did not appear in its film version. The 'double movement of containment and resistance' that characterizes the 'culture of the popular classes', as Stuart Hall put it in his 1971 essay (referred to in the introduction to this book), had become more than apparent in the popular musical imaginary soon after independence.

A different conception of 'voicing of the popular' in cinema came from the work of the filmmaker Ritwik Ghatak from the 1950s, who brought in strong social critique through soundtrack and sonicscapes that reflected the aesthetic positionings around music in the period of the IPTA's active work in Bengal. Standing apart from commercial cinema yet becoming popular with mass audiences, Ghatak's films, notably *Komal Gandhar* (E Flat), his use of folk music forms, voicings, and choice and mode of use of instruments projected an aural imaginary through templates that were unusual yet strongly rooted.

I have also attempted to demonstrate how such a radical moment in twentieth-century history brought out contradictions that were both aesthetic and political that then got organizationally interpreted, mechanically or linearly, driven by contingencies of political praxis and organizational discipline. Without going into whether particular positions that were adopted during the period of the IPTA tradition's history in the 1940s and 1950s were 'correct' or 'wrong', I contend that the musical repertoire as well as the debates and circumstances around its creation brought forth a range of issues that govern the relationship between music and politics that go beyond the historical moment itself, and are highly relevant to our times. Defining political music or protest music in terms of its functions, and function taking precedence over form, are tendencies in left political movements the world over that, I believe, stifle creativity as well as make the protest song less effective over time. It is evident from the repertoire I have analysed in this book that it is often not possible to locate the exact function that singing a song or playing music fulfils, especially a function that can be directly related to the objectives of political mobilization. In one of the few analytical pieces that attempt to classify protest songs in the American tradition, R. Serge Denisoff laments,[1] from a purely functional point of view, the demise of the 'magnetic' protest song (which is openly mobilizational and hence adopts forms that are suited to the purpose), and the rise of the 'rhetorical' protest song that relies on emotional appeal and is hence considered by him to be less politically effective. I argue that with the multifarious challenges posed by politics as well as the differing histories and realities of different societies, it is highly limiting to proscribe creative possibilities through narrow understandings of function. In other words, it is not only music *in* politics but music *as* politics, and the understanding that political movements have to incorporate music (or art in general) as a concrete expression of the politics in itself that will help resist attempts towards straitjacketing of the creative process.

Finally, I believe that a significant part of the music that is analysed here, precisely because of the astounding range it contains as well the fact that it was produced at the crucial transitionary moment between colonialism and independence, continues to be relevant in our times. The IPTA was formed in the backdrop of famine and war, and it is hardly surprising that the songs written then are eminently suitable for interpretation and renewed performance in current situations of hunger and conflict. In my own experience of performance, the poignant '*Jaane waale sipahi se poochho*', '*Din khoon ke hamaare*', Sheela Bhatia's *Heer* about the Bengal famine, and the upbeat '*Pachhapanamtatte*', with contemporary instrumentation, have become popular with audiences on their own terms, not merely as historical record.

In the last year (2016), as debates on nation, nationalism and identity have erupted once again in India, and questions of '*azaadi*' have been debated, these songs, I believe, remain relevant, in both political and aesthetic terms.

Note

1 Denisoff (1968).

Bibliography

Aadnani, R., 2006, *Beyond Rai: North African Protest Music and Poetry*, The Free Library, available at http://www.thefreelibrary.com/Beyond Rai:NorthAfricanprotestmusicandpoetry.-a0148481229 (last accessed on 25 August 2015).

Ali, A. and N.M. Rashed, 1977–78, 'The Progressive Writers' Movement in Its Historical Perspective', *Journal of South Asian Literature*, Vol. 13, No. 1/4, Miscellany.

Attali, J., 1977, *Noise: The Political Economy of Music*, Minneapolis: University of Minnesota Press.

Baké, A., 1953, 'The Impact of Western Music on the Indian Musical System', *Journal of the International Folk Music Council*, Vol. 5: 57–60.

Bakhle, J., 2005, *Two Men and Music: Nationalism and the Making of an Indian Classical Tradition*, New York: Oxford University Press.

Ballantine, C., 1984, *Music and its Social Meanings*, Johannesburg: Ravan Press.

Bardhan, G., 1992, *Rhythm Incarnate: Tribute to Shanti Bardhan*, New Delhi: Abhinav Publications.

Barker, T., 2015a, 'Individualism, Collectivism, and Otherness in Protest Music: The American Civil Rights Movement and the Counterculture', available at https://www.academia.edu (last accessed on 20 June 2015).

——, 2015b, *Protest Music and the American Counterculture*, available at https://www.academia.edu/2914071/Protest_Music_and_the_American_Counter_Culture (last accessed on 10 May 2015).

Bennett, T., S. Furth, L. Grossberg, J. Shepherd and G. Turner (eds), 2005, *Rock and Popular Music: Politics, Policies, Institutions*, New York: Routledge.

Bharucha, R., 1983, *Rehearsals of Revolution: The Political Theatre of Bengal*, Calcutta: Seagull Books.

——, 1990, *Theatre and the World: Essays on Performance and Politics of Culture*, New Delhi: Manohar.

Bhatia, N., 2004, *Acts of Authority/Acts of Resistance: Theatre and Politics in Colonial and Postcolonial India*, Ann Arbor: University of Michigan Press.

Bhattacharya, B., 2013, 'People's Art or Performance of the Elites?: Debating the History of IPTA in Bengal', *Rupkatha Journal on Interdisciplinary Studies in Humanities*, Vol. V, No. 2: 178–88.

Bhattacharya, M., 1971, 'The IPTA in Bengal', *Journal of Arts & Ideas*, No. 2, January–March: 5–22.

Biswas, H., 1967, 'A Glorious Heritage', in H. Biswas (ed.), *Folk Music and Folklore (An Anthology)*, Calcutta: Folk Music and Folklore Research Institute, Vol. I: 165–75.

——, 1983a, 'Jibon Silpi Jyotiprasad', *Journal Emporium*, Nalbari.

——, 1983b, 'Ujan Gang Baiya', *Anustup*, Kolkata.

——, 1990, 'Axom Aru Bongor Lokasangeet Samiksha', *Journal Emporium*, Nalbari.

——, 2002a, 'Gananatya Itihasor Ekhon Pramanyo Dolil', in B. Khataniar *et al.* (eds), *Hemanga Biswas*, Guwahati: Lokayat Prakasan: 56–73.

——, 2002b, 'Aahok Akou Aami Ekotar Setu Bandhu (Asomor Gananatyo Aandolonor Eti Smoroniyo Ghotona)', in B. Khataniar *et al.* (ed.), *Hemanga Biswas*, Guwahati: Lokayat Prakasan: 74–85.

——, 2008, 'Bharotiyo Gananatya Sanghar Tritiyo Raijjwik Sonmilonor Sompadokor Pro-tibedon', in P. Majumdar (ed.), *Hemanga Biswas Rasanawali*, Assam: Publication Board: pp. 923–94.

Biswas, H., 1955, 'Foreword', in H. Biswas (ed.), *Jilikabo Luitore Paar*, Assam: IPTA: 923–94.

—— (ed.), 1967, *Folk Music and Folklore (An Anthology)*, Vol. I, Calcutta: Folk Music and Folklore Research Institute.

Bloch, E., [1954] 1986, *The Principle of Hope*, translated by N. Plaice, S. Plaice and P. Knight, Oxford: Blackwell.

Booth, G.D., 1993, 'Traditional Practice and Mass Mediated Music in India', *International Review of the Aesthetics and Sociology of Music*, Vol. 24, No. 2: 159–74.

——, 2008, *Behind the Curtain: Making Music in Mumbai's Film Studios*, New York: Oxford University Press.

Booth, G.D. and Terry L. Kuhn, 1990, 'Economic and Transmission Factors as Essential Elements in the Definition of Folk, Art and Pop Music', *The Musical Quarterly*, Vol. 74, No. 3: 441–38.

Booth, G.D. and B. Sharpe, 2014, *More Than Bollywood: Studies in Indian Popular Music*, New York: Oxford University Press.

Bose, F., 1959, 'Western Influences in Modern Asian Music', *Journal of International Folk Music Council*, No. 11: 47–50.

Bowen-Struyk, H., 2001, *Rethinking Japanese Proletarian Literature*, Chicago: University of Chicago Press.

——, 2006, 'Introduction: Proletarian Arts in East Asia: Quests for National, Gender and Class Justice', *Positions: East Asia Cultures Critique*, Special Edition, Vol. 14, Issue 2, Fall: 251–78.

——, 2007, 'Proletarian Arts in East Asia', *The Asia-Pacific Journal*, invited essay based on the introduction to the special edition: *Proletarian Arts in East Asia: Quests for National, Gender and Class Justice*.

Burke, P., 1981, 'The "Discovery" of Popular Culture', in Raphael Samuel (ed.), *People's History and Socialist Theory*, London: Routledge.

Carruyo, L., 2005, 'La Gaita Zuliana: Music and the Politics of Protest in Venezuela', *Latin American Perspectives, Venezuelan Exceptionalism Revisited: New Perspectives on Politics and Society*, Vol. 32, No. 3, May: 98–111.

Chakravartty, G., 2007, *P.C. Joshi: A Biography*, New Delhi: National Book Trust.

Chatterjee, P., 1986, *Nationalist Thought and the Colonial World: A Derivative Discourse?* London: Zed Books.

——, 1993, *The Nation and Its Fragments: Colonial and Postcolonial Histories*, Princeton: Princeton University Press.

Chen, S.W., 2007, 'The Music Industry and Popular Song in 1930s and 1940s Shanghai: A Historical and Stylistic Analysis', unpublished PhD thesis, Department of Film and Media Studies, University of Stirling, available at http://storre.stir.ac.uk/bitstream/1893/202/1/shanghai.pdf (last accessed on 12 April 2013).

Chen, X., 2006, 'Reflections on the Legacy of Tian Han: "Proletarian Modernism" and Its Traditional Roots', *Modern Chinese Literature and Culture*, Vol. 18, No. 1, Spring: 155–215.

Chowdhury, S., 1989, 'Remembering Hemanta-Da', available at www.salilda.com.

Cowley, M., 1980, *The Dream of the Golden Mountains: Remembering the Thirties*, New York: Viking Press.

——, 1992, 'Feasts of Unnaming: Folk Festivals and the Representation of Folklife', in Robert Baron and Nicholas R. Spitzer (eds), *Public Folklore*, Washington: Smithsonian Institution Press: 263–305.

Damodaran, S., 2008, 'Protest Through Music', *Seminar*, August.

Damodaran, S., 2014, 'Understanding the Relationship Between Art and Social Movements: Towards an Alternative Methodology', in Wiebke Keim, Ercüment Çelic, Christian Ersche and Veronika Wöhrer (eds), *Global Knowledge Production in the Social Sciences: Made in Circulation*, Aldershot: Ashgate Publishing.

Dasgupta, R., 2005, 'Rhyming Revolution: Marxism and Culture in Colonial Bengal', *Studies in History*, Vol. 21, No. 1: 79–98.

——, 2014, '"The People" in People's Art and and People's War', in G. Chakravartty (ed.), *People's 'Warrior': Words and Worlds of P.C. Joshi*, New Delhi: Tulika Books.

Degirmenci, K., 2006, 'On the Pursuit of a Nation: The Construction of Folk and Folk Music in the Founding Decades of the Turkish Republic', *International Review of the Aesthetics and Sociology of Music*, Vol. 37, No. 1: 47–65.

Denisoff, R.S., 1968, 'Protest Movements: Class Consciousness and the Propaganda Song', *The Sociological Quarterly*, Vol. 9, No. 2: 228–47.

——, 1983, *Sing a Song of Social Significance*, Bowling Green: Bowling Green University Popular Press.

Denning, M., 1996, *The Cultural Front: The Laboring of American Culture in the Twentieth Century*, New York: Verso.

——, 2004, *Culture in the Age of Three Worlds*, New York: Verso.

Dewri, P., 2012, 'The World Is a Stage; the People Are its Players: The Music of the IPTA in Assam', presented at a seminar 'Awaaz Do', Sahmat, September.

Dharwadker, A., 2008, *Theatres of Independence: Drama, Theory, and Urban Performance in India since 1947*, Iowa City: University of Iowa Press.

Donaldson, C.R., 2011, 'Music for the People: The Folk Music Revival and American Identity, 1930–1970', PhD dissertation,Vanderbilt University, Nashville, Tennessee.

Drott, E., 2011, *Music and the Elusive Revolution*, Berkeley: University of California Press.

Dunaway, K.D., 1987, *Music and Politics in the United States, Folk Music Journal*, Vol. 5, No. 3: 268–94.

Edmunds, N., 2000, 'Music and Politics: The Case of the Russian Association of Proletarian Musicians', *The Slavonic and East European Review*, Vol. 78, No. 1: 66–89.

Eisler, H., 1978, *A Rebel in Music*, Berlin: International Publishers and New York: Seven Seas Books.

Elliot, R., 2011, 'Public Consciousness, Political Conscience and Memory in Latin American *nueva canción*', in David Clarke and Eric Clarke (eds), *Music and Consciousness: Philosophical, Psychological and Cultural Perspectives*, Oxford: Oxford University Press.

Eyerman, R. and A. Jamison, 1998, *Music and Social Movements: Mobilizing Traditions in the Twentieth Century*, Cambridge: Cambridge University Press.

Fay, L., 1980, 'Shostakovich versus Volkov: Whose Testimony?', *Russian Review*, Vol. 39, No. 4: pp. 484–93.

Fay, L.E. (ed.), 2004, *Shostakovich and His World*, Princeton: Princeton University Press.

Frackman, K. and L. Powell (eds), 2015, *Classical Music in the German Democratic Republic: Production and Reception*, New Delhi: Camden House.

Frith, S., 1989, *World Music, Politics, and Social Change: Papers from the International Association for the Study of Popular Music*, Manchester: Manchester University Press.

——, 2007, *Taking Popular Music Seriously*, Aldershot: Ashgate Publishing.

——, 2008, 'Why music matters', *Critical Quarterly*, Vol. 50, Nos 1–2: 165–79.

Frolova-Walker, M., *Music and Soviet Power, 1917–1932*, Woodbridge: The Boydell Press.

Ganguly, A., 2002, 'Citybeats: Urban Folk Music in Late-Modern Calcutta', *Sarai Reader 02: The Cities of Everyday Life*, New Delhi: Centre for the Study of Developing Societies.

Garabedian, S., 2005, 'Reds, Whites, and the Blues: Lawrence Gellert, "Negro Songs of Protest," and the Left-Wing Folk-Song Revival of the 1930s and 1940s', *American Quarterly*, Vol. 57, No. 1: 179–206.

Gasparotto, M., 2011, 'Curating la Nueva Canción: Capturing the Evolution of a Genre and Movement', Rutgers University Community Repository, available at http://dx.doi.org/doi:10.7282/T3CN72B1 (last accessed on 21 May 2015).

Ghatak, R., 1954, *On the Cultural 'Front'*, Calcutta: Ritwik Memorial Trust.

Ghosh, A., 2002, 'Revisiting the "Bengal Renaissance": Literary Bengali and Low-Life Print in Colonial Calcutta', *Economic and Political Weekly*, Vol. 37, No. 42: 4329–38.

Gong, H., 2008, 'Music, Nationalism and the Search for Modernity in China, 1911–1949', *New Zealand Journal of Asian Studies*, Vol. 10, No. 2: 38–69.

Gopal, P., 2005, *Literary Radicalism in India: Gender, Nation and the Transition to Independence*, London: Routledge.

Grabs, M. (ed.), 1978, *Hanns Eisler: A Rebel in Music: Selected Writings*, London: Kahn and Averill.

Gramsci, A., 1971, *Selections from the Prison Notebooks*, New York: International Publishers.

Guiat, Cyrille, 2003, *The French and Italian Communist Parties: Comrades and Culture*, London: Frank Cass.

Gutkin, I., 1999, *The Cultural Origins of the Socialist Realist Aesthetic, 1890–1934*, Chicago: Northwestern University Press.

Habib, I., 1998, 'The Left and the National Movement', *Social Scientist*, Vol. 26, Nos 5–6: 3–33.

Hall, S., 1981, 'Notes on Deconstructing the "Popular"', in Raphael Samuel (ed.), *People's History and Socialist Theory*, London: Routledge and Kegan Paul.

Heller, L., 1997, 'A World of Prettiness: Socialist Realism and Its Aesthetic Categories', in Thomas Lahusen and Evgeny Dobrenko (eds), *Socialist Realism Without Shores*, Durham: Duke University Press.

Homberger, E., 1979, 'Proletarian Literature and the John Reed Clubs 1929–1935', *Journal of American Studies*, Vol. 13, No. 2: 221–44.

Hujuri, R., 2014, 'IPTA in Assam', PhD dissertation, Department of Folklore, Guwahati University, Assam.

Jalil, R., 2014, *Liking Progress, Loving Change: A Literary History of the Progressive Writers' Movement in Urdu*, New Delhi: Oxford University Press.

Jones, A., 2001, *Yellow Music: Media Culture and Colonial Modernity in the Chinese Jazz Age*, Durham: Duke University Press.

Jones, S., 1999, 'Chinese Ritual Music under Mao and Deng', *British Journal of Ethnomusicology*, Vol. 8: 27–66.

Jussy, S., 2005, 'Left Movement in Kerala and the Commencement of a Literary Movement', *Social Scientist*, Vol. 33, Nos 11–12: 29–42.

Karat, P., 1973, 'The Peasant Movement in Malabar 1934–40', *Social Scientist*, September.

Koenker, D.P., W.P. Rosenberg and R.G. Suny, 1989, *Party, State, and Society in the Russian Civil War: Explorations in Social History*, Bloomington: Indiana University Press.

Kun, J., 1995, *Audiotopia: Music, Race and America*, Berkeley: University of California Press.

Laing, S., 1986, *Representations of Working-Class Life: 1957–1964*, Houndmills, Basingstoke: Macmillan.

Lipsitz, G., 1994, *Rainbow at Midnight: Labor and Culture in the 1940s*, Urbana: University of Illinois Press.

Livingston, T.E., 1999, 'Music Revivals: Towards a General Theory', *Ethnomusicology*, Vol. 43, No. 1: 66–85.

Long, P., 2008, *Only in the Common People: The Aesthetics of Class in Post-War Britain*, Newcastle-upon-Tyne: Cambridge Scholars Publishing.

Mally, L., 2003, 'Exporting Soviet Culture: The Case of Agitprop Theater', *Slavic Review*, Vol. 62, No. 2: 324–42.

Manuel, P., 1988, *Popular Musics of the Non-Western World: An Introductory Survey*, New York: Oxford University Press.

———, 1993, *Cassette Culture: Popular Music and Technology in North India*, Chicago: University of Chicago Press.

———, 2010, 'Thumri, Ghazal, and Modernity in Hindustani Music Culture', in J. Boer, F. Delvoye, J. Harvey and E. Nijenhuis (eds), *Hindustani Music: Thirteenth to Twentieth Centuries*, Delhi: Manohar.

———, 2013, 'Democratizing Indian Popular Music: From Cassette Culture to the Digital Era', in Ravi Sundaram (ed.), *No Limits: Media Studies from India*, New Delhi: Oxford University Press.

Mao Tse-Tung, 1977, 'Talks at the Yenan Forum on Literature and Art', in M. Tse-Tung, *On Literature and Art*, Peking: Foreign Languages Press: 1–39.

Menon, D., 2001, 'Lost Visions?: Imagining a Left Culture in the 1950s', in Alice Thorner (ed.), *Land, Labour and Rights: Ten Daniel Thorner Memorial Lectures*, New Delhi: Tulika Books.

———, 2007, *Caste, Nationalism and Communism in South India: Malabar 1900–1948*, New York: Cambridge University Press.

Middleton, R., 1990, *Studying Popular Music*, Philadelphia: Open University Press.

———, 1993, 'Popular Music Analysis and Musicology: Bridging the Gap', *Popular Music*, Vol. 12, No. 2: 177–90.

———, 2006, *Voicing the Popular: On the Subjects of Popular Music*, London: Routledge.

Mir, R. and A.H. Mir, 2006, *Anthems of Resistance*, New Delhi: India Ink.

Mitra, S., 1980, 'Progressive Cultural Movement in Bengal', *Social Scientist*, Vol. 8, Nos 5–6: 115–20.

Mittler, B., 2010, '"Eight Stage Works for 800 Million People": The Great Proletarian Cultural Revolution in Music – A View from Revolutionary Opera', *The Opera Quarterly*, Vol. 26, Nos 2–3: 377–401.

Moore, C., 2008, 'Socialist Realism and the Music of the French Popular Front', *The Journal of Musicology*, Vol. 25, No. 4: 473–502.

Moro, P., 2004, 'Elite Music and Nationalism in South and Southeast Asia: How Music Becomes Classical', *Journal of Southeast Asian Studies*, Vol. 35, No. 2: 187–211.

Myrsiades, L. and K. Myrsiades, 1999, *Cultural Representation in Historical Resistance: Complexity and Resistance in Greek Guerrilla Theater*, Lewisburg: Bucknell University Press.

Namboodiripad, E.M.S., 1986, 'Half a Century of Marxist Cultural Movement in India', *The Marxist*, Vol. 4, No. 2.

Naregal, V., 2008, 'Marginality, Regional Forms and State Patronage', *Seminar*, No. 588.

Nelson, A., 2000, 'The Struggle for Proletarian Music: RAPM and the Cultural Revolution', *Slavic Review*, Vol. 59, No. 1: 101–32.

Neog, S.C., 2001, 'Axomot Progotisil Sanskritik Andolon: Bharotiyo Gananaya Sangha', Guwahati: Bani Mandir.

Oja, J.C., 1988, 'Composer with a Conscience: Elie Siegmeister in Profile', *American Music*, Vol. 6, No. 2: 158–80.

———, 1989, 'Marc Blitzstein's "The Cradle Will Rock" and Mass-Song Style of the 1930s', *The Musical Quarterly*, Vol. 73, No. 4: 445–75.

Olwage, G., 2008, *Composing Apartheid: Music For and Against Apartheid*, Johannesburg: Wits University Press.

Patel, G., 2002, *Lyrical Movements, Historical Hauntings: On Gender, Colonialism and Desire in Miraji's Urdu Poetry*, Stanford: Stanford University Press.

Pillai, P.G., 1975, 'Deshabhimani Study Circles: Literary Movement in Kerala', *Social Scientist*, Vol. 4, No. 2: 56–60.

Pearson, D., 2009, 'A Critical Defense of Socialist Realism: Shostakovich's 5th Symphony versus the Shoddy Scholarship of Anti-Communist Re-Interpretation', *New Zealand Journal of Asian Studies*, Vol. 10, No. 2: 38–69.

Pietaro, J., 2010, *Out of the Red Megaphone: The Modernist Protest Music of a Lost Age*, Durham: Duke University Press.

Pradhan, S., 1979, *Marxist Cultural Movement in India, Chronicles and Documents (1936–1947)* and *(1947–1958)*, Vol. I, Calcutta: Navana.

Pradhan, S., 1982, *Marxist Cultural Movement in India, Chronicles and Documents (1936–1947)* and *(1947–1958)*, Vol. II, Calcutta: Navana.

Pradhan, S., 1987, *Marxist Cultural Movement in India, Chronicles and Documents (1936–1947)* and *(1947–1958)*, Vol. III, Calcutta: Navana.

Radice, W., 2008, 'Keys to the Kingdom: The Search for How Best to Understand and Perform the Songs of Tagore', *University of Toronto Quarterly*, Vol. 77, No. 4: 1095–109.

Ranade, A., 2002, *Hindustani Music*, first reprint, New Delhi: National Book Trust.

Raphael, S., Ewan MacColl and Stuart Cosgrove (eds), 1985, *Theatres of the Left, 1880–1935: Workers' Theatre Movements in Britain and America*, London: Routledge and Kegan Paul.

Reuss, R.A., 1979, 'Folk Music and Social Conscience: The Musical Odyssey of Charles Seeger', *Western Folklore*, Vol. 38, No. 4: 221–38.

Reuss, R.A. and J.C. Reuss, 2000, *American Folk Music and Left Politics: 1927–1957*, Lanham: Scarecrow Press.

Robbie, L., 1989, *My Song is My Weapon: People's Songs, American Communism, and the Politics of Culture, 1930–1950*, Urbana: University of Illinois Press.

Rosenberg, Neil V. (ed.), 1993, *Transforming Tradition: Folk Music Revivals Examined*, Urbana: University of Illinois Press.

Ross, A., 2004, 'Unauthorized: The Final Betrayal of Dmitri Shostakovich', *The New Yorker*, September.

Sailaja, K., 1998, 'Popular Cultural Movements in Andhra: A Study of Progressive Writers Association and People's Theatre of Arts (1940–50)', PhD thesis submitted to Department of History, School of Social Sciences, University of Hyderabad

Sarkar, S. and T. Sarkar (eds), 2008, *Women and Social Reform in Modern India*, Bloomington: Indiana University Press.

Schwarz, B., 1965, 'Soviet Music since the Second World War', *The Musical Quarterly*, Special Fiftieth Anniversary Issue: 'Contemporary Music in Europe: A Comprehensive Survey', Vol. 51, No. 1: 259–81.

———, 1972, *Music and Musical Life in Soviet Russia, 1917–1970*, New York: W.W. Norton.

Scott, H.G. (ed.), 1935, *Problems of Soviet Literature: Reports and Speeches at the First Soviet Writers' Congress*, Cooperative Publishing Society of Foreign Workers in the USSR.

Sen, S., 2008, 'The Art Song and Tagore: Settings by Western Composer', *University of Toronto Quarterly*, Vol. 77, No. 4: 1110–32.

Sitas, A., 1987, 'Class, Nation, Ethnicity in Natal's Black Working Class', in *The Flight of the Gwala Bird*, Durban: Madiba Press.

———, 1989, 'Traditions of Poetry in Natal', in *The Flight of the Gwala-Gwala Bird*, Durban: Madiba Press.

———, 1990, 'The Voice and Gesture in South Africa's Revolution: A Study of Worker Gatherings and Performance-Genres in Natal', in *The Flight of the Gwala-Gwala Bird*, Durban: Madiba Press.

———, 2007, *The Ethic of Reconciliation*, Durban: Madiba Press.

Storey, J., 2009, *Cultural Theory and Popular Culture: An Introduction*, London: Pearson Longman.

Subramanian, L., 2006, *From the Tanjore Court to the Madras Music Academy: A Social History of Music in South India*, New Delhi: Oxford University Press.

Swiderski, M. Edward, 1979, *The Philosophical Foundations of Soviet Aesthetics: Theories and Controversies in the Post-War Years*, Dordrecht: D. Reidel Publishing Company.

Taruskin, R., 2000, *Defining Russia Musically*, Princeton: Princeton University Press.

Tham, Gje, 2009, 'The Influence of Socialist Realism on the Yellow River Piano Concerto', PhD dissertation, University of Alabama, available at www.gradworks.umi.com/33/69/3369772.html (last accessed on 6 June 2013).

Tharamangalam, J., 1981, *Agrarian Class Conflict: The Political Mobilization of Agricultural Labourers in Kuttanad, South India*, Vancouver: University of British Columbia Press.

Tharu, S. and K. Lalita (eds), 1991, *Women Writing in India: 600 BC to the Present*, Volume 1, New York: Feminist Press.

Titus, J.M., 2006, 'Modernism, Socialist Realism, and Identity in the Early Film Music of Dmitry Shostakovich, 1929–1932', PhD dissertation, Ohio State University, available at https://etd.ohiolink.edu/ (last accessed on 26 February 2013).

Tragaki, D., 2007, *Rebetikoworlds*, Newcastle-upon-Tyne: Cambridge Scholars Publishing.

Treece, D., 1997, 'Guns and Roses: Bossa Nova and Brazil's Music of Popular Protest, 1958–68', *Popular Music*, 16 (1), pp. 1–29.

Turino, T., 2003, 'Nationalism and Latin American Music: Selected Case Studies and Theoretical Considerations', *Latin American Music Review*, Vol. 24, No. 2: 169–209.

——, 2008, *Music as Social Life: The Politics of Participation*, Chicago: University of Chicago Press.

Vaughan, J., 1960, *Soviet Socialist Realism: Bases of Marxist–Leninist Aesthetics (Osnóvymarksístsko-léninskoiestétiki)*, Moscow: State Publishers of Political Literature.

Volkov, Solomon (ed.), 1979, *Testimony: The Memoirs of Dmitri Shostakovich*, London: Hamish Hamilton.

Warnaby, J., 1995, 'A New Left-Wing Radicalism in Contemporary German Music?', *Tempo*, New Series, No. 193, German Issue: 18–26.

Weber, M., 1967, *The Rational Foundations of Western Music*, Carbondale: The Southern Illinois University Press.

Weidman, A.J., 2006, *Singing the Classical, Voicing the Modern: The Postcolonial Politics of Music in South India*, Durham: Duke University Press.

Wilson, E., 2006, *Shostakhovich: A Life Remembered*, Princeton: Princeton University Press.

Willet, J., 1964, *Brecht on Theatre: The Development of an Aesthetic*, London: Methuen.

Williams, R., 1981, *The Sociology of Culture*, Chicago: University of Chicago Press.

Zhdanov, A., 1935, 'Soviet Literature: The Richest in Ideas, the Most Advanced Literature', in H.F. Scott (ed.), *Problems of Soviet Literature: Reports and Speeches at the First Soviet Writers' Congress*, New York: International Publishers.

——, 1998, 'From Speech at the First All Union Congress of Soviet Writers 1934', in V. Kolocotroni *et al.* (eds), *Modernism: An Anthology of Sources and Documents*, Chicago: University of Chicago Press: 524–26.

Index